·On the Water·

ABBOT PUBLIC LIBRARY
235 Pleasant Street
Marblehead, MA 01945

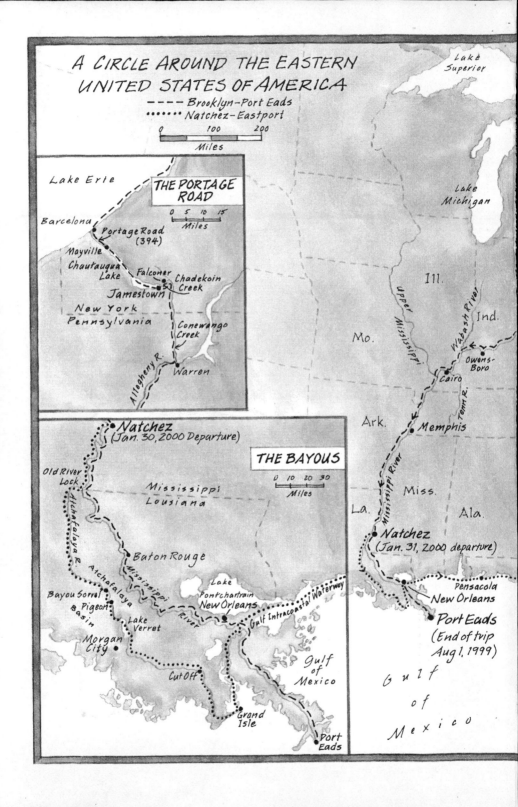

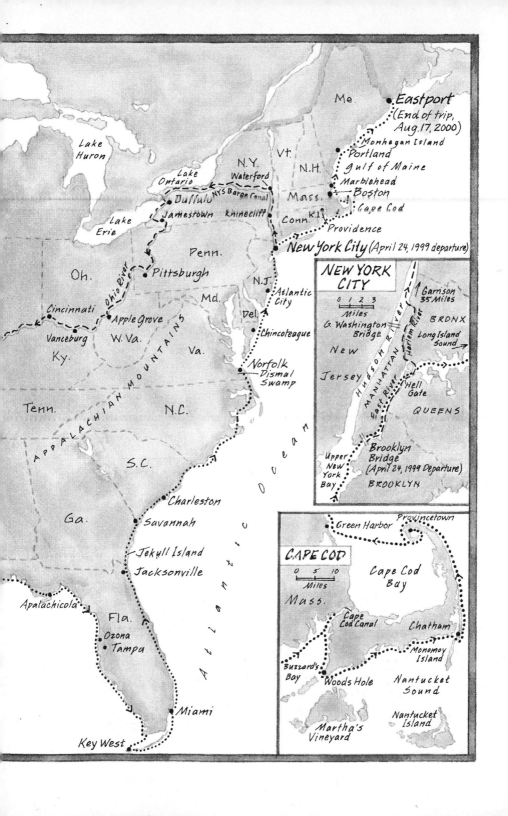

· On the Water ·

DISCOVERING AMERICA
IN A ROWBOAT

Nathaniel Stone

Illustrations by Elizabeth Stone

BROADWAY BOOKS
NEW YORK

A hardcover edition of this book was published in 2002
by Broadway Books.

ON THE WATER. Copyright © 2002 by Nathaniel Stone. All rights
reserved. No part of this book may be reproduced or transmitted
in any form or by any means, electronic or mechanical, including
photocopying, recording, or by any information storage and
retrieval system, without written permission from the publisher.
For information, address Broadway Books, a division of
Random House, Inc.

PRINTED IN THE UNITED STATES OF AMERICA

BROADWAY BOOKS and its logo, a letter B bisected on the diagonal,
are trademarks of Random House, Inc.

Visit our website at www.broadwaybooks.com

Book design by Jennifer Ann Daddio

Map illustrations by David Cain

Illustrations by Elizabeth Stone

The Library of Congress has cataloged the hardcover edition as:
Stone, Nathaniel.
On the water : discovering America
in a rowboat / Nathaniel Stone.
p. cm.
1. United States—Description and travel. 2. Stone,
Nathaniel—Journeys—United States.
3. Boats and boating—United States. I. Title.
E169.04 .S77   2002
917.304'93—dc21   2002018489

ISBN 0-7679-0842-2

BVG 01

TO THE MEMORY OF PARKMAN SAYWARD—

MY GREAT UNCLE PAT

· Contents ·

· Leg Two ·

· Author's Note ·

THE FIRST BOAT I ever built swamped immediately. I built it out of a shipping pallet picked from the trash at my mother's wood-stove shop, scrap plywood from behind the garage, and, for flotation, stray Styrofoam I'd collected along the shore. My skills with tools included hammering screws as if they were nails and trimming plywood with a coping saw. I was eight years old.

That was about the time, as I remember, I started looking out of windows. Out the kitchen window to a harbor deserted in winter by all but lobster boats, a vision of adventurous freedom cut short each morning by my sullen departure for school. And out the windows of classrooms as the minutes plodded by, to scenes of playgrounds and neighbors' rooflines beyond wooden fences. But I was never rebel enough to occasionally ask the teacher for a bathroom pass, slip out the side door, and disappear over one of those fences.

I was no rebel at all, in fact. Far from it. I was just a geographical deviant, always thinking of someplace new, usually near water and re-quiring, of course, a boat. My favorite book was the world atlas, and it still is. I can't help wondering what it's like to live on the Belcher Islands in Hudson Bay, and whether the Rio Grande is running at El

Paso, and how the rapids are on the Olenek River as it descends to the Laptev Sea.

I was twenty years old before I slept in a tent, and twenty-two when I first paddled a canoe. I was a late bloomer when it came to anything adventurous, and it's important for me to say so in case anyone gets the wrong impression that the trip described in this book required anything more than the skills and conditioning of most any outdoor enthusiast. I think of it myself as a weekend rowing trip, extended. But it was also, to me, another chance at the schoolyard fence, and once I hopped over it, I never looked back.

Nathaniel Stone
Zuni, New Mexico, February 2002

· Leg One ·

· I ·

A Perceptible Wake

"WHAT STREET ARE WE AT?" I call up to a jogger who's been watching as my strokes against the river's current overtake his strides along the promenade. He glances to his left, where one of the lesser architectural canyons of Manhattan is marked by a street sign just out of my view.

"One-hundred-and-tenth Street," he reports. A moment of silence as we acknowledge each other in self-propulsion.

"How far are you going?"

I search the riverscape briefly, then look back to him: "Bourbon Street!"

A blank look. He carries his momentum through a few more strides while I take a couple of strokes. And then suddenly he smiles and punches a fist up into the air.

It is spring on the Harlem River. As I row northward, people fishing from the granite seawall cast their lures and hooks on silken strands that sing out across the water. The way the weighted barbs arc across the blue April sky you'd think the aim, spiderlike, was for the opposing shore of the Bronx. Then, reels spent, they lose their flight and softly plunge into brown, working water, and the slackened filaments follow, sighing across the river's surface. There are others too,

3

families and friends, who sit on city benches, talking and laughing, or reading, or with their eyes closed and faces tilted up to the spring-warm sun. Some lean against the green metal railing with their fore-arms, hands clasped, looking down at the river, or beyond the river to the Bronx, or, as I pass by, at me. Young children wave to me through the bars of the railing. One boy is too tall to look below the handrail, but too short to look above. He stretches his legs for the upper view, then stoops for the lower and waves. Some call out to ask where I'm going, and I tell them "New Orleans!" or "the Gulf of Mexico!" One man with a thick city accent corrects me, pointing south: "You're goin' the wrong way, man! New Orleans is *that* way!" He won't be the last to say so as I proceed up the Hudson toward Albany, and west along the Erie Canal toward Buffalo, five hundred miles of rowing without an inch gained toward the gulf before finally swinging the bow southward toward the land of the Cajuns.

Already the palms of my hands have opened up to the deepest layers of skin. Two months before setting out I started training on a rowing machine in hopes of building my calluses, but the machine doesn't mimic the feathering of the oars, and any toughness I had has been blistered, ruptured, then slowly worn away as if the trip itself has had a word with me: "Now let me show you what I meant by cal-luses." The chafing is exacerbated by the rubber grips of my second-hand oars. The parallel fine ridges of rubber tread, presumably once soft, have been hardened by exposure to the sun and slowly pare my hands to their epidermal base. Yet just two weeks and 140 miles from here, at Watervliet, near Albany, I will be given a piece of 80-grit sandpaper with which I'll scour smooth the ridges of my leathered palms.

"WHAT POSSESSED YOU?"

A question I was frequently asked over six thousand miles of row-ing. The phrasing rarely wavered, and the verb choice was consistent.

It's enough to say that I'm possessed by a love for water and by a fascination with boats. Had I been raised in farm country I might have ridden a horse from Butte to Bar Harbor, but I grew up along the coast of Massachusetts, and the first boat I was ever in by myself was an inflatable dinghy with the wooden oars of a skiff. It was the summer of 1975 and I was seven years old, and I still remember my newfound sense of independence as I struggled to coordinate the two unwieldy oars through the translucent cold below. Two snapshots were taken of me that day. In the first, preserved in the family photo album, I am seated, oars idle in the oarlocks, blades in the water, grinning at the camera and with arms raised in a cheer. In the second picture, with oars not quite synchronized but leaving a perceptible wake, I am rowing away.

Add to my love affair with boats and water a passion for geography. I spent uncounted hours as a child poring through the family atlas, distracted from the center of the universe that was my hometown by the idea that someone, at the same moment, was living in such exotic outbacks as the Zuni Indian Reservation in New Mexico, or along the simple crosshairs of Leola, South Dakota, or at the end of the dead-end road to Candelaria, West Texas. At some point, when I was perhaps ten, while studying the Mississippi River, the Great Lakes, and their outlet down the St. Lawrence to the sea, it occurred to me that the right combination of blue watery veins on the atlas maps might provide a narrow yet unbroken channel between the North Atlantic and the Gulf of Mexico. From Lake Erie I traced the dead-end Sandusky, and eyed the Maumee River, which very nearly kisses the Wabash, a tributary of the Ohio. To the east, heading inland from Lake Ontario, the Genesee's shared geological roots with the Allegheny tempted me. I discovered, though, that they too are divided, with headwaters some five miles apart, as one drains toward the Atlantic and the other toward the Gulf of Mexico. Just cousins.

I traced west through the pages of the atlas, past, for my purposes, riverless Michigan and Indiana, and arrived by finger at Chicago. There I discovered I'd been right to mount the quest, for parallel to both the Adlai E. Stevenson Expressway and the partly filled Illinois and Michigan Canal runs the thirty-mile thread of the Chicago Sanitary and Ship Canal. Though I imagined a gapingly wide sewage gutter plied by oceangoing ships with foreign flags, a canal is a canal, and by Joliet, heading south, it becomes the Illinois River, bound for the Mississippi. Despite this technicality of American engineering, and with Nova Scotia, New Brunswick, and a bit of Quebec included, I've thought of the eastern United States as an island ever since.

A final seed of motivation was planted shortly after the day of my college graduation when, as I bade farewell to extended youth, I was diagnosed with chicken pox. While friends celebrated and planned their next steps, I sat at home for three weeks, let my whiskers grow into a beard I was not allowed to scratch, and read. I became immersed in *Lone Voyager*, Joseph Garland's biography of Howard Blackburn, a late-nineteenth-century Gloucester fisherman. While fishing for halibut in January on Newfoundland's Burgeo Bank, Blackburn and his dory mate, Thomas Welch, were separated from their mother schooner, the *Grace L. Fears*, by a blizzard. When the blizzard gave way to night and a cloudless gale, the two could see the lantern lights of the schooner on the windward horizon, but they were unable to row their lumbering dory against the waves. By morning they had been blown out of sight of the *Grace L. Fears*.

The two men took turns bailing for their lives as the gale continued, and in doing so inadvertently bailed from the boat Blackburn's woolen mittens, which he'd tossed into the salty bilge to keep them from freezing solid while he worked. Soon, as Welch weakened in the cold, Howard's fingers grew frostbitten and useless. With rowing for the coast his only hope, he forced his fingers around the handles of the oars. In twenty minutes they were frozen claws.

On the second night, with the gale unabated, Thomas Welch died of exposure. With his frozen partner as company and ballast, Blackburn managed to continue bailing with his lifeless hands. At dawn of the third day the wind eased and he started rowing north toward the coast of Newfoundland, some sixty miles away. For two days and a night Blackburn continued on, his fingers worn bare to the bone on the wooden handles of the oars.

Amazingly, Blackburn reached the desolate coast, and happened to find an abandoned, roofless shack in which he spent a night fighting his lethal desire for sleep. The following day, after attempting to remove Welch's corpse from the boat and losing it to the salty depths, Blackburn set out again in his dory and headed west along the rugged coast in search of help. On the fifth night after Howard Blackburn and Thomas Welch were lost on the wintry sea, Blackburn was rescued when he landed near a settlement of impoverished fishermen, who over the following months nursed him to digitless health.

After returning to fame in Gloucester and a venture as a successful tavern owner, Blackburn grew restless and taught himself to sail despite the limited usefulness of his hands. After several solo transatlantic crossings in smaller and smaller boats, he embarked in 1902 on a circumnavigation of the eastern United States by sail. He cruised his gaff-rigged sloop, *Great Republic*, up the Hudson River, travelled westward across New York on the Erie Canal, then sailed the Great Lakes to Chicago. Eight decades before I had stumbled across it in an atlas, Blackburn traveled the Illinois and Michigan Canal to the Illinois River, and was soon headed down the Mississippi for the Gulf of Mexico.

Upon rounding Florida and reaching Miami, Blackburn had nearly had enough. Among other obstacles, his deep-draft vessel had regularly encountered the shallow depths of Mississippi sandbars and the shoals of the Gulf coast. After running hard aground near Miami, he sold *Great Republic* and with characteristic determination replaced it with a twelve-foot rowing boat. Blackburn managed, with a leather strap around each wrist, to row another two hundred miles up the coast of Florida, at which point he'd had fully enough, and took a steamer back to New England.[1]

Yet Blackburn had thought of the island too. I was entranced. I pulled out my road atlas, with its detailed representation of American rivers—the book most often by my side—and studied the route and possible alternatives. By the time I had finished *Lone Voyager* I'd decided that the ideal nonmotorized vessel, for its shallow draft, carrying capacity, and ability to progress in wind or calm, was a rowing boat. And over the following seven years, years spent discouragingly far from navigable water, my bedtime reading was often from the atlas. I wondered how many miles I could row in a day, and for how many days on end.

I had plain adventure in mind, to be sure. I imagined camping along riverbanks, dodging coal barges, and simply being in a boat on the water. But there was more to it than boyhood fantasy, and it's not enough just to add that I wanted the physical challenge. Over a period of several years, in a recurring dream of descent into darkness, I found myself following narrow, wooden, rickety stairs, dimly lit, perhaps by a hanging bulb, to a musty cellar, which in turn led through a trapdoor or some gaping hole to other stairs and other cellars, one below another. In variations of the dream I followed tunnels borrowed from Edgar Allan Poe—ever constricting but not dead-ending—or ventured into darkened water through which I dived headlong, uncertain whether the bottom was feet or fathoms below. Sometimes I carried a light that emitted a murky glow, then died. Other times I had enough light only to say the darkness was not absolute.

The dreams were tense, yet void of fear. I was not running from anything, but was being drawn toward some unknown, in cellars and tunnels and oceans never fully plumbed. To me, they suggested an inner search for something more, perhaps, for something richer, more off-centering than what my everyday, familiar routines allowed. It was true, I'd been treading water, wondering what was next, and waking up in the morning had become more of a habit than an opportunity. Days were becoming forgettable; they blended too quickly in memory. It was time to derail the train, jump off, and walk into the nearest forest. Not that the dreams alone motivated me to set off rowing, but they reflected, amid my work for one bureaucracy and then another, a need and desire to step, as Robert Frost titled one of his poems, "into my own." In a culture of acquisition and enlargement, I felt an impulse to stop, step back, observe, and live by my wits and material minimums.

And so I decided that I would row the circuit I had traced with a finger as a boy, the same orbit that captured the sailing Blackburn, a circumnavigation whose point of departure would evolve into a point of return. For the real meaning of circumnavigation lies not just in movement from Point A to Point A, but in the opportunity to mark change in oneself at two different times in the same place. The beginning becomes the end as we labor, react, create, flourish, or suffer to make it so. In short, to answer the question that was to become so common, nothing possessed me. I possessed myself.

The route would begin in New York City and lead to the Gulf of Mexico, following a series of waterways including the Hudson River, the Erie Canal, and Lake Erie. With a nod to those merchant mariners, including Blackburn, who'd claimed the Great Lakes were as treacherous as any oceans they'd sailed, I would search for the simplest portage from Lake Erie toward the Allegheny or Ohio. The Ohio leads to the Mississippi, and the Mississippi gives way to the Gulf. And, if I made it that far, I would row the Gulf coast to Key West, and the Atlantic coast back to Brooklyn.

In a rented sandstone farmhouse on the Zuni Indian Reservation, where I'd spent the previous few years teaching and running the local newspaper, I saw a magazine advertisement for a rowing shell I thought would be appropriate for the trip, and with a description of the route, sent off a request for a brochure. Soon I received a letter from the company offering the use of one of their boats, a sleek scull with a sliding seat and long oars, for my endeavor. I was ecstatic. As I stood outside my local post office, where tumbleweeds often roll down the main road until they get caught up in some wire fence, and four hundred miles from the nearest body of open water, the trip had suddenly become a reality. I left my job with the newspaper and headed east.

The Beginning of a
Nearly Breathlike Habit

THE RECLUSIVE FRACTION OF MYSELF wished to set out
unannounced, anonymous, the way you live your life when guided
purely by your own interests and motivations. Or the way one refuses
help when help is needed, stubbornly, martyr-like, trapped by the idea
that success is tainted by a second set of fingerprints. On the last night
before setting out I stayed with a friend in Manhattan in his one-room
apartment in a four-story tenement on Mott Street. The following
morning I sat in the apartment's rear window, wide open on one of
the first warm days of spring, waiting for the phone to ring, hoping to
hear that one friend or another had managed to borrow a car to transport the boat from Mott Street across the Brooklyn Bridge to Old
Fulton Street. Alternative modes of transportation were considered: a
taxi driver might have been willing, for a small fortune no doubt, to
lash the boat to the top of his cab. A grocery cart could have been
discreetly borrowed to tote the thin vessel down the sidewalks of
Houston Street to the East River. Or, with enough help, I could have
just carried it, and all its gear, to the water's edge.

Looking down from the window, I studied the scull, which lay in
the middle of a courtyard strewn with urban debris: old bicycles, a
rotting picnic table, rain-soaked cardboard boxes. Rectangular slate

slabs that once contributed a certain refinement to the space were now cracked and overgrown. Long and slip-streamed, and freshly white, the boat was incongruent, the only object in the yard with an imminent mission, its greatest days still to come. And yet I could not, in studying it, have begun to appreciate what lay ahead in the rowing, what intimacies would evolve between me and my craft. In the corner beside me my gear sat packed in three brightly colored waterproof bags. The disassembled components of the boat's sliding seat lay jumbled like oddly shaped logs in a wood pile, and the long oars, with butt ends to the floor, reached with their spooned blades toward a corner of the ceiling. If I was mentally prepared for this trip, I realized, it was largely because I hadn't fully realized what I'd bargained for.

The phone rang, and a friend reported that her brother had offered the use of his truck, and that their parents would also be there to see me off. Another phone call, to ask how many people were expected, so that the right amount of bread, cheese, and other goods for a picnic could be bought. My reclusiveness was put in check.

Two hours later a riverside restaurant near the Brooklyn Bridge had offered the use of their floating dock in response to a last-minute request, and several snapshots of departure were etched in memory. The first was a scene of the naked boat descending slowly on several shoulders from the restaurant's patio to the dock. It was low tide and the wooden stairs descended steeply into the water, and required a lateral step across the murky river to the dock. Already a picnic of bread, cheese, sausage, and red wine had been spread out on a cloth on one corner of the wooden float, and bottles of water and wine were opened. One friend, in a photographer's off-center stance, focused on the hoisted boat and clicked. Across the river at South Street Seaport, the towering masts of the *Peking*, among the last of the clipper ships to round Cape Horn, were dwarfed by the buildings of the financial district, the foundations of which must surely have been funded in part by her cargoes.

Another scene, as I stood at the end of the dock, was of the river itself, whose slow drift northward was marked against the skyline beyond. The tide had turned as if the Brooklyn Bridge, which framed my view to the right, had expended a liquid breath and was now inhaling, carrying anything on it north.

An image of a group of friends, sitting and lying on the dock in the early afternoon sun. Some had only just met for the first time, and some shook hands and were reacquainted for the first time in years. Someone brought a bottle of champagne to christen the nameless boat. The bottle would have crushed the boat's miniature bow, so I popped the cork and stood pouring, drenching the foredeck. The champagne stained the wooden decking and found its way between the planks into the river.

Finally the boat, which rested near the dock's edge, was packed. My gear was tied in place, the oars were set in their oarlocks, and there was nothing left to prepare. I half wished to stay there, lounging, talking, dozing, eating, yet it was an event designed to send me away, not keep me, and I'd already missed an hour of favorable tide. Just as one decides, in a moment, to get out of a warm bed, I announced that I ought to go. Wearing a pair of white gym shorts and a moth-nibbled brown sweater bought in a Minnesota thrift shop a decade before, I turned away from the river to say, with all eyes watching, an awkward thank you and good-bye. My thanks was partnered with apprehension, for only I knew of the corner I'd had to cut in the inevitable rush of last-minute planning: I'd never before set foot in this boat. Thus my first day's goal of rowing beyond the bounds of greater New York City rested upon smaller goals, the first of which was to row out of sight before, if it had to happen, I lost a grip on an oar and tumbled into the April cold.

I recall a final scene, a two-minute movie, of sliding the boat off the end of the dock and into the river, and pulling it alongside. The hull, even loaded with gear, danced lightly on the water, and I warily set one foot in the boat, and then, with both hands on the oars for stability, pulled my other leg in and shifted my weight to sit squarely on the sliding seat. A moment later I was shoved away from the dock. I was afloat, tense, gripping the oars and watching to see that the blades were feathered, horizontal to the water's surface. Until I found my own balance, they would be my crutches. With a twist of my wrists the blades were then opened for a stroke. I faltered, corrected the heeling, and slowly turned the boat toward the river, my eyes shifting from the boat and its balance to cameras and familiar faces. Another moment in the lifelong process of learning to say good-bye. And then a stroke, uneven but effective, and the boat surged forward. And a second stroke into the current, which carried me around the floating restaurant, whose window-side patrons smiled, waved, and pointed, calling attention to me. I smiled back, then watched as the dock and those who knew me disappeared behind the restaurant. I was afraid to let go of an oar even long enough to wave. The tide was stronger than I'd anticipated, and within a dozen strokes I passed through the shadow of the Brooklyn Bridge, and into the light beyond.

I'd aimed on this day to get past the outer bounds of New York City, to row beyond the urban range to where I might find a safe place to pitch my tent for the night. I had no more than a vague idea of what self-accommodations the riverfront would allow. In fact—a confession—I'd planned virtually nothing of the trip beyond the day of departure and the combination of a suitable boat and gear. I would not map out my every move, and there would be no itinerary. I didn't want to be expected and I had no message to deliver. I'd been stuck in my future for most of my life, always, as the tribe had trained me to do, looking forward, planning, thinking ahead, then wistfully recalling the past and events that I'd never had the presence of mind to truly attend. So much of my life spent counting down, it made me lose a breath to think of the time I'd wasted, scanning narrow horizons, getting ready for change and progress. Now I would simply row, come what may. Although, as it turned out, at the last minute before leaving Brooklyn, where my throat felt scoured with sandpaper (the first symptom of a cold that I'd kept secret to avoid any suggestion that I delay my departure), a friend of a friend gave me directions to a river-front house in New Jersey where I would be welcome should I want a place to stay. "Watch for the Italian flag," I was told.

With the bridge behind me and the corporate skyline of New York to my right, I thought of stopping to take a picture but feared that in reaching for my camera, stuffed within a bag behind me toward the bow, I might lose both my balance and the camera to the river. Row further, we'll get a picture later, I told myself, much in the same way I'd bypassed highway exits, needing to make a call, yet unwilling to stall momentum.

On an impulse I started to count out strokes, thinking to count my way through fifty. I'd done the same while training on the rowing machine in increments of twenty or fifty or a hundred to help distract myself, and I'd closed my eyes while counting to avert them from the slow passing of time displayed on a digital readout in front of me. But now on the river I caught myself, knowing that if I tried to count my way through the miles to come, a distance to the Gulf I could hardly comprehend at this rowing pace, the trip would become an unbearable exercise in tedium; this watched pot would never boil. Once I'd started counting, however, the numbers followed automatically with each stroke, and resolving to not count out so many as ten strokes, I had to either stop rowing or else distract myself. In what would become perhaps the single most important decision of the trip, though it too was made on an impulse, I refused to stop rowing and resorted in a near panic to saying the alphabet out loud in reverse. I had noted with certainty no more than the seventh stroke by the time I worked my way through V, U, and T. Trained to count, my mind would tease me for months to come by simply noticing a stroke and giving it the number one, but the same mind would come to resist the quantification of experience.

As the Manhattan Bridge and then the Williamsburg Bridge passed above me, Roosevelt Island, a long stripe of land, presented the choice of which of its two shores to follow and my first verbal exchange on the water. Barely audible above the sounds and wake of his diesel-powered tanker, a ship captain called out as he passed me heading south, "Stay to the right!" But I had already committed to the western shore, the Manhattan side of Roosevelt Island, and after a brief and failing attempt to redirect the boat against the strong current and around the southern point of the island, I resigned myself to whatever would be the greater dangers of this channel. I called back weakly to the observing captain, "It's too late!" and soon saw that his wake was rebounding tumultuously off the island's seawalls. I took careful strokes as the boat rocked unnaturally and buried its bow in the waves, and the current carried me through.

I hadn't known that while the East River flows north on an incoming tide, the Harlem River, supplied from the north end of Manhattan by the incoming Hudson, flows south. The two meet halfway up Manhattan's eastern shore at a three-way intersection called Hell Gate, around 96th Street, and, after a brawl, resolve their dispute by draining east into Long Island Sound. Though I kept my bow pointed toward the mouth of the Harlem and pulled hard on the oars, visual fixes on land told me I was making little progress, and worse, being drawn toward the sound. I realized that I should have hugged Manhattan's shore where the current's rate is decreased and even reversed by its friction with land, yet I'd already drifted so far out that the two rivers easily engaged me in their dispute. Great systems of swirling water collided and frothed and lost track of themselves. I pulled harder, but with caution, realizing that in a stubborn attempt to beat the tides I might lose my balance amid the twisting flow. Marking inches of progress against the shore, I aimed for the southern point of Ward's Island, which guards the mouth of the Harlem. There I might at least get out of danger, and if lucky play my way on eddies upstream. The swirling, imploding pools created by each stroke of the oars flowed behind me in pairs, churning, contorted by the fascinating currents of this watery intersection, and blended into its larger scheme. Finally, by the shore of Ward's Island, so close I scraped an oar blade on a submerged ledge, and gaining small fractions of a boat length with each stroke, I made my way into the narrow Harlem River, crossed easily to its Manhattan shore, and took what advantage I could of its eddying periphery.

Over my shoulder, while watching for fishing lines and emerging detail around the furthest, gradual bend in the stream, I saw the lone jogger trotting north along the promenade. I gained on him with each surging stroke, glided at his speed, and then fell behind as my momentum was stalled by the weight of my body sliding aft. I studied the oars as they flexed with each stroke and levered the boat through the water. My heart was thumping full bore, my hands chafing, and I was utterly content, even incredulous to find myself, twenty years on from a childhood curiosity, rowing north from New York City on my way to the Gulf of Mexico. With the elegant reach of the oars for propulsion and the water behind the stern gently boiling with each stroke, the jogger noticed the bow passing into his view, looked fully down at me, and, as he waved, I called up to ask him where we were.

IMAGINE YOURSELF sitting in the scull, facing aft, as if on the sterndeck of a ferry as you watch its wake. What lies ahead of the boat is behind you, over your shoulder. Your view while rowing is of the place you left, where you last said good-bye. The boat is heading north and you are facing south. To your right is the skyline of Manhattan Island, a riverbound reef of human thought, aspiration, and industry expressed through architecture. The starboard oar is in your left hand, and port is in your right. Pull on the left oar and the boat bears right, toward Manhattan; pull right and the bow swings left toward the Bronx. It seems that everything is reversed, except that when your body moves forward with the stroke, the boat moves forward too. To hike a distance equivalent to this rowing trip, I would have had to walk twice across the country—backward.

The boat is seventeen feet, nine inches long. Its prow rises little more than a foot above the water's surface, its stern perhaps ten inches. It is double-ended and sleek like a kayak. Like a child's plastic toy motorboat, it is constructed of two molded shells: the bottom hull, with a partial skeg—a fixed fin toward the stern to track the boat through the water—and the top, which provides narrow decks fore and aft that dip bathtublike to form a center cockpit, where I sit. The two shells are glued together, and the watertight space between is accessed through a porthole in each deck. By itself the hull weighs forty pounds, less than the small bag of concrete you might have hefted to your shoulder, or about the weight of a five-gallon bottle of water. Had I not been raised in the Massive Era of Chevy Impala station wagons, the boat might not feel so small. Yet with my own weight and that of my gear, which is piled haphazardly in the limited space of the cockpit, the stern deck of the boat dips notably underwater as I reach my body aft for the beginning of each stroke. As the river endeavors to pull me down for a peek within, it occurs to me that perhaps my first error was in choosing a boat from the safety of the landlocked New Mexican high desert.

A single black aluminum beam, half the length of the cockpit and set on two footings along the centerline, provides tracking for a sliding seat. The seat rolls freely, fore and aft, on three sets of two-inch wheels. At the aft end of the beam, a set of footrests with adjustable straps provides a brace against which to push with your legs for each stroke of the oars. Attached perpendicularly to the bottom of the beam is an aluminum pipe, which, with a few exhaust-pipe bends, acts as an outrigger to hold a set of oarlocks over the water eighteen inches beyond the gunwales. Imagine you're sitting on the seat and looking at the aft end of the beam, where a bracket is bolted upright to the beam between the two footrests. In your peripheral vision you can see the outriggers to your left and right. Now imagine two braces, straight tubes of black aluminum pipe, which reach like the hypotenuses of a triangle from the supporting bracket outward toward the ends of the outriggers, to which they are attached with C-clamps. The ensemble resembles a crossbow aimed toward the stern. Yet, where the cross-

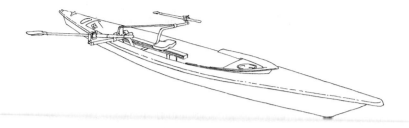

bow would send an arrow back toward the Brooklyn Bridge, the oars, with oarlocks for fulcrums, lever the hull toward Albany.

As you row, the sliding seat expands the range and power of the stroke by incorporating the use of your legs. Thus, not only does it extend the duration of each stroke in comparison to fixed-seat rowing, as in a regular dinghy or rowboat—the arms reach further toward the stern for an extended stroke—but a longer, more powerful pair of oars can be applied with efficiency. A scull, put differently, has a longer stride than a standard, fixed-seat rowing boat. Or say the wing cadence of a heron compared to that of a gull. The oars themselves, each one nine and a half feet from the grip of the handle to the blade's grip of water, are made of varnished yellow basswood, light and strong.

The spoon-shaped blades grab the water in a four-count cycle that begins with the catch, and is followed by the stroke, the release, and the recovery. You start from an easy sitting position on the sliding seat, with your legs straight and your feet strapped into the footrests. Then, as if reaching to touch your toes, oars in hand, pivot your torso at the hips toward the stern. While reaching, a slight pull of your feet against the footrest straps and a contraction of the legs draws you aft on the sliding seat. The rubber grips of the oars—as simple as those on a child's tricycle—are held lightly but surely within your fingers, and as you push the handles aft, the blades sweep forward through the air toward the bow, almost out of your view and ready to plunge. With your body now cocked in a horizontal crouch, ready to pull, drop the blades in the water. Do not force them but instead, as I would later be instructed, "just let them find their depth."

The stroke begins, cricketlike, with your legs. Push against the footrests and your body slides toward the bow. Keep your arms straight out; you are pulling, yes, but only by hanging on, letting the legs alone power the blades. As you continue driving with the legs, open your back from its toe-reaching position, so as to sit up, with the spine straight, and broadly contract your lateral and deltoid muscles. As the back opens and the legs approach full extension, now pull your arms toward your chest and finish where your thumbs graze your ribs. The sounds of the stroke emanate from beneath you, where wheels and bearings enable your slide, and from within you as you exhale one breath, and from the blades of the oars, a mere two square feet of sculpted wood façade that have so disrupted the indolent water that the hull surges forward through a boat length and a half of the river's surface.

Given the merest assistance the blades release themselves from the water. Press down slightly on the handles of the oars while gently twisting the grips toward you a quarter turn. In an elegant instant the spooned blades abandon the stroke and feather into nearly horizontal forward flight toward the next catch.

Release leads to recovery; remember, reach for the toes and slide into a crouch on your way to the catch. It also marks the beginning of the hull's glide, a nearly silent report on the technique and power of your last stroke, the sculler's equivalent to the long arc of a hurled baseball, an echo of your own self. It is here, as the boat glides on the liquid rind of the earth, and you slide slowly aft for the catch, that you are most likely to fall possessed into rowing. Here your gaze becomes fixated by the churning pools left at each release, or by the feathered blade in silent flight above the reflecting water (and the blade sheds estuarine tears, which drop one by one like the first melt from a frozen roof), or by the wake of the hull, which contracts the water's reflection of the sky as the boat accelerates with each stroke, then loosens its hold as the momentum ebbs, flattening the image.

Once in steady rhythm the movement of the blades becomes metronomic, entrancing. The sound made below the surface reports efficiency: near silence indicates the blades have cut too deeply, while loose splashing tells of a shallow catch. Catch, stroke, release, recovery: the beginning of a nearly breathlike habit, a cycle that will be completed more than eight thousand times on this first day alone.

My pop-up tent is stored in a waterproof version of a seabag, which has room also for a sleeping bag, an inflatable mattress, and a small pillow. In a second bag, a waterproof duffel, I've brought five T-shirts, two pairs of gym shorts, a pair of light cotton pants, and the motheaten sweater. In addition, I have a fleece pullover, a wool hat and gloves, and long underwear, all to confront the remaining cold of late spring. Should I need to present myself in more than gym shorts and a T-shirt, I carry a pair of clean canvas shorts, a light wool Pendleton shirt, and a new pair of canvas shoes. Also in the duffel are two cameras, one an old single lens reflex, a scuffed and dented victim of my previous negligences, and the other a pocket-sized point and shoot.

In a third bag, a rubberized but not quite waterproof carryall with a zippered top, is a first aid kit, a Primus stove in its own plastic container, a compact set of pots, a frying pan, a bottle of cooking oil, and a dull variety of food that includes spaghetti, dried noodles, dried apricots, and a few apples. Also within are my toothbrush and related items, a flashlight, a pocket knife, and two Allen wrenches for adjusting the sliding seat, footrests, and oarlocks.

A fishing rod lies along the length of the cockpit, and otherwise there is little room for more than my bags and several gallons of water. On this first day I have lashed the bags into the boat, fearful that I would lose them to some rogue wave or breaking wake, or, worse, to a capsize. I will soon grow lazy about this, however, as the gear seems to stay in its place. In the remaining space by my feet and beneath the center beam, a handheld bilge pump lies next to the fishing rod. A bright-orange boxy life preserver, a five-dollar special, is stowed near to the seat. The truth is that I don't wear it because it would interfere with the completion of the stroke, where the knuckles of my thumbs graze my ribs. Thus my vanity is spared. A heavy sponge helps mop the boat dry, a white canvas hat keeps the sun off my face, and a yellow rubber raincoat will shed most of the rain.

The scull has two enclosed storage areas, one beneath the foredeck and another beneath the aftdeck. I can access neither while rowing, and so use them to store the nonessentials: four foam blocks the size of bricks should I ever wish to transport the boat cartop; a groundcloth for protecting the bottom of the tent or for covering the tent in case of leaks; a small tackle box; a supply of camera film, matches, and flashlight batteries; half a roll of duct tape for temporary repairs to the hull; a spare oarlock. I also keep a journal and an address book, and such weighty classics as *Middlemarch*, which I envision reading while resting in the boat beneath a shading willow.

OVER MY RIGHT SHOULDER I hear the sounds of tools and metal, and of men talking, at first unintelligible and faint, yet unmistakable amid the urban hum as even the slightest notes of human voice carry over the water. I had not paid much attention while planning to issues of personal plumbing and now, somewhat pressed for time, I row toward a dilapidated wooden pier, a makeshift marina with several docks, one half submerged and half stripped of its decking, all still rafted together from winter storage. The voices become clearer; several men are working on a partially disassembled engine set up on a stand at the end of the pier. A short distance away another is kneeling, hammering nails into the crooked wooden runway that leads from one of the docks. In the background and looking my way, several women sit at a painted blue picnic table with two young boys, perhaps eight and ten, not quite playing by their sides.

Adjacent to the marina is a shallow cove of marsh grass, the merest trace of natural riverfront along Manhattan's shore. The marina scene is what I might have expected to find along some rural stretch of the rivers ahead. Several oil drums converted to trash cans sit on one dock, and a stack of old tires, presumably used as boat fenders, sits on the corner of the pier. The young man hammering notices me out of the corner of his eye, turns toward me on his knees, and watches as I approach. I begin to call out to him, then catch myself, take a few more strokes to bring myself within speaking distance and look again, half over my shoulder. With the sun behind him and the brim of his baseball cap pulled low, I can see little of his face. Suddenly uncertain about my choice of greeting, I opt for "Hey!" And receive from him silence, but attention. Should I have said "Hey there" or "Hello"? It is unclear whether one section of a patchwork building beyond the picnic table is a store, and if so whether it has opened for the boating season. "I'm looking for a place to buy something to drink," I tell him, as I slowly spin the boat to face him more directly. I hope that a purchase will soften my imminent request for facilities.

"Sure," he says, standing. "Tie up over there." He points to the edge of dock guarded by trash barrels, and walks down the runway to take my lines. At this point I have gotten into the boat once, and I've rowed it for a couple of hours, but I've never stepped out of it. I aim to do so knowingly, to imply competence, and discreetly test how best to shift my weight from the sliding seat to the dock.

"Where're you headed?" he asks.

"New Orleans," I respond with some hesitance. I'd called out the same answer with exuberance earlier to those I'd seen fishing along the riverfront, just as you might have hollered anything at all from the safety of a passing school bus. But now I'll have to explain myself. New Orleans, I tell him, eye to eye, yet chin down, as if it were an uncertain lie.

"You're going to New Orleans—in *that*?"

I nod.

"So," he pauses, "where'd you start?"

"The Brooklyn Bridge," I answer, "a few hours ago." He studies me for a moment, then turns and calls up to the men working on the engine.

"This guy's rowing—*rowing*—to New Orleans!" he exclaims.

"Better you than me!" says one with a smile.

Soon relieved of my primary purpose, and having been given a can of ginger ale out of what may or may not have been a store, I am invited by the most gregarious of the three women to sit at the worn picnic table, scattered with cans of beer and packs of cigarettes, while the men go back to work. She's heavyset with tightly fitted black pants, a red T-shirt, and a black zippered fanny pack around her hips. With a short auburn haircut, a ready smile, and a slew of questions about the trip, she appears game for whatever the whimsical world may choose to present. Her two less certain companions across the table appear to be understudies. One of them, perhaps Rod Stewart's long-lost twin sister, drifts between focused and forthright questions about my personal life and muffled delirium as her head hangs down slightly to the side, hovering above her arms on the table. The third, who smiles constantly, sports a brown bobbed haircut, an oversized denim jacket with sleeves rolled back, and a smouldering cigarette.

"So," asks the woman with the fanny pack, "what do you eat?"

"Well, I've got spaghetti, dried soup, I might catch some fish—" I pause as I can see she's already focused the next question.

"How're you going to cook all that?"

"I've got a stove in the boat."

"You've got a stove in your boat?"

"It's a little camping stove. It's small."

"So," she begins to summarize, "you're gonna eat spaghetti and soup"—she searches—"and what else?"

"Fish, maybe."

"And fish. That's it?"

"Well no, I'm sure I'll be able to find other things to eat too."

She holds my eye for a long moment, then turns to the woman with the cigarette. "Did you hear that? Are you listening to this? You should be paying attention to what's going on here! This guy is going to row his boat to New Orleans—that's in *Louisiana!*—and he's going to eat fish he catches on the way!" She stares in silence for added effect, then looks at me, stands, and takes a few steps toward the end of the pier for a clearer view of the boat.

It's funny how one thing leads to another, but then food is a seed of many interests. During the thirty minutes we've been talking I've glanced often at the water, wondering when the tide will shift. An ebbing Harlem River would assist me toward the Hudson, yet the Hudson itself would then be flowing seaward against my northerly aim. Not knowing what lies ahead I feel the urge to leave, and start to say so by shifting my legs from beneath the table to the other side of the bench, a physical hint at departure prior to standing up to say thank you and good-bye. The fanny-pack lady is standing already, however, now taking pictures with my small camera, and then, in a slightly stunning moment, I find her sitting in my frozen lap, facing me, with hands on my shoulders and eyes closed, attempting to gallop like a child on a motorized horse for which her mother will not give her fifty cents, self-engaged in a fantastical, arrhythmic rhapsody of human longing. "Yeah Baby!" she cries, swinging one arm up in the air as if riding a bull. Spring on the Harlem River, indeed!

She continues to have her way as I sit passively, awkwardly glancing at her friends, who seem pleased, though not surprised, by this unexpected entertainment. The Rod Stewart look-alike is laughing so hard she again is unable to keep her head up. Across the pier the men, much to my relief, appear thoroughly amused and continue working on the engine. What's in that fanny pack anyway? "Look at me!" she exclaims to no one in particular, though I can hardly help looking myself. Her exuberance, tidelike, will soon ebb, I hope, and it does.

Thus initiated to the human element of the trip—and standing at the first opportunity—I thank them for their company and make my way toward the boat. As I walk across the pier, one of the men steps away from the engine, and in mock discretion with a smirk on his face says, "Hey, I don't know if you can find any room in that boat, but you're welcome to take them with you!"

THE HARLEM RIVER leads suddenly west to the Hudson like a narrow corridor to a great hall. I've driven across the Hudson many times, from the Berkshires toward Albany, and from Manhattan to New Jersey. But now I will see it for the first time as it really is, not just a landscape seen momentarily from a highway bridge. The river is more than just a fleeting suggestion of escape and adventure. To me, its broad sweep fading into distance is a question, *Who are you?* Stripped of your conventions and routines, and of your titles and reputation, without a résumé, solitary and spare, what remains of you? And implicit in the question is an invitation to those of us who've found ourselves stuck in rush hour traffic on the George Washington Bridge, watching as our imagined selves disappear around the furthest bend in whatever craft seems most Odyssean. Come on, says the river, take a detour into yourself. Leave your car behind. Your Post-it notes will wait.

Was I out to find myself? A question I would occasionally be asked, and which would always smart with its condescending tone. But maybe the answer was yes. Not that I was lost or wayward. Perhaps I was out to find more of myself. Or else just to be on the water, alone within the natural world from which, or within which, we've emerged.

Now I can see it, beyond the soaring Henry Hudson Bridge, which crosses the mouth of the Harlem to connect Manhattan to the Bronx, and beyond a low, swinging train bridge. Still on the protective Harlem, I watch as waves on the mile-wide Hudson surge and tumble, failing to keep up with the wind that created them. It is late afternoon, and the Columbia University boathouse is nearby; prudence suggests

I should wait there for calm before heading onward. But I feel I've waited long enough. I pass beneath the swinging bridge and row a slow, surveying circle. If I were to lose my wits about the trip I would likely do so here, intimidated by the vast river that dwarfs a tanker heading south. Yet with an eye over my western shoulder I steadily pull myself and the boat into a new current.

THE HARLEM RIVER is quaint compared to the gaping Hudson, the breadth of which is proclaimed looking south by the nearly mile-wide George Washington Bridge, whose catenary tracks the eye in a sweeping inverted arch across the river—*river* as it's called, and so I'll call it. In fact the lower Hudson, from Troy south to the sea, is not a river but an estuary, and I will row its flooding tides nearly all the way to the eastern outlet of the Erie Canal. Mindful of the consequences of losing my balance—I am uncertain in the waves whether I would be able to climb back aboard were I to fall out—I follow the eastern shore of the Hudson, rowing a dozen feet from where staccato waves are breaking on a shoreline of crushed rock, the bedding for a set of rails that guides passenger trains to northern rivertowns with such Old World names as Sleepy Hollow, Ossining, Poughkeepsie, Rhinecliff, Stuyvesant, and Rennselaer. My slight bow pounds through the waves with each stroke of the oars as the blades nearly vanish in the river's silted water, and occasionally a well-endowed crest floods the foredeck and sends a portion of itself over the forward coaming, designed to keep the cockpit dry. Watching for the sun's descent and wondering how long I have before dusk, I plot a crossing of the broad river toward the towering basalt Palisades of the New Jersey shore. There I hope to find protection from the still-gusting northwest wind.

Now is as good a time as any, I decide, for the rocky eastern shore offers no cove or beach but instead carries straight to the horizon. During a lull in the wind I pull hard on my starboard oar and the bow swings northwest into open water. Gripping tightly, I concentrate on the vital mechanics of each stroke: feather the blades for stability over the water and they slap against the rising crests; pivot for the catch and plant them surely but carefully in the shifting liquid; pull the stroke, allowing one blade to grip soundly in the trough between two waves while the other plows beneath a crest and is suddenly, as the wave passes, released into air. I falter sideways in my balance, but recover. The stroke is followed by release, and the hull's speed ebbs through the buffeted glide.

Toward the middle of the river I see a red navigation marker, the only point of reference to divide the crossing, and I aim for it as the merest token of safety. Though the space between me and the railroad bed widens visibly minute by minute, the Palisades seem no closer, and I wonder at what point the far embankment will become a safer destination than the one I've left behind. Unfettered by the shoreline, the wind on the open river seems to have increased, and a wave rebounds squarely off the starboard bow, expands into spray as it gains altitude, and showers across the boat as if to taunt me for having ever attempted to reach the New Jersey shore. I glance at the bilge pump lying near my feet, and row on. Downriver I can once again see the skyline of Manhattan, which had been briefly hidden by the rise of Harlem, and the slowly shrinking towers of the financial district suggest the distance I've come from the Brooklyn Bridge.

At last within the cool and placid shade of the Palisades, the glassy water allows my trifling wake to dissipate unimpeded, and across the river the remaining light reflects against the bluffs of Yonkers in autumnal glow. A distant pane of glass slowly catches the deepening fire, blooms starlike for a dozen strokes in even flame, then dies. A brief echo of the solar repetition. In dusk the smaller details blend into larger shapes of land and water and sky, and, uncertain of the remaining distance to the welcoming Italian flag, I monitor the uninhabited shoreline for a spot to camp. An occasional patch of sandy beach invites a landing, and here and there I can see where I might fit the tent on near-level ground between boulders that had been shed by the cliffs above. But I continue on up the river, and soon after I've conceded that the light of day has vanished entirely, I catch the glow of a floodlight beyond a slight protrusion of the shore. Minutes later I see the green, white, and red flag, illuminated as it gives shape to a wakening breeze, and marking the end of the day of departure.

That night before turning out the lights I see myself in the bedroom mirror. I wonder, having finally set out, if I might see something new, something in my eyes, but there is nothing I haven't seen before. Across the river the lights of Dobbs Ferry, not twenty miles from the brilliance of New York City, suggest little more than a village, and it is easy to imagine the night view of a hundred years before.

· 3 ·

A River-long Neighborhood

MEET ANYONE ON THE HUDSON, it seems, and you're part of a river-length neighborhood. I start, by chance, with architects, with a senior architect at Sneden's Landing, and the junior architect who lives down a footpath in the house next door, a rower himself who commutes to his office across the river with a set of oars on all but the most tempestuous days. A dinner at one house leads to a barbecue the next day, where I meet a Croatian architect from Croton-on-Hudson, who with her husband invites me to spend the night on my way further up the river. She meets me the following day at Ossining, after an early southwest wind helped sail the boat up the Dutch-named Tappan Zee—once the Tappan *Sea*, by the village of Tappan—where the river broadens for nine miles. I am taken in, doors are freely opened, and I am repeatedly invited to "make myself at home." In Zuni, in western New Mexico, I was once told by a friend that "the way it used to be, if a traveler came to your door you would take him in. It didn't matter what time of day it was. It could be eleven at night. If you didn't have much food you still fed him. People trusted each other, and out here you were happy to know whatever news the person had. You wanted to hear about where he was coming from and where he was going. Now we lock our doors and want to know what someone is trying to sell us."

The past is usually idyllic, of course—"back in the good ol' days"—and aside from the occasional marvels of modern medicine and technology, we often think of the present as an overall degradation of living. And yet I'm finding "the way it used to be" right here, right now on the Hudson. Human curiosity about one another, a root source of hospitality, is timeless. I am, as my Zuni friend had described, invited to sit and to drink: "What would you like? We have water, milk—prune juice!—and a couple of sodas." I'm offered the use of showers in which, stripped of all defenses, uncertain of my position, and yet allowed into one of the most private enclaves of any home, I feel humbled by trust. Whatever I might have to thank someone for—and the range of assistance will steadily diversify over the course of the trip—it is for trust of inclusion that I feel most indebted. There is really not much more one person can do for another upon first meeting than to say, *Come in.*

On each of the first days of rowing, the northwest wind rises steadily by midday and carries through the late afternoon, making northerly progress difficult, if possible at all without swamping the boat. The fourth night of the trip is the first night spent in the tent, at the head of the beach at Croton Point Park, which juts out from the eastern shore of the Hudson like a comma to demarcate the northern reach of Tappan Zee from the southern end of Haverstraw Bay. The point includes not only the site of the largest oyster shell middens in the eastern United States, but also the more recent and hulking midden of the Westchester County dump. The regional dump is now closed and its unnaturally even grades, vented to release combustible gases, are planted with grasses and wildflowers.

The sleep that finally falls over me ends abruptly as I wake with a start in fear I've overslept, and that wind will have the better of my day once again. In the previous two days I'd managed nine miles and four miles, and although I have no particular schedule for the trip, I've reasoned that I should eventually be able to row thirty miles a day and still have a chance to look about in river towns along the way. I also have in mind the goal of reaching the Gulf of Mexico before August as an attempt to avoid some of the summer heat along the rivers. I unzip the tent to find that the sun has not yet risen, but treat every zephyr of wind as a threat and am rowing by six, hands and bare toes chilled in the cold air.

In the late morning as the wind gathers I reach the waterfront at Garrison, a lovely setting across from West Point, where a riverside park with a gazebo is shaded by weeping willows. Not a municipal park, square and sectioned and marked with restrictive signs, but a small lot donated for public use by a local resident. A cluster of adjacent buildings hints of Main Street, though the road itself is no more than a cul-de-sac, at the end of which, perched on a slight hill overlooking the river, is a general store. I buy a newspaper and sit on the gazebo bench while a small class of elementary school students is let into the park for recess. A mile or two inland, I am told at the store, is the main town of Garrison, while this small area seems content to remain unto itself.

I'd been encouraged downriver to look up Bob Boyle of Garrison, a Hudson River historian and, since the 1960s, a noted and successful opponent of a variety of land developers and polluters. Bob first fought against the planning of a nuclear power plant slated for the base of Storm King Mountain, across the river near West Point. The end result was a victory both for local grass-roots environmentalists and for American environmentalism in general, as it set a legal precedent for a citizen's right to sue on behalf of the environment itself. One successful fight led to other fights, and Bob had been described to me before I met him as the Rachel Carson of the Hudson.

We sit beneath a maple tree while he tells me about a challenge posed since the late 1940s by General Electric, whose Hudson Falls plant farther upstate had been leaking and dumping 1.3 million pounds of highly toxic polychlorinated biphenyls, or PCBs, into the river. General Electric, by its own admission, was increasingly aware of the dangers of PCBs, whose carcinogenic nature had already been noted by the late 1930s. Yet the fledgling environmental protectionism of the several decades following World War II, when PCB-formulated lubricants were used to produce a variety of electrical equipment, including refrigerators, had not yet evolved to confront such pollution. Thus, while GE knowingly polluted the river, it broke no environmental law.

Because of the relatively heavy weight of the chemical, it has not been flushed out to the diffusing sea as one might hope, but has settled at the bottom of the river, from which it rises quite literally through the food chain. The question remains of whether amelioration should be left to the river's natural ecological processes, such as they are in the face of poisonous intrusion, or whether the river should be dredged where the PCBs are particularly concentrated. Moreover, would dredging actually succeed in removing the toxins, or remove only a portion while stirring up the rest, thereby setting the river's own response back several decades? And if dredging is the answer, who should bear the cost?

Bob tells me that a river is like a person's life, with a beginning, a middle, and an end. From anyone else this might sound like the text from a condolence card, but from him, with his let's-get-on-with-it voice, weathered face, and reputation as a heavy-hitting eco-slugger against the largest utilities and corporations, I take the simile with me. I also take a health advisory brochure from the New York State Department of Health, focusing on "Chemicals in Sportfish and Game, 1998–1999." It reports that "Women of childbearing age, infants and children under the age of 15 should not eat any fish species from waters listed below," including the Hudson. From the Troy Dam, near Albany, south to Catskill, about thirty miles, citizens are warned to eat no fish except for American shad because of PCBs. From Catskill to the Verrazano Narrows Bridge, near open ocean, the advisory warns against more than one meal per month of any of the following: American eel, Atlantic needlefish, bluefish, carp, goldfish, largemouth bass, smallmouth bass, rainbow smelt, striped bass, walleye, white catfish, or white perch.

I'm left with a question that will linger: how to determine whether a refrigerator, or a car, or a computer so improves the quality of one's life that the environmental costs of its production and maintenance are justified? It's the pollution we don't see that helps keep the economy humming and that allows us to ignore that question. But now, on the Hudson, though I cannot see the PCBs, I know their story and cannot recall that refrigerators, though unfailingly convenient, have ever been fundamental to my happiness. Who, for that matter, can look back and ask, "Whatever would have become of me without my Ford Fairmont?"

So I leave behind my dreams of trolling for fish along the rivers, and on an evening departure from Garrison the long, exhaling breath of the northwest wind is all but expended as the cooling air approaches a moment of barometric balance. Yet still there is a breeze, faint as the whispering between lovers that drifts into sleep, so delicate it makes no sound, stirs no water, and is sensed only as the slightest brushings of cool air over skin. As the last light of dusk gives way to a full moon rising over the hills of Garrison, I pull my way toward open water, away from the shadowed shoreline and into lunar light. There is no other sound but the sounds of rowing, of the plunging of the blades into blackened water, of the seat in slow rhythm along its track, and of the wind, its velocity equal to and created by my own speed, blowing past my ears. To my left, facing aft, a dusting of lights marks the village of Garrison, and to my right the granite walls of West Point, fairly glowing in the moonlight, defined against the evening sky, windows lit from within, slowly but perceptibly drift in their relation to the brightening stars above. The distant blasts of an airhorn, like the call of an elephant, echo up the river, announcing the approach of a passenger train from the city, and soon the deeper drone of its wheels and engines rolls up the river too.

West Point guards a rare bend in the river's course, a mile-long S looking north, and as I row toward its eastern shore to take advantage of the bend's speeding effect on the tide, I look over my shoulder and see at first only lights, red and green bow lights and a white stern light, and then begin to hear a droning diesel. Minutes later I can make out the dark mass of a boat, probably a tanker. We are at opposite ends of the S; the ship is ahead of me heading south, and soon we'll pass. Aiming to row with certainty outside its channel, I pull toward a shoreline of bare cliffs that I've been told descend vertically to the deepest point along the Hudson. I pull harder as we approach each other, perhaps two hundred yards apart. I hope to pass unnoticed, not only to avoid his silent or muttered rebuke for my lack of navigation lights—it hadn't occurred to me that I might row at night—but to spare him the mystery of a man rowing the river on an April night. Are there others, he would have to wonder, and if so, ahead or behind?

Whether I've been spotted I cannot tell, but now we've passed and I watch as the ship slowly bears eastward to follow the contour of the channel. I look for the moon to show me its wake, more curious than concerned, and glance over my shoulder as the upper bend of the S straightens to the north. And then, electrifying, the brilliant beam of the ship's spotlight exposes an aisle of water and shoreline off its port side, sweeps downriver toward Garrison, holds its position, then reverses toward me, stopping momentarily as the captain scans the shoreline. Did I show up as a small yet constant tick on his radar screen, or was my white hull lit by the moon? The beam shifts toward me again but still I pull long and powerfully, my adrenaline abetted by the sound of the pools sent broiling with each stroke, and shift my exhilarated gaze between my surging wake, the still shoreline by which I've been learning to gauge speed, and the light itself, whose source magnifies as it swings toward me. And then, as I wonder what to do once discovered—how much can I say with a distant wave?—the light is extinguished, and I've evaded all but the most ambiguous entry into the ship's log.

Somewhere in the bend I pass the point at which the "Great Chain" of two-foot iron links, each weighing 150 pounds, was stretched across the river during the American Revolution. It was a tedious—imagine forging a quarter mile or more of such heavy links—yet ingenious attempt by colonists in 1778 to stymie the threat of British domination of the Hudson corridor, which would have isolated the forces of the northern colonies from those to the south and west. If the chain, pulled taut just feet below the river's surface, did not cause a fatal leak in a British warship, it might at least reef a hull long enough for the delivery of dispiriting blows via cannonfire, and discourage additional attempts at navigation. No British captain was ever so embarrassed, however, as the young Americans succeeded by other means in containing royal warships to the south. Now, at West Point, on a bluff facing north on the Hudson, a fence of two dozen of the original links memorializes the colonial resolve to achieve independence from England.

Now a musing breeze stirs the river's surface and the moon reflects in patches of uncountable shimmering tiles. The river has straightened and West Point is dead astern, and to my left, though drawn by the sounds of bantering voices and music, I pass the lights of Cold Spring. Within several miles the mass of Pollopel Island, little more than a thimble of land a quarter mile off the eastern shore, becomes discernible. Pollopel is more commmonly known as Bannerman's Island, after Francis Bannerman, a Scottish-American dealer in used military equipment. After buying the island in 1900, Bannerman designed and built a castle in old Scottish style to use as both an arms warehouse and a summer retreat. Sold to the state in 1967 and gutted by fire in 1969, the building and its grounds are now abandoned. I pass within a hundred feet of the castle itself, can see stars through its burned-out windows, and, as the hull thumps on a rock below, am easily dissuaded from calling it home for the night.

Farther up the river, I edge close enough to the wooded shore to notice a small group of boys, judging by their chatter, walking along the water's edge, shaded from the moon. I can't make out details, but can see that they've stopped and are watching me and the boat as we pass in near silence. "Hello," I call out, but am met with neither reply nor movement, and I row on into the night.

· 4 ·

Two Paths Cross
in a Small Kitchen

EVERY SO OFTEN you just walk around a corner and you're in the right place at the right time, and you marvel at the fact that if you hadn't forgotten the keys that morning, or if you'd stepped on the gas to make it through that yellow light, you would have missed the beat. Blind luck. Or you may say it's fate, that the Grand Plan made you forget the keys so you'd still be in the pharmacy when your future husband came along and started sniffing the shampoos.

In the riverside village of Rhinecliff, a quiet hamlet without even a gas station, I ask a man repainting the wooden trim of the corner café whether he knows of a pay phone nearby. He tells me I can use the phone in his art studio next door, and when I return to thank him we get to talking. He reaches out his hand and tells me that his name is Alan; he is perhaps in his late forties, with slightly graying blond hair beneath a worn canvas baseball cap. He's wearing a pair of old sneakers, khaki pants that display the drips of other painting jobs, and a white T-shirt. With his bucket of paint, a job half done in satin white, and the blossoms of a fruit tree beneath a spring blue sky reflecting in a large window of the café, Alan is central to the idyllic scene that he creates, in part, by the time he gives to a passing stranger. I get the sense that it doesn't matter whether he finishes painting today or tomorrow, that if a hawk were soaring on a thermal overhead, he would notice it and stop to watch. He tells me that he was a rower himself, back in college, and with the ease with which he offered the use of his phone he invites me to spend the night with his family in Rhinebeck, the larger town just up the road.

The following morning I am sitting alone at a small kitchen table drinking tea. I study the children's artwork on the walls, and am distracted for a moment by the chickens I see through the window, strutting and pecking—an unusual sight in what some would call a high-dollar town. For the first time on the trip I have the purest sensation of being in the present, and I sit quietly absorbing the details around me, astonished to find myself drinking tea out of this porcelain mug, sitting at this table, in this kitchen, in this neighborhood. How it all could have led to this, from the events of my life ten years ago to the events of my life ten days ago, I haven't the faintest idea. My presence here seems on one hand so overwhelmingly random— why not the kitchen at the next house, or in a town across the river?— and yet so natural that it almost seems meant to be.

Alan is married to Michelle, a petite woman with a craze of black hair and seemingly boundless energy. He has walked the children to school—the family car is used only by necessity—and Michelle talks to me from across the kitchen. She fills the kettle, stacks dishes, which clatter, and talks about her children, Stella, the youngest, and Isaac. *Stella by Starlight*, I think to myself, and soon learn that Isaac can play it for his sister on the violin. He is ten years old.

When Michelle looks at me she looks me dead straight in the eye. The movement of her mouth makes the sounds, but it's her eyes that deliver the meaning. As we talk amid her activity I get the sense that wherever she's looking she is totally focused on me, and she includes my name in almost every sentence. She steps outside to the backyard for a minute with a stack of plates from breakfast. Now she is framed, from where I sit, within two panes of the window. I cannot hear her as she brushes scraps of food onto the ground, and it seems for a moment that I am watching a silent film through the glass. The chickens, which saw her coming, peck frantically. She leaves the dishes on a wooden table in the yard, which is where they get washed in the summer. The neighbors, whom I first thought of this morning when the roosters crowed before sunrise, must think they're nutty. Yet I already count Alan and Michelle and their two children among the sanest people I've ever met. They seem to have a real genius for living, each one.

My particular awareness of the moment persists, a feeling that I have rarely experienced in the routines of my previous life. A sense of fate, I conclude, goes hand in hand with the unexpected, the surprising, and the new. What if I had somehow been able to plan this visit, if Alan and Michelle were friends of friends? Would I still feel the same way, not only pleased to be here in company and safety, but mystified by my presence and at the same time struck by a sense that there's nowhere else, in this moment, for me to be?

It's a big house, a Victorian, with tall ceilings and tall doors, and plenty of rooms I haven't seen. But so far everything has happened in the kitchen. This is where Isaac put his shoes on before going to school, and Stella brushed her long brown hair while fighting back grins. Now the kitchen door opens and I expect Alan the moment I hear the latch. But it is not him. Instead I see an old woman step carefully, methodically, through the door, turn to close it, and step into the kitchen. I feel as though another actor has appeared on the stage. I can't tell if she's seen me through her large shaded glasses, which were last in style in 1976, and which seem once again in style on her. She is an unexpected presence.

She has beautiful, curling, untamable black hair and dark skin. I try to guess where she's from: India? No. But certainly from Asia, from the middle of the world. She's dressed in a bathrobe and soft slippers, which drag slightly with each of several steps until she has taken center stage on the wooden floor. She then speaks with a South African accent, and I am riveted. Turning to Michelle, whose back has been to the kitchen door, she says, "Good morning, darling. How are you today?" How many mornings, I wonder, over how many decades, has she said the very same thing? For it is now clear that she is Michelle's mother.

"Marcina!" cries Michelle. "I'm fine, Marcina! How are you?" Marcina is still standing in place—frail, but regal.

"I'm very well, darling, thank you."

"Marcina, we have a guest! I want you to meet Nat. He spent the night last night in Isaac's room. Nat's rowing a boat up the Hudson, and Alan found him down by the river!" I stand up and greet her. Marcina looks at me through her glasses. I get the sense that she'd fully absorbed my presence by the time she'd closed the door. She reaches out her hand and says, "It's so very, *very* nice to meet you."

"You must be from South Africa." I couldn't wait to say it.

"Yes, I am from South Africa. Do you know South Africa?" she says, the way an aged Queen Susan the Gentle might have asked me what I know of her world of Narnia. I tell her that at the age of twenty I'd bought a plane ticket without a plan, aiming to travel through this land of apartheid—some of whose laws were still in place—which might also instruct me in the realities of our own American, pre–civil rights apartheid. By chance before leaving I'd met the daughter of an Afrikaans woman living in Johannesburg, and the son of a Xhosa family from a village near Umtata, in what was then the "homeland" called Transkei. I stayed with each family, and taught in the village school.

At the time, Nelson Mandela had just been freed. He'd given a speech in Umtata, and I could not keep myself away from the private reception that followed in a library adjacent to the auditorium. In a room in which I could see clusters of people standing and talking, Mandela stood alone. He had grown up near Umtata, and perhaps his pre-presidential presence was not a big deal. Or else people were shy. I recognized a singular opportunity and introduced myself. I recall that we talked about education, but what I remember above all is his height, his flawless posture, and his reserved yet boundless pride.

I glance through the window at the chickens strutting around outside. I'd first lived with chickens in the village, had washed the freshly laid eggs. There had been no running water, no electricity. The day was over when the light was gone. Two of my worlds have intersected.

"Please, sit down," she says, and we both sit at the table, with its one side to the wall. "So you know South Africa," she says wistfully.

Marcina is tricontinental—of Malaysian, Afghani, African, and Scottish background—as well as tritheistic, with connections to the Muslim, Jewish, and Christian faiths. She is the daughter of Zainunissa "Cissy" Gool, an early opponent against both male domination of South African politics and the growing movement of apartheid laws in the 1930s. Gool was a leader of various political organizations, and in 1938 became president of the Non-European United Front, which represented a wide variety of coalitions, including the African National Congress, in the fight against racist government policies. Also in 1938 Gool was elected to the Cape Town City Council, on which she served for twenty-seven years. Ironically, the South African government under Jan Smuts instead turned its attentions toward the fight against fascism in Europe, while continuing to lay the foundation for its own fascist society at home. Cissy Gool died in 1963 of a heart attack, or one might imagine of a broken heart, two years after the government, Nazi-like, required South African women of non-European descent to carry passes as a method of apartheid control.

Michelle explains most of this. Marcina, who had washed Gandhi's feet when he stayed with her family on visits to Cape Town, fills in the gaps, sitting with a ballerina's posture on the kitchen chair. With her story told, Marcina is silent. She casts a sighing glance out the window, looks back to me, and with the voice of a girl says, "And then we came to America. It was all a very long time ago."

"Marcina," says Michelle, setting a tea cup on the table in front of her mother, "would you sing Nat the song you made up when Stella was born?"

"Yes," she says, without the slightest hint of shyness. "It's a simple song, something to tell Stella about where she comes from." She stands up, facing me. I'm reminded of the manners of schoolchildren in the village, and my surprise when, having asked my first question to the class, the boy who first raised his hand stood up to give his answer. I feel awkward now to be the audience, to be seated when Marcina is standing. Where is she as she's singing? On a ship, as her children look through the deck railings, or so it seems as she gazes through her dark glasses out the window, her voice careful with every note.

Over the ocean and very far away,
I left my country on a summer's day.
The ship was in the ocean, waiting
  In the bay.
I took my family and we sailed away.

And we went over the ocean
And very far away,
Until we came to the USA
And there we stayed.

It is a migration song, as American in nature as the national anthem. She sits down. I thank her and tell her that the song was lovely. Michelle fills her mother's tea cup from a porcelain kettle, then fills mine and her own. She sits at the table too.

"So tell Marcina about your trip!" says Michelle. I summarize the route. Marcina has only one question.

"And what does your *mother* think of this?" I reassure her that this is nothing; my brother's planning to sail a boat around the world.

Alone. It's a good answer, which usually leads to more questions about my brother. Marcina doesn't buy it.

"She must be *very* worried." I tell her I call my mother often from pay phones.

"Have you spoken with her today?"

I pause. "No."

"Well then I think you should call her right now." Three minutes later I am speaking with my mother through an orange rotary telephone mounted on the wall near the kitchen door. Marcina and her daughter sit at the table drinking tea.

Alan returns from walking Isaac and Stella to school. I'm invited to spend another night, but say I ought to continue on. As Alan will soon be walking back to his studio, he asks me if I'd like to join him, and I am soon packing my duffel and heading with him out the front door. Marcina follows us out to the driveway, still in her robe and slippers. I tell her what a pleasure it was to meet her.

"And it was a very great pleasure to meet *you*," she says in her genteel accent, bred on the stage of one of the great modern dramas of political consciousness. "I hope we'll meet again some day." Marcina, unforgettable South African, matriarch of this family, with her sunglasses and wild hair, standing at the end of a gravel driveway, self-possessed and free.

"I hope so too," I tell her.

Alan avoids the roads, and we follow a path that weaves between pastures and through woods several miles to the river. Already the breeze has risen from the northwest and small whitecaps texture the water, miniature avalanches down the faces of waves. We launch the boat and shake hands, watching each other as I force my way, bow pounding, upriver, and he sits at the edge of a granite wharf until, when I can just barely make out his figure, he stands and walks away.

· 5 ·

Remember This

To me the very idea that I would set out on a trip like this seems natural. Others ask me why or how. "Don't you get lonely?" they wonder. Some surmise that I must have been abandoned by a wife, that I must need time alone, time to figure things out. But I always reply that anyone could do it. It's a weekend camping trip extended, notable only for its distance. No permits are needed, just moderate expertise in a boat and relatively simple gear, whose price tag, even if I hadn't been given the use of the scull, would be less than that of the average college sophomore's used car. This is no exotic adventure beyond the range of the average water or wilderness enthusiast. No newly discovered coastline will be charted; the nearest Coke machine will rarely be more than eleven miles away. The canoe hanging in the neighbor's garage, if launched on the nearest seabound creek—and most creeks *are* bound for the sea if the rains have been generous—is a ticket to a journey of any length.

Eventually people's questions sink in, and I begin to ponder what stepping stones I could point to and say, *that's* where it started. Or, without *this*, I might have taken the trip, but with friends. Or, if not for *that*, it might never have occurred to me. Perhaps only the children of royalty, once they become kings and queens, can say with certainty why their lives evolved as they did, for they had so little choice.

But if I had to choose one defining memory of myself as a child it would be of an autumn afternoon, walking home from the school bus stop, plaid lunch box in hand, after another day of kindergarten. I was walking along the left-hand side of a neighborhood street, guided by the curb, with houses and yards to my right, and thickets and woods immediately to the left. My Keds kicked through the fallen leaves, mostly maple, and my eyes followed the meandering patterns of sand and soil beneath, sculpted by the runoff from the last time it had rained. I don't know why, but I stopped beneath the reach of an apple tree, where a path disappeared into the woods, and looked down it to a landscape I still remember as if I had seen it this morning. My feet were planted amid the colors of the papery leaves—New England leaves are most beautiful when dying and shedding—the tree sifted the sunlight in a pattern as still as the tree itself, and my shadow was cast slightly to one side. I looked down the path and was lost for a lingering moment, lunch box hanging in one hand, and heard myself mouth these words: "Remember this." I was five years old. To this day I don't know where those words came from, but I knew then that they could lock any moment in memory. This is my earliest recollection of presence, isolated from past and future. Moments later I took another step and continued kicking onward through the leaves up the road, a boy bound to the future on the first rungs of the long ladder of formal education.

I also recall sitting in the top of a birch tree looking out to the harbor in the distance. I was eleven years old and it was Thanksgiving, and the house was full of people: relatives, friends, my parents, my two older siblings. What was I doing in the tree? I don't remember it as play, not the way two cousins would go climb a tree together. It was simply where I wanted to be. Someone noticed out the kitchen's bay window and took a picture, which is now in the family photo album. One might say I remember this because of the snapshot. But in fact I have two versions of this memory. One is in the still photo, in which I see myself from afar. There I am in the tree as the photographer— my mother?—saw me. The other is a movie of my climbing the tree, one I'd never climbed before and would never climb again. The movie ends when I've nearly reached the top, perch myself as comfortably as possible on the slender limbs, and look through the bare branches to the harbor.

In a third image I am older, just out of high school. I had set out on a short voyage along the coast of Maine, from the mouth of the Sheepscot River to Bass Harbor. I was in a simple, double-ended twelve-foot skiff that I'd built out of plywood with my brother and father and that was designed to be either rowed or sailed. I don't re- member whether I had at the outset an aim to do one more than the other, but off Fisherman's Island, near Ocean Point, the wind died, and I recall taking down the short mast and sail, pulling out the oars, and setting them in their locks. And I distinctly remember my sudden resolve, in the posing and acceptance of a challenge, to sail no further on the trip, but just row.

In thinking about what has led me to this point, it is these three memories that surface out of tens of thousands. If the moment be- neath the apple tree, and the minutes in the birch tree, and the days of rowing the skiff had never happened, might I still be here, now, with a pair of oars approaching the junction of the Hudson River and the Erie Canal? It is impossible to say. But to answer the question of why I, of all people, am the one rowing this scull, I return without think- ing to these memories, to an experience of absolute presence in na- ture, to my preference for a birch tree amid a family celebration, and to the moment in a dying wind that I chose to define myself through rowing.

AT A MARINA south of Albany I pull in to find a pay phone, and before calling, stop to chat with several men who are halfway through the afternoon drinking shift at the bar. They'd seen me through the bay windows overlooking the Hudson as I'd rowed in and are curious to know where I'm headed. I tell them, then wait for what I'm sure will be variations on common responses. Thus far I've been told, in cruder terms, that I must be *disrupted* in the head, that I must have lost my *effluences*, that I must have *didym* the size of watermelons. Now, however, I'm simply told that I must have a lot of questions I need to answer. After making my call in an entranceway to the bar I exit to the parking lot, only to remember ten steps later that I need to make a second call. As I enter the hallway again I am privy to the conversation underway.

"... all the way to the Gulf of Mexico?" asks one. "He'll never make it that far."

"Not in that," argues another.

"I don't know," says a third. "He's made it this far already. And that's a hundred forty miles." I save my call for later, and step quietly back out through the door, wondering which of these men motivates me most.

I'VE HEARD ABOUT the Hudson River and the Erie Canal for longer than I can remember, but reaching the junction where they meet is less than the grand event that I'd vaguely anticipated. The canal is simply a left turn to the west—a right turn from my perspective—like Wayside Road off Main. In fact the turn is marked by a large sign in white letters on highway green: One white arrow points to the left for west, and another to the right, for north:

⇦ ERIE CANAL
SYRACUSE AND BUFFALO
CHAMPLAIN CANAL ⇨
WHITEHALL AND LAKE CHAMPLAIN
SPEED LIMIT 10 M.P.H.

If I'd wished to circumnavigate New England I would have headed north on Lake Champlain and the Chambly Canal to the St. Lawrence River, out the St. Lawrence to the Atlantic and around New Brunswick, west across the Gulf of Maine and back to Brooklyn. Another time, I think, as I arc the boat westward into the Erie Canal, which promptly leads to the first of a flight of five locks that lift or lower boats a total of 169 feet within a mile and a half. The thirty-five locks on the canal between the Hudson and its western outlet to the Niagara River and Lake Erie are all 300 feet long by 43.5 feet wide. Each stretch, or pool, between locks varies in elevation, and as Lake Erie is higher than the Hudson, most locks heading west will raise me, ultimately from 1.3 feet above sea level at Waterford, the eastern end of the canal, to 572.4 feet at Tonawanda, at the Niagara River. Yet mapped out across a page, the canal generally rises until Rome, New York, where it reaches 420.4 feet, then falls to 363 feet at Baldwinsville, then climbs again to its end. On graph paper the canal hints of southwestern mesas, rising and falling in clear terraces. Or one might think of these pools, some less than a mile long and others more than thirty miles between locks, as liquid stepping stones across the topography of upstate New York, from Waterford in the east to Tonawanda, 337 miles to the west.

I reach the first lock at Waterford immediately after turning into the canal. It is full, level with the next pool, 33.5 feet above me. The lock is the centerpiece of a Waterford town park—a weekend spring fair is underway—and after tying up to a dock and climbing a long set of cement stairs from the base of the lock to its observation deck, I watch as several other boats, local runabouts with outboards, transit in both directions through the chamber. I introduce myself to the lock-keeper, a man in his mid-thirties with long blond hair, tint-adjusting prescription glasses—they are semishaded on a glare-producing over-cast day—working blue jeans, and a denim jacket. He carries a clip-board and a small wad of cash from having collected locking tolls paid by those in the motorboats. Self-powered boats like mine lock for free.

He comes across as engagingly shy and gentle, though I guess that he's listened to his share of heavy-gauge rock and roll. He tells me that when I'm ready he'll lock me through slowly, as the filling of the chamber is turbulent and might flip me and the boat.

Back on the water the lock is imposingly tall; its two mammoth steel doors closed against each other, holding back a tide 33 feet deep by 43 feet wide, and 300 feet long—enough water, if it were suddenly released, to wash me back into the Hudson. I've been told to stay back from the doors as enormous underwater valves will be opened for the lock to drain to my level. That current in itself might topple me. I watch as the canal begins to flow, and soon find that a moderate stroke into the current holds me in place.

Locking itself is elegant in its simplicity. Since I am heading upstream, the lock is drained through its valves until its water level is at my level. Then the heavy gates, like the Doors of Durin, swing open as if on their own impulse, though one could easily imagine a pair of Tolkienesque dwarves assigned to the task, each one leaning into a door with his weight, but no strain. I row into the huge chamber, sidle up against one wall, and choose one of the ropes that hang down to help boaters keep from banging into one another as the lock is filled. My boat is most stable when both oars are in the water, however, and as I am alone in the chamber now I wish to confront the imminent surging of water while floating freely, away from the walls, but decide to not ask the lockkeeper to bend the rules.

Then the doors shut. They close with a low boom that resonates throughout the lock, and moments later the water appears to have suddenly reached its boiling point, welling from within as the upstream valves are opened. At first the tops of trees are all I can see of the surroundings, yet slowly their trunks come into view as the water rises gradually like a great elevator, taking me up with it. For a moment I can imagine that the water is instead stationary, and it's the rest of the world that is moving, slowly falling away around me. The up-

stream doors are then opened and I've been graduated to the canal's first pool heading west.

The Erie Canal is in fact a series of natural rivers, lakes, and dug canals. Looking at a detailed road map one can see its various names heading west: the Mohawk River (which I am now rowing), Oneida Lake, the Oneida River, the Seneca River, Cross Lake, and the Erie Canal, which ends at the Niagara River, the tail of Lake Erie that plunges over Niagara Falls. First constructed in 1825, the canal evolved over nearly a century as a route for commercial shipping, and was repeatedly rerouted and deepened in response to competition from railroads. Its current iteration was completed in 1917. It branches north to Lake Ontario along the Oswego Canal, south to Cayuga and Seneca Lakes on the Seneca-Cayuga Canal, and, now behind me, north to Lake Champlain on the Champlain Canal. The canals altogether are known as the New York State Barge Canal, no longer commercial but increasingly recreational. So early in the season, only a week after the Erie was reopened after its winter closure, I share the canal with seasonal nomads on sailboats and live-aboard powerboats, returning from winter months spent in warmer climates, headed for such Great Lakes ports as Rochester, Buffalo, Toronto, and Cleveland. The masts of the sailboats have been lowered and stowed on deck in order to clear the bridges that will come.

Howard Blackburn traveled the Erie Canal in his sloop and, unable to sail on the narrow channel, had no choice but to have the boat towed, which at first he did under his own power.

I had to tow the boat forty miles myself before I could get anyone to take her in tow. Then Captain Howard came along with two light boats. He agreed to tow me to Buffalo for thirty dollars. He carried a crew of three men besides himself and four mules.

One man and two mules would tow the boats for six hours. Then they would run the boats alongside of the canal, when the driver and two mules would come on board, and the other driver with the two fresh mules would take their places and tow us for another six hours.[2]

My own expectations of the canal are pleasantly contradicted and reshaped. I had imagined that much of it would be lined with the rotted husks of a former age of industry and commerce, and that the canal itself would be filthy. Instead I row through broad valleys of patchwork farms and between banks overgrown with leafy trees and thicket. Carp broil the water in mating ritual and a variety of fish jump in the evening calm. Several miles west of Fonda I come across a small inlet hardly large enough for turning the scull around and bordered by gardens of vegetables. A painted plywood sign announces:

KANATSIOHAREKE MOHAWK COMMUNITY
RE-ESTABLISHED 1993

Until now I have only heard about Indian communities trying to retain authorship of their continuing histories despite both the coercions and allures of American culture, but I have never heard of a tribe trying to re-create itself. Curious, I land the boat at a weathered pier no longer than the boat itself—Norman Rockwell might have painted a boy sitting at its end, bare legs crossed, with a homemade fishing pole and a straw hat—follow a path to a paved road, and cross the road to two large white houses, perhaps old farmhouses. One is a bed and breakfast and the other contains a gift shop, both owned by the tribe. In the gift shop I meet Tom Porter, the founder of the community, a warmly rugged man on a mission to make sure that the horses are fed, the prayers are revived—some of the community are currently engaged in a fast elsewhere on the community's four hundred acres, once Mohawk land and now reacquired—and the language is practiced. After talking for a bit in the gift shop, which includes Zuni, Hopi, and Navajo jewelry from the southwest, Tom invites me upstairs to the second-floor apartment he shares with some of the twenty members of Kanatsiohareke—pronounced, as a brochure explains, "Ga-na-jo-ha-lay-gay" and translated into English as "The Clean Pot"—most of whom are from the six tribes of the Akwesasne further north in New York. A large kitchen expands into a larger dining room and two bedrooms. But "dining room" is too formal. It's the center of living, defined by a large table and surrounded by an assortment of chairs. There is already food on the table: the remains of the last meal, the beginnings of the next meal, meals that overlap.

It is late morning and Tom says that I must be hungry with the miles already behind me today. I am reminded of Zuni, a culture whose hospitality revolves around food, where the first thing likely uttered to a stranger after basic pleasantries is "Come eat!" Or, if you've missed the sitting, then "Go eat!" For there's almost always still food on the table. Tom offers me tea, a banana, a bowl of Cheerios, and a burrito, and our conversation turns to issues of language and teaching at both Kanatsiohareke and Zuni. I'm lucky to have shown up when I did, for he comes and goes between the kitchen and a bedroom as he prepares to make a trip north. I know few Indians (I use that term intentionally, not only because it's the one commonly employed among the tribes I know in the southwest, but also because describing Sandias or Isletas or Cherokees as natives of a land named after an Italian explorer is not much better) in the East and am surprised to find an accent similar to the one I know among Indians in New Mexico. In the background, in another room, I hear a language entirely foreign to me, as the Zuni language had once been foreign, incomparable to anything I'd ever heard. It had been my pleasure in Zuni, as it is again now, to know that in such a culturally homogenized society native languages unintelligible to me still live on.

Back on the water I come across such towns as Canajoharie and St. Johnsville which, though they may have lost their sense of original purpose once provided by bustling trade along the canal, now offer the subtle richness of rural life and hints of a new economy based on the increasing recreational use of the water. At Canajoharie I am surprised by the local library's collection of twenty-one Winslow Homer oil and watercolor paintings, many of which I recognize. Occasionally I camp by the locks themselves, whose buildings are usually set on several manicured acres. Often when I come across a lock with no traffic the lockkeeper is mowing the lawns instead. Picnic tables and grills invite those on boats and others visiting by car to spend several hours, although camping is not permitted. This evening, however, I have been unable to find a clearing along the canal where I might safely pitch the tent, and continue rowing until I arrive at a lock at dusk. The lockkeeper has already gone home for the day and the grounds are empty, but a local road runs alongside the canal, and I'm both reluctant to upset the lockkeeper should he see my tent in the morning and concerned about what late-night visitors I might have. In the remaining light I row across the canal, now perhaps two hundred yards wide as each lock is paired with a dam, to a rocky beach with woods and fields beyond. It appears to be a park with playing fields on the left and walking paths through the woods on the right. Even though it is now empty and the nearest house looks about half a mile away, I wander quickly along some of the paths and return to the boat with an inexplicable feeling that I would not be alone here. I return across the canal to the lock and set up my camp on the most remote corner of the lawn, confident at least that I will wake up well before anyone arrives in the morning. I'll test fate here rather than take my chances with late-night visitors.

As on most other nights I decide to not bother cooking anything with my Primus stove and set of camping pots. So far in nearly three weeks I've cooked only twice, once with an open fire. I'm simply too tired at the end of a day of rowing to want to go through the routine of boiling water, cooking, then cleaning up. If eating on the trip were a social as well as a practical event I would feel differently. But I've been rowing an increasing number of miles per day—twenty-six miles today, yet it was only three days ago that, in rowing thirty miles, I finally exceeded the distance I covered on the adrenaline-assisted day

I left Brooklyn—and I've begun thinking of food more in terms of caloric need than taste. I finish a box of granola bars and an apple, and delve at length into a jar of crunchy peanut butter served on saltines. Granola bars will soon prove too expensive for my limited budget, and before long generic peanut butter and saltines, and apples, which keep well, and sometimes a can of sardines as an evening treat, will dominate my menu.

An hour after having landed for the second time by the lock, I've eaten and pitched my tent, and after checking on the boat a second time I crawl into my nylon home with a sleeping bag one size too small. Before zipping the tent closed I happen to look across the canal, where a flickering white light, a flashlight behind bushes and beneath trees, reports the movement of the hand that is carrying it. Who knows, I think—I might be missing the great love of my life, or the local entomologist out hunting for some rare katydid that has long eluded his specimen collection. But I was right. I would not have been alone. My instincts are becoming honed as weather, people, navigation, and my own abilities and limitations present a nearly constant flow of questions. Some are easy to answer with mere precedential judgment. I learned on the Hudson, for example, that the largest tankers pose little threat with their rolling wakes, while a half-planing twenty-foot pleasure boat is not only capable of swamping me with its tighter, breaking wake, but that the man in control is, generally, neither likely to notice me nor interested in slowing down. Yet instinct, with which we're born, runs deeper than the judgment we acquire with all of its learned biases. It was not judgment that urged me back to this side of the canal, but instinct, which I had the good judgment to heed. These animal instincts are perhaps just as present within us as they ever have been, yet as we create worlds in which we feel safe—an instinct in itself—we seem to need them less and less. However, like unexercised biceps suddenly put to use they are quickly tuned when needed.

The following day I row thirty-four miles—my longest day yet—to Sylvan Beach, at the east end of Oneida Lake. I'd been warned about Oneida as far back as Waterford, where I'd learned that every year on the open expanse someone is caught fatally unawares by sudden winds that whip the lake into a frenzy of breaking waves. It is twenty-one-miles long by perhaps five wide, and if its shape on a map were a cloud in the sky I would see a tailless sperm whale heading east. The daily northwest wind I'd faced on the Hudson has continued while rowing the canal, yet even when it comes head on it never raises more than wavelets. But I've assumed all day that the same wind I've hardly noticed on the canal must have thrown the lake into havoc, and by five o'clock when I first see Oneida's broad horizon I deem it unrowable. Its swells even penetrate the canal until they're quelled as they rebound off the banks.

I'm tired, but know that wind from most any point west tomorrow will yield the same result, and so decide that I will row this leg of the trip at night. I expect the lasting breeze to die as the sun sets, and hope that the lake's surface will quickly calm. In the meantime I'll rest, eat, walk about. Sylvan Beach is primarily a summer community, and when the weather turns warm it blossoms in the form of a full-time carnival along one stretch of beach. Motorboats are tied up to a cement wall that borders the canal, which leads by a side channel to a small marina filled with pontoon boats. The carnival is a village unto itself of flashing lights and sound and throngs of people on this Saturday night. From the canal I can see children with huge paper cones of cotton candy, a merry-go-round, and beyond that a roller coaster from which young people scream in delighted fear.

Reluctant to leave the boat in such a public place, I row through to the end of the canal and brave my way onto the open lake long enough to round a corner to where the beach continues on the south side, which seems strictly residential. Surely I'll find someone who won't mind if I pull the boat up on their lake frontage. As it turns out many of the homes are still closed up from last winter, and after securing the boat above the water I cross a vaguely private lot between two houses with boarded windows and enter the streets of a neighborhood. The sun has almost set as I fall into conversation with a middle-aged man working in his garage, in front of which a restored 1965 Mercury Comet glows deep green in the ebbing light. His name is Rich Ziezio, a firefighter nearing early retirement. By the time we've taken a slow walk around the car, with a look inside the immaculate trunk and beneath the hood, he has taken a keen interest in the trip, and insists that I take a bag of supplies from his kitchen cabinet: spaghetti, some cookies, freeze-dried soup, and a bunch of bananas.

Upon returning to the boat I meet an older woman I'd asked along the road about local diners. The one she'd recommended had already closed, as she'd feared. She's come down to see the boat and find out whether I've managed to get myself fed. I ask whether she knows Mr. Ziezio and show her the bag of his groceries. I tell her I'm planning to head out tonight so as to beat tomorrow's wind.

"I live right there and I'd like to send you on with something. It won't take me a minute." She looks at me like she's a runner waiting for the starter's blast. I smile and thank her, and say I'd appreciate it. Fifteen minutes later, after we've made a trip to her kichen, she and several of her neighborhood friends escort me back to the boat. The wind has steadily died with the loss of its solar source and already the lake has begun to relax, although large swells still texture the horizon. I stow my gear carefully as I'm sure to take some water over the bow, and stop for a half moment while repacking Rich's bag, in which he had discreetly placed a twenty-dollar bill. It seems at times that this is a trip of angels. I pack it away and turn to shake hands with those near me, who then wave me on as I row into the coming night.

I keep my bow straight into the remaining breeze and swells and head northwest toward the northern edge of the lake. I hope to avoid other boats, particularly police boats, as I still have no proper navigation lights beyond a bright flashlight. Slowly the lights of Sylvan Beach become smaller, and the clear, moonless sky is lit with stars. Within half an hour I have approached to within a quarter mile of the north shore of the lake. The breeze has died completely and I nose the bow west toward Brewerton, whose lights still lie beyond the horizon. I can see the glow of Syracuse to the southwest, and mark my progress in the dark night as much by the slow passing of radio towers on the south side of the lake as by bonfires burning along the sparsely settled northern shore. Voices carry across the water, telling here of families with young children, and there of couples spending the weekend together, and sometimes report more boisterously of younger partyers, perhaps local high school or college students with the weekend chance to be themselves unattended.

I have recently acquired my first injury, not debilitating at the moment, but potentially, I fear, the end of the trip. I've developed in my left wrist what I can only guess is carpal tunnel syndrome, or tendonitis. I'm hoping that it's merely a matter of technique, and during the day had studied my wrists during each stroke and noticed that my hands bend slightly upward from the wrists as I pull. I have tried to focus on keeping them straighter and am reminded of doing so now as they protest the long, repetitive day. Increasingly, no matter the amount of water or food I consume, I stop for short breaks and lean back on my bags with the oar handles tucked under my knees for stability. When I feel the growing weight of sleep I force myself up and, with the plural pronoun I've always used when speaking to myself, say dully out loud, "Well, we can't stay here all night."

I reach Brewerton at two o'clock in the morning, and despite the lights of several marinas can hardly see where I might land and pitch my tent. I am so tired I am tempted to do so beneath a willow tree in what is obviously someone's backyard. Yet I keep searching and finally stumble into a patch of grass beside a public boat ramp. Ten minutes later I am deconstructing the tent, whose poles of various lengths I'd numbly set in the wrong positions. Another five minutes later, and fifty-five miles from the lock where I last camped, I fall soundly asleep.

———

THOSE UNDER THEIR OWN POWER and on long trips, and those with unusual boats are of particular interest to lockkeepers, who by and large attend to local runabouts they see on a regular basis. I am always asked at each lock about my route and am often told about others who've gone before me. I hear of a Chinese-Canadian who left Toronto on a raft constructed entirely of other people's trash. It was powered by an outboard engine, but even that had been reconstructed from abandoned parts. The last any lockkeeper knew, the man, who'd headed east on the canal, had made it as far as Virginia. Another man passed through in a canoe with his dog and all of the domestic belongings he could carry; his wife had left him in New York City, and he'd decided to return by paddle to his hometown of Buffalo. I hear of other canoeists too, as well as kayakers, and I seem to be a near-novelty for having a pair of oars. I'm frequently asked, "What kind of kayak is that, anyway?"

The most astonishing story is of a man who also rowed with oars, but in a canoe. I was told by one of the first lockkeepers I met that he was on his way from the salt waters of Coney Island to the mouth of the Yukon and the Bering Sea, along the west coast of Alaska, but he didn't make it. The story continued to evolve several locks later, yet became only more difficult to believe: I was told that the man got sick somewhere in the Yukon Territory, only weeks from achieving his goal. So several years later he returned to Coney Island and started again. I find the story more unlikely with each telling. What would prompt the man to return to his starting point once recovered from illness, rather than just continuing on? Imagine, rowing from New York City almost all the way to eastern Siberia, one of the longest possible lengths of the North American Continent, almost making it, and then starting the same route over again. I sense that the truth has been victimized as in a game of telephone, especially since no one seems to know what became of the man after he rowed through their canal the second time.

As I ROW THROUGH ROCHESTER I pass through the intersection where the Erie Canal crosses the Genesee River, which I'd once hoped might be my portage route, as the headwaters of the Genesee lie just miles from those of the Allegheny. Yet as I rowed closer I was told about waterfalls along the Genesee, and came to appreciate that I would not make it far up that river before it became a rushing mountain stream. So I continue on, keeping my eye out for a way to get myself and the boat over the divide that separates the St. Lawrence River drainage basin from that which flows to the Gulf of Mexico. Several options, I see on a map, will be available along the shores of Lake Erie.

I ARRIVE AT LOCKPORT, NEW YORK, shortly before the lock-keeper's five o'clock closing time and am lifted forty-nine feet through two locks in a row to the final stretch of the canal. The upper lock is protected by two sets of doors for safety, as the water beyond is contiguous with the Niagara River and Lake Erie. I have little choice but to continue rowing, as the canal is now bordered on each side by twenty-foot cliffs created when the canal was dug through a section of the Niagara escarpment, a massive reef of sedimentary rock stretching in an arc from as far east as Rochester, New York, to Wisconsin. As dusk passes I resolve to continue beneath a rising moon until I reach the end of the canal. Now 492 miles from Brooklyn, which I left twenty-six days ago, I row between Tonawanda and North Tonawanda, joined by the last bridge across the canal. Late at night there is no one fishing from bulkheads, no motorboats puttering by, only an occasional car, and now a police car at an idle speed over the bridge. The canal just simply ends where the Niagara River, perhaps a mile wide, rolls quietly by.

I had been unable in the dark to spot any place remotely hospitable for a tent along either canal bank of the Tonawandas, and so turn the corner into the mild but steady current of the Niagara River, along whose banks the city of Tonawanda has a long, narrow park between the river and a road. I have little doubt that camping is not allowed, but at a boat ramp decide to row no further and pitch my tent as far as possible from the light of the nearest lamp pole.

Perhaps an hour later I am suddenly awakened by a bright light shining through the fabric of the tent, followed by a man's voice.

"Hello! Tonawanda Police. Who's in there?"

"My name is Nat Stone," I say with what lucidity I can muster, but before I can explain any more he continues on.

"Well there's no camping allowed in this park."

"I'm rowing a boat from New York City to the Gulf of Mexico. I just rowed out of the Erie Canal an hour ago and couldn't find any other place to camp. My boat's pulled up on the ramp." The light fades as he aims it in the direction of the boat. I welcome his momentary silence as a sign of capitulation.

"Well," he pauses, "I guess it'll be all right." I promise him that I'll be gone first thing in the morning.

"All right," he replies. "I'll let the next shift know."

But I am not gone first thing in the morning. I awake at sunrise to a conversation between two women out for their morning walk, and one woman seems to have raised her voice more than necessary: "Well I *know* they don't allow campers in this park!" Fifteen minutes later, with the tent crudely stowed in its bag, I am back on the water, still groggy with sleep as I begin the day's repetition.

· 6 ·

The Cool Flowering
of Light Below

I DO NOT STOP AT BUFFALO as the wind and water are calm on this slightly hazy day, and I've feared Lake Erie's tempestuous reputation as the worst among the five great and ornery siblings. Blackburn himself had commented that the Great Lakes were more dangerous in his view than any of the oceans he'd sailed, as one can batten down the hatches and be blown safely for days on end in an open ocean gale, but you won't be blown far on any Great Lake before drawing upon some wave-pummeled shoreline, with the nearest safe harbor characteristically out of reach. Erie especially, as the shallowest of the five, plays tricks on the unsuspecting mariner. Its average depth of ninety feet, combined with the likelihood of strong and sustained winds, can turn a glassy surface to outrage between lunch and dinner. If Oneida Lake had deserved caution, Lake Erie now deserves utter respect, and as I scan the shoreline leading south from Buffalo into the fading contour of its western arc, I recognize that which I'd gleaned from the road atlas years before while studying possible routes: Lake Erie offers few safe harbors along its shoreline. I'd heard from a Coast Guardsman along the Hudson that the southern shore of the lake consists largely of steep bluffs above rockbound beaches and cliffs rising straight from the water. Be careful when setting out, he'd warned, and be prepared each day to either make your destination or return to where you started, as there may well be no options in between. Indeed, as Blackburn warned, "Once out in the lake a little wind will do, for it seems that only a hat full of wind is enough to kick up a bad sea."[3] As I look more directly toward a blank horizon, only the lack of salt in the water confirms that this is not a great bay opening up to an ocean.

So I row past Buffalo, and marvel at the clarity of the lake's water, which even along the cityfront reveals details of the rocky bottom twenty-five feet below. I'd been under the impression that the Lakes in general were polluted to the point of national embarrassment and am again pleasantly surprised as I had been by the pastoral serenity of the Erie Canal. Though cautious upon reaching the first expanse of truly open water on the trip, I drift away from land in a straight-line shortcut across the arc of the shoreline. Slowly the basin of the lake deepens, and the pale boulders that minutes before had been reassuringly visible below me are now obscured by the depth of the water, which bends the sun into bouquets of softened light, shimmering and pulsing as the water's surface, a liquid lens, is brushed by the wind. It's these depths of water that hold my heart in both fear and love, water too deep to see any further than the cool flowering of light below. Where is the bottom? How far down? What's there? A place I'm afraid to go, because it's lonely and because I don't know what I'll find there, afraid that I might be changed. And yet it's the depths that fascinate me. They lock my gaze downward, as if into a dream in which I am merely Existence struck by its own mystery, with no help offered from Purpose or Reason, who observe with mocking smiles from a nearby bench.

Several miles out from shore I stop for a drink of water and eat a package of saltines with peanut butter. Though I am watchful for any change in the weather, it feels safe to rest for fifteen minutes in compensation for the previous night's brief sleep, curtailed by the early morning pedestrians. I check the horizon for squalls and motorboats, and register several small craft drifting, probably fishing, no less than a mile away. Deep on the northern horizon, toward Ontario, another boat, its wake exaggerated in mirage and its engine silenced by the distance, traces the straight line between water and sky. I look below me into the muted depth, and am lost for a moment in the greenish light, then shift focus and see myself reflected, peering down from a boat in the sky. I lay back on my bags, and with the oar handles tucked under my knees for stability, I doze as deeply as my instincts will allow.

I row for two days along the Erie coast, newly mesmerized by the flight of the blades, as the clear water fully reveals the span of their submerged catch. Along the Hudson and Erie Canal they had been partly obscured by the silty translucence, yet now the full reach and power of the stroke are exposed, as are the threadlike, lower stems of the upper whirlpools, which peel off the stroking blades like wildly twisting, molten wineglasses blown out of water. The line of the shore repeats a wavelike alternation between steep bluffs and even taller, stratified mounts, sixty to seventy feet in height and nosing bluntly out into the lake. In the humid haze on the second day I can see no more than five or six miles ahead of me, and in slow, funereal procession the peaking promontories reveal themselves and drift somberly past me as if they would continue without end.

Occasionally a stream empties itself through a break in the shoreline, and here and there a slight indent in the coastline, combined with breakwaters, offers a harbor. Otherwise the shore is as uninviting as I'd anticipated. Several times when rowing too close to land I find myself amid a constellation of boulders just barely submerged, and deposit small bits of the boat on some of these rocks as an acceptable toll to pay for the calm weather. Yet I can easily imagine the troubles I would face should a strong wind pick up from the north.

Having found that the simplest overland route to the Mississippi River drainage basin will lead me on Route 394 to Chautauqua Lake, I arrive at Barcelona, New York, in the late afternoon as the heavy, silent humidity gives way to growing clouds and muttering breezes.

Relieved to have safely reached my furthest lakeside destination, I paddle slowly across the small harbor, constructed outward from a slight depression in the shoreline with a combination of stone jetties, and land on a short strip of sand at Duff Monroe's Marina. My plan is to walk or hitchhike to the nearest lumberyard, purchase the minimum materials required to give life to my mental sketch of a two-wheeled boat dolly, and somewhere along the way, perhaps at the lumberyard, acquire the loan of a small arsenal of tools. I will need two two-by-fours, a set of lawn-mower wheels and one axle, a handful of nails, a handsaw, a drill, and a hammer. From this I will fashion a two-wheeled gurney on which to rest the boat, whose bowline will be tied to the strap of my duffel bag, which I'll wear around my chest.

Though I've rowed thirty-five miles today I am eager for such a constructive adventure into some town, and set out to ask for permission to leave the boat on the beach. With a couple of leaps over driftwood and across patches of green that might include poison ivy, I step up to the gravel parking lot of the boatyard, whose corrugated aluminum sheds, sailboats cradled in drydock, all manner of anchor chains and masts, and the occasional forlorn hull, could keep any boat fanatic occupied in observation and imagination for hours. As I try to determine which building contains the marina office, a weathered man with wire-rimmed glasses, in his early fifties and with a gray beard, walks purposefully across the yard. I ask whether he knows if the further building contains the office.

"That's it," he confirms, and by his manner of stopping to look at me I know he is more than a marina customer here to scrape copper paint off the bottom of his weekend cruiser. "What do you need?" he asks.

"I've got a rowing boat pulled up on the beach"—I turn halfway toward the boat, pointing beyond the weeds—"and I'd like to ask permission to leave it there for a few hours."

"Sure, that'll be fine right there. But you better tie it up. It's supposed to blow." He speaks with such authority that I don't dare ask whether I should double check for permission in the office.

"So where're you heading?" he continues.

"The Gulf of Mexico."

"Which way are you going?" He asks this as if he's made the run many times and is wondering if his favorite route is mine too.

"Well," I begin, aware that I may be on the edge of uttering the single most ridiculous thing he's heard all week, "I'm planning to go overland from here to Chautauqua Lake, and from there down to the Allegheny." He looks at me as if I have more to say but don't know it. I pause, then continue: "I'm actually looking for a lumberyard. I need to build a dolly so I can pull the boat."

"Then follow me," says Duff Monroe.

Without another word between us I follow him to a large storage shed, all but emptied for the summer, and into its cavernous shade. Several orphaned sailboat masts and a range of wooden blocks and metal frames for supporting and bracing hulls for winter storage lie strewn across the earthen floor. In a far corner one of the masts, whose confusion of shrouds and halyards is vined around its length, rests with one end on the ground and its middle lashed to a metal-framed version of what I'd intended to build, complete with inflatable tires.

"I built this for moving masts around the yard," says Duff. "All the boats are in the water now and you're free to use it if you want. Your hull should fit on it nicely." I express amazement that within minutes of stepping ashore I've been offered a ready and superior version of what I'd intended to build. Inflatable tires, for one, had been beyond my budget, and I hadn't been relishing the prospect of the clatter of plastic mower wheels over nine miles of pavement.

"You'll be going to Mayville if you're going to Chautauqua. I drive that way twice a week in my truck. I'll pick it up and bring it back." He describes the marina where I should leave the dolly. I'd thought from time to time over a period of weeks about how I would build such a thing, and while rowing had scribed blueprints in my mind for a contraption whose need I'd anticipated years before. As we free the mast from the dolly and wheel it out of the shed, Duff points to a picnic area where I can camp for the night if I wish and hands me the key to the shower.

Still eager to wander the streets of any given town, I secure the boat and walk inland, and what altitude I gain heading up the paved hill gives me, looking back toward the lake, a reminder of the security of dry land. The earlier breeze is maturing into a steady wind, which textures the vast expanse of water with the crests of breaking waves, erupting and fading brush strokes of white on blue-gray, a Winslow Homer painting brought to life. Within a half mile I reach what little there is of Barcelona, where two rural roads intersect near a scattered cluster of older houses on unfenced grassy lots, as if the choice presented by the crossing of two routes had simply been too much for passing migrants, and so they settled here. The intersection is served by a convenience store where I find cheddar-filled wheat crackers in plastic wrappers, six to a twenty-five-cent pack. After eating two of these while loitering in the empty parking lot, I return inside and, with the remaining change in my pocket, buy two more.

The wind increases throughout the evening. I pitch the tent in the picnic area that Duff had pointed out, and although I normally don't bother staking my tent to the ground, I secure it from every point available to brace it against the wind and likely rain. That done, I tour the yard and its drydocked hulls, mostly sailboats, but some powerboats too. Aside from utilitarian skiffs, powerboats have never captured my imagination. A favorite exception is my twelve-foot fisherman's skiff with classic sheerline, built in 1980 by a Maine lobsterman named Tarbox for $310, with half a bushel of herring bait thrown in for my lobster traps, and powered by a fifty-pound Evinrude. Otherwise, despite my boyhood fascination with cars, and a continuing regard for the ingenuity behind the design of the internal combustion motor, I've all but lost my interest in engines. And what's left to love about a powerboat? The faster they go, the less effect the water has upon their hulls as they skim across the surface, and the remaining motive is simply speed, getting from here to there, for whatever reason, to fish at a favorite spot, to dive on a wreck, or for no reason at all. And they require virtually no skill. A recent kindergarten graduate, given fair weather and an elementary knowledge of navigation buoys ("keep the red ones to your right when going home, kid") can go a long way before the tanks run dry. But put him in a sailing dinghy with the same weather and the same understanding, and he'll soon be capsized or otherwise befuddled. I consider myself lucky to have grown up with a father who was a collegiate rower, and an older brother who loves to sail, for if one's first experience on the water is easy speed, there's no obvious incentive to ever pick up a paddle, or wonder how it's possible to sail a boat faster than the wind.

Every hull suggests its own adventure, and I can entertain myself for hours on end given a boatyard full of cradled hulls to wander through. Deep-bodied, broad-beamed ketches make promises of landfall beneath billowing clouds among South Sea Island volcanoes. Deep-keeled, carbon-fiber thoroughbreds, essentially fifty-foot surfboards with hundred-foot masts, dare solo sailors to surf down forty-foot rollers at thirty knots across the landless desolation of the Southern Ocean. And wooden classics, Herreshoff sloops and Concordia yawls, hint of laps across San Francisco Bay on a broad reach and of August ventures among the islands of coastal Maine. It's the smaller boats, however, that stir my deeper curiosities, which inch for inch tend to embark upon the greater adventures. The shallow draft of a Beetle Cat or kayak, while capable on open water, invites exploration of tidal backwaters and remote rivers, and their limited size requires improvisation and resilience in the face of added exposure to wind and spray and sky. I'd rather paddle a restored canvas-on-cedar canoe down the Neosho River, though I know this tributary to the Arkansas River only from a map, than cross the Atlantic on a cruise ship. In the way that the architecture and the setting of every house speaks to a style of domesticity, every boat suggests a manner of exploration, and for the price of imagination I've owned a handful of the hulls in Duff's yard before I return to the tent, which is now convulsing in the wind. That night I occasionally wake as the maturing gale whistles around the metal sheds and rings taut boat halyards against metal masts.

· 7 ·

Mayville by Nightfall

THE NEXT MORNING in a light rain blowing on the continuing wind I hitchhike the couple miles from Barcelona to Westfield, New York, with Budda, a local apiarist and upstart ostrich farmer, whose shotgun lies propped against his pickup's bench seat after a morning turkey hunt. He hadn't heard a single turkey, and I tell him I am reminded of a time I came across a wild turkey without even looking for one. I was in the fifth grade and returning home from a fall weekend with my collegiate brother in Vermont, riding Greyhound and reading *Where the Red Fern Grows*, the first book to ever make me cry.

The bus gently heaved from side to side on an uneven road just straight enough for the then national 55-miles-per-hour speed limit. I can only imagine what the bus driver and his victim each saw the moment before impact, but I heard the smashing of glass and felt the bus swerve drunkenly as we came to a stop along a gravel shoulder. I was sitting toward the back and stuck my head around the seat in front of me to look down the aisle, where I saw a fairly flustered turkey strutting toward me. It stopped, seeming to realize that there were no empty seats, and swaggered back to the front. The driver, perfectly on cue, as if a company memo had arrived just that morning to add a wild turkey clause to his job description, pulled open the door, and the

71

ruffled beast, annoyed by having hailed the wrong bus, strode pompously, never looking back, into the late autumn woods.

"It lived?" Budda demands.

"Yes!" I insist, feeling some regret at having told such an unlikely, nevertheless true, story. Budda laughs, and I laugh too, imagining what Budda would have done if *he'd* been the bus driver.

Budda drops me at a breakfast diner, and I follow my two-dollar eggs-with-toast special with a trip to the Westfield library to read the news, all the while hoping for a clearing in the weather. At the library I meet a retired man, now a photographer by avocation, who asks me for help in searching the Internet for a birding site with his own images of two rare birds, including the stygian owl, whose presence in the United States he'd been the first to photograph. We get to talking about my trip, and, as he is a local and knows the route ahead of me, he offers to drive me part way to Mayville to study the hills of my hike; this is the first time I've scouted any part of the trip. We quickly become lost in conversation about birding and rowing, and from the elevation and speed of a Jeep, the hills pass below us unthreateningly. "This is pretty much it," he says when the slopes of the road begin to flatten; "a few more miles and you'll be at Chautauqua Lake." I point to a red-roofed farmhouse and say optimistically, "Okay, when I see the red roof I'm pretty much home."

Late that afternoon, despite no change in the weather beyond a slight, unpromising lapse in the rain, I wheel the dolly to the edge of the parking lot near the beached boat, assemble my gear in a pile on the ground, and lift the slim vessel to its first step across the eastern continental divide. With a spare length of yellow line I lash the hull to the dolly like a seesaw to its fulcrum and stow my gear within the cockpit. I remove the shoulder strap from my duffel bag and clip its ends together. I will use it as a harness over my shoulders and around my chest to pull the boat, and connect it to the boat with two feet of the bowline. Expecting something to be out of balance, I try on the harness and find that the contraption's center of gravity is slightly and favorably ahead of the dolly's axle and that the bow rests easily on the strap around me. Perhaps a steeper incline will shift the balance too far from the stern and send the bow skyward, but I'll make adjustments later if necessary.

Pleased with the initial outcome of this long-anticipated overland traverse—true, I've taken hardly a step, yet my only real concern thus far has been the equipment I would need, not the walk itself—I make a farewell tour to the far end of the boatyard, which blends into sandy beach washed by the still-seething lake. It was by chance that I'd found the fabled expanse of Lake Erie in a serene mood long enough, by a matter of mere hours, to pull the sixty-odd miles from the outlet of the Erie Canal to Barcelona and the first steps inland. With that distance fully behind me, I lose myself, with the weight of the bow still hanging from my shoulders, looking out across the water, which, though burdened by its own weight, mimics the surging currents of wind.

Now pressed for time if I wish to reach Mayville by nightfall, I turn from the lake, and in so doing diverge for the first time from Blackburn's route. He had headed farther west on Lake Erie, north on Lake Huron, around the hump of Michigan south to Chicago, and via canal to the Illinois River and upper Mississippi. It wouldn't have occurred to him to take my inland route, for even if he had managed to arrange transport for his twenty-five-foot *Great Republic* for the nine miles to Mayville, he would have gotten only so far as Chautauqua Lake, which feeds several creeks to the shallow waters of the upper Allegheny. Blackburn's crossing would, in fact, have had to continue to Pittsburgh before he'd have found water sufficient for the draft of his sloop. I, of course, had considered following Blackburn's route through the Great Lakes, but remained unsettled by accounts of the lakes' infamous weather. So our paths will not cross again until Cairo, Illinois, where the Ohio River meets and surrenders to the Mississippi, its stronger cousin.

Reassuringly, though previously unknown to me before I actually saw it, the sign marking the exit from Duff's yard and pointing toward the intersection at Barcelona and beyond, reads "Portage Road" in reflective white on green. I can only begin to imagine what Indian, French, and perhaps English explorers and traders have gone before me. How far had they traveled and to what purpose? Surely I am not the first to leave Lake Erie on Portage Road bound for the Gulf of Mexico, but I might at least claim, if nothing else, the least purposeful and least profitable venture of all, ordered by no chief, funded by no king, fueled in part by processed cheddar cheese on crackers wrapped in plastic.

The road soon rises in a steep swell of pavement, and my only choice aside from giving in to the weight of the boat and ebbing backward toward the lake is to dig in with short strides and pull, and to optimistically ignore the fact that my load's weight against the climb is greater than I'd anticipated. With the muscles in my legs soon burning, the hill flattens and I spin within the makeshift harness, now walking backward to try new muscles. Though I've walked perhaps a mere hundred yards of the nine miles to Mayville, I note with satisfaction the gain in elevation, which reveals the breaking lake beyond the roofs of Duff's boat sheds. I turn again, and soon cross the empty intersection at Barcelona without obeying the stop sign. A quarter mile further to the south the pavement rises again in a gentle arc across Interstate 90, which starts near Boston's Chinatown and carries fully across the country to Seattle. I'd driven this road in my first car, a trembling $900 special, purchased despite a bashed-in rear door and bald-to-the-wire tires from two slick-haired, pot-smoking cousins clad in black leather in Providence. "Mind if we smoke?" one had called from the backseat as I was shifting on a test drive into fifth, with my college sweetheart sitting next to me. "No, go ahead," I replied, expecting cigarettes. Despite making my first major purchase amid a flutter of red warning flags, I drove that car hitch-free for fifty thousand miles, including those now stretching east and west of this bridge. As I cross a trail of my former self, whom I now see zooming west toward an unknown future in New Mexico—had I even noticed this bridge? had my gas tank been too full to bother stopping for a look at the lake?—I continue south on a newer journey, whose long path I'll someday cross again in reminiscence.

Few drivers seem to take note of this odd gypsy getup, but instead stare straight ahead, as if pretending to not see an unalluring hitchhiker. Consigned to oddness, and with leg muscles in a steady first-degree burn, I look down and walk a mile or two to Westfield, through an intersection at a trot, and toward increasing steepness. Two miles later I realize that the Jeep ride up the hill had been lost on me, though maybe the lesson is that the only way to appreciate a hill you're about to walk is to walk it. I stop only to take a picture of a bronze-green plaque on a granite boulder, so nestled amid bushes that I wonder what year it was the last time anyone had noticed it, let alone read it:

THE OLD PORTAGE ROAD
BUILT BY CELORON IN 1749 WHEN HE
EXPLORED AND CLAIMED THIS REGION FOR
FRANCE. FOLLOWED AN INDIAN TRAIL AND
CROSSED THE HIGHWAY AT THIS POINT.
IN 1753 IT WAS REBUILT BY THE FRENCH
FOR MILITARY PURPOSES.

How to shift from the details of the present to a storied past? From my cut-rate blue canvas shoes with red rubber soles, from a passing beige Chevrolet driven by a mother of two—one of whom, with tousled blond hair, peers out at me through the rear window—and from the endless crust of pavement along the sandy shoulder of the road? How, amid the banal safeties of the American here and now to construct an imagined past of exploration, of colonization, and of being colonized, upon this very landscape? The present lies less in its date than in its detail, which obscures what once was, or was not, much in the same way that it's difficult to recall the look of a vacant lot after a house is built, after it's finally been tamed, sodded, and occupied. What might the plaque read a century from now?

THE OLD PORTAGE ROAD
WHOSE ETYMOLOGY, THOUGH ONCE
OF INTEREST, IS NOW FORGOTTEN.
LAST PAVED IN 2087 BY THE CHAUTAUQUA
COUNTY HIGHWAY DEPARTMENT,
AFTER THE OLD ASPHALT BECAME
WEATHERED AND CRACKED.
DRIVEN BY AMERICANS COUNTLESS MILES;
TO BE REPAVED WHENEVER FUNDING IS AVAILABLE.

The hill steepens along a succession of slow curves, and I soon learn I should not expect any encouraging waves from passing drivers. One car full of high school–aged kids does offer a communiqué out the back window of their white sedan, yet its ambiguous enunciation, something along the lines of "Blehwaaahha-you-blaaaaah . . ." quickly fades into a Doppler void and may have been followed by a question mark. I am left stumped except for my response of a dumb smile and a half wave.

Soon after, while walking forward, I hear a car pull up behind me and turn to see a tall, lanky man with rimless glasses and an easy smile step out of a burgundy four-door and quickly catch up to me on foot. Seeming to recognize my need to keep walking and perfectly adapting himself to my step, he says, "I just had to ask where you're coming from and where you're going!" I've taken to walking alternately forward and backward as far as a certain goal, such as a light pole or a road sign, and when I spin within my harness to now walk backward, he spins too for the same view. "I think I know the answer to this," he says after we've traded nutshell stories about ourselves—he is a local high school teacher on his way home from work—"but would you accept help in pulling your boat?"

Already since arriving in Barcelona I'd received four generous offers from those I'd met with trucks, including Duff and Budda, to help me transport the boat to Mayville. I'd been warmed by these invitations, which told me that I was not on my own if I didn't want to be, and yet I had stubbornly insisted that while I welcomed and often craved human association during the trip, the work would have to be mine alone, a full possession of the physical and psychological challenges of rowing and, for nine miles, walking. These nine miles, I know, would haunt me to no end if I'd thrown the boat in the back of Budda's truck.

So I'd said thank you, but no, to each of these offers, and yet am doubly touched by this schoolteacher's willingness to help pull the boat himself. I will say no again, but now feel that in doing so I am rejecting his interest to participate, if only briefly, in the trip. "Well, I really appreciate your offer," I reply, "but I want to do it under my own power." It's a need that he understands, though he may have outgrown it himself a long time ago. After walking another ten minutes with me, he says he will be on his way. We shake hands and he turns back to his car. Though I did not accept his grip on the boat, his company and conversation have helped distract me from my protesting muscles for half a mile, and before long the grade of this first hill eases. With Lake Erie still in the background I stop long enough to take a picture of the boat next to a road sign warning trucks heading toward Westfield to "Use Low Gear, 6% Grade, 2 Miles."

From successive stages in my climb I am given broad views of Lake Erie, still churning, a fluid description of the wind, and though from even higher points the lake is obscured by trees, I would have known without ever having heard of Erie that something—an enormous valley, or ocean, or inland sea—was beyond the furthest range of pines, past which, looking down, I can see only sky. I finally reach

the house with the red roof and revise its significance. It had signaled in my mind the end of climbing when, I now discover, it ought to have represented nothing more promising than "Beginning of really long hill." Not the steepest, but not nearly the shortest, and its division by thirty or so light poles is both help and hindrance. I alternate walking forward and backward and am disheartened each time I turn around to see that the distance between me and the red roof seems unchanged.

The rain increases with the decrease in light, but within four and a half hours I at last arrive in Mayville on Chautauqua Lake. I chance upon Webb's Restaurant for a dinner celebration of crossing a continental divide that I myself had hardly noticed that day in the Jeep. Wearing a yellow slicker that left the bottom of my canvas shorts dripping wet, along with soggy black cotton socks and soaking sneakers, I park the boat in a space next to a white Cadillac in front of the restaurant and notice the attentive glances of some diners inside. Minutes later, ready to ignore my budget for an hour, I am seated and questioned by my neighbors at the next table about the trip. I inquire about camping and am asked by an older, white-haired man in a blue blazer with a royal-looking crest on the breast if I see the unlit house through the window and across the street by the lake. Yes, I do. "You just go around back, by the water, and you can stay there." Are you sure? "Sure I'm sure! I own it!" And so I become the guest of Paul Webb, who with his wife started a hot dog stand after the Second World War, and now owns the restaurant and attached motel, as well as an adjacent candy factory and summer guest houses. Relieved to have found a place to stay, I eat a full meal in dry seclusion from the weather, yet from time to time study the wind through the willows by the lake and the rain sweeping at angle through the cold light of the street lamps.

With halfhearted optimism that the weather might dry up a bit before I pitch my tent, I kill time watching hockey playoffs at the bar and playing pool in the next room with two Texans up on business. Waiting my turn out in a high-backed leather chair, I notice the barkeep look into the pool room, then turn back to say, "Yeah, he's still here." A moment later, as I stand up wondering who could possibly be looking for me, Mr. Webb appears in the doorway. "My wife and I came down to open up the house for you," he says. "It's cold out there and it's not going to stop raining."

We venture across the road and find Mrs. Webb already on a quick clean up of what they perceive as a mess—the house hadn't been opened after the winter—and what I consider palatial. As I try to express my gratitude, standing in a doorway between Mrs. Webb, who is busily tidying up in the living room, and Mr. Webb, who is checking cabinets in the kitchen, Mrs. Webb steps toward me and whispers, "He was in Patton's Third Army. He helped capture twenty-nine men. We married before the war and I waited for him here. Started as a hot dog stand!" I feel charmed as I flip through my invented, mental scrapbook of their lives, with hand-colored snapshots of a meeting, a marriage, good-bye and war, and a stand in a roadside parking lot. Charmed to be here, in their care, and not alone under the partial protection of some willow tree in the adjacent park, where I might easily have camped unnoticed that soggy night.

· 8 ·

A Riverbed of
Polished Stones

WITH CLEAR SKIES and a growing northwest breeze, I head down Chautauqua Lake, a far reach of the Mississippi drainage basin, whose waters are mostly bound by way of New Orleans for the Gulf of Mexico. I wonder, if a single drop of the lake could be isolated, what its story would be on its route to the sea. How many outboard engines would it help cool? How many municipal water systems would it enter through massive intake pipes, being released downstream days or weeks later. Would it sneak quickly back to the current by way of a dripping faucet or end up in a ten-gallon aquarium filled with guppies? If a drop could evaporate and remain a drop, how many times would it be reconstituted as rain falling again near the headwaters before completing its route more than two thousand miles to the gulf?

Still near the head of the lake, I stop by the house of Roy Harvey, whom I'd briefly met the day before. At fifty-something, Roy is an author and retired Chicago television and radio producer, whose gentle yet authoritative voice reminds me of a National Public Radio correspondent, though I haven't asked him whether this guess is founded. On an impulse, with his wife next to him at the door, Roy asks whether I'd like company for several days, and I say I would. He looks to his wife with a smile, recognizing a missed step. She smiles back. An hour later we are both on the water, Roy in a yellow kayak. The wind has grown to a steady fifteen to twenty miles per hour in our favor, and we sail and surf and paddle the eighteen miles or so to Jamestown, New York, where the lake narrows into Chadekoin Creek.

For more than five hundred miles I have had, on balance, neutral current. I'd had the moderate assistance of incoming tides on the Hudson, yet the wind largely against me. The currents of the Erie Canal, sometimes with me and sometimes against me, were negligible. Yet within minutes as Chautauqua Lake narrows into the creek, a current develops and I am soon able to drift at the same rate that I'd been rowing. Thus far the landscape had passed by only as a direct result of work—when I stopped rowing the passing of the shores stopped too. It's a strange sensation now to see the trees drift by themselves in relation to me and the cumulus clouds above. Like an astronaut in a space capsule I can take one stroke of the oars, or even no stroke, and keep gliding, as if, through sheer repetition, I have overcome the laws of friction. My mind races ahead to recalculate the mileage I might cover in the coming weeks, and, while optimistic that this current will continue, sometimes abating, sometimes increasing, through to the gulf, I feel a bit of shame that I will have to do so much less work than I'd imagined. I might spend days just drifting and still make twenty miles. Such fanciful notions we're willing, against better intuition, to adopt. I tell Roy that at this rate we should make the Pennsylvania border by the end of the day. We would, in fact, make it over the border by the end of the day. But not this day.

Chadekoin Creek seems largely forgotten the way it runs beneath Jamestown's short city bridges. Old brick buildings whose factories once depended upon its flow have now been inhabited by other businesses depending more on telephone and electric lines for their income. The foundations of these buildings often form the embankments of the creek, whose flow I imagine is a quaint bit of history for those who work within, if not unnoticed altogether. The natural riverbanks are steep and shaded by overhanging trees, and as often as not the views of the city consist of dumpsters at the backs of minimalls, chain-link fences guarding the lots of used car dealers and the like. The city is turned away from the source of its water. But the banks are tall enough that all of this can be ignored, and the world of the drive-thru and the world of the creek, though forty yards apart, are different worlds altogether.

Occasionally the cityscape gives way to stretches of neighborhood and people's backyards, but even then Roy and I are rarely noticed by anyone other than a surprised dog barking out a nervous warning. Steady rains have swollen the creek and here and there leafy trees have lost their grip and fallen across the water until caught in other branches. Sometimes two trees have each lost their hold and lean into each other, forming an inverted V for us to pass through, sometimes followed immediately by other obstructions. Roy is able to weave smartly beneath and around such obstacles, yet though my shell is as narrow as his kayak, I need room also for the outriggers and the oars. If I proceed bow-first I will have difficulty controlling my speed and will have to row with my head over my shoulders, one then the other, back and forth, so as to steady my aim through the narrow channels. So I swing the boat around, bow upstream, rowing against the current so as to maintain a stationary position, gauging the movement of the hurried water, anticipating its effect on the hull, sizing up the width of the gap between the tree trunks. Roy waits for me in an eddy below and minutes pass by as I plan my move. I fear that in hooking either outrigger or an oar blade not only will the boat be capsized, but, worse, a blade will catch on the bottom below and snap as the rest of the rig and boat are forced onward by the current. These are not my oars, and a replacement set would cost me all that I have left for the rest of the way to the gulf. Breaking an oar is simply not an option.

Finally I feel that the passage I've imagined is also likely. It's the feeling I've waited for before diving from a high dive, after having once nearly dislocated a shoulder doing so. I take a final stroke to position the hull in the current which then carries me as I push the oar handles outward so as to bring the blades in, and the oars are parallel to the shell. We've sucked in our stomach, the boat and I. We drift half a dozen feet before entering the makeshift tunnel, and at the last minute I push the handles out further to bring the blades in even closer to the hull. I close my eyes as the branches give way around me, an outrigger nicks a stump and the hull shudders, and with squinting eyes in case more branches are to come, I look up, chin still to my chest, and swing the blades back to take a stroke and stop the boat in clear water. Ripped leaves are littered across the baggage, in the bilge, and on me. A small amputated branch is lodged in the rig. I am inwardly elated to be facing such an unanticipated series of challenges. Each one is different and provides a single opportunity for a solution, and I am glad to have not known about it in advance, for improvisation is at its purest when unexpected.

The next set of snags follows immediately. A dam of broken tree trunks and branches lies in the middle of the creek, which splits around it. Roy has passed successfully to the left and once again waits for me. Yet his route, while straighter, is also narrower, and after once again studying and plotting for minutes on end, I choose the longer, arcing route for its breadth, though I will have to sneak a single stroke midway through to favorably reposition the bow in the twisting current. At certain points no further planning will improve your lot. You have to let go, release what grip you have on the larger elements, and give in to the currents of time, or emotion, or water, and just be carried as best you can, lucky along the way if you can plant a quick but shifting stroke, or grasp a branch, to help the currents, or fates, see you through. And so again I stop rowing, watch as the hull follows the route I'd aimed for, manage a meager yet limb-dodging stroke, close my eyes and duck my head when necessary, and emerge newly showered in green.

On the occasional straightaway down the creek I row bow-first and marvel again at my speed past land. Here and there a branch drapes down to the water and I slip beneath it and manage an unobstructed bend at full speed. Yet the natural obstacles are not alone. We come to a bend so sharp that the creek pools before accepting the new direction, and the lessons learned thus far do not apply. The question now posed does not involve fitting our boats between tree trunks and branches, but fitting beneath a bridge, for the creek has risen to within a foot and a half of the supporting steel girders. Roy and I confer while floating safely on the eddying pool, which is bordered by the chain-link fence of a junk car lot, ten feet tall and running clear to the end of the bridge. No option for portage there. Across the creek we would have to exit the boats onto a stubby bank—no easy feat for either one of us—negotiate a route through patches of poison ivy, and stop traffic after carrying the boats over a waist-high cement wall leading to the bridge. Roy tells me he's been hospitalized twice for poison ivy. Which leaves one option.

I pull out into the current, align myself stern-first, facing the bridge, and after a strong pull upstream I lay back on my gear, looking beneath the bridge to scout whether I can see the bottom of the girders. Check. My body and the hull should fit beneath. Though my wake is carried away beneath the bridge, the hull, like a boy walking against an escalator, remains in place. I take another stroke and lay back again, this time gauging whether the tops of the oarlocks, the highest points of the scull, and taller than my lying body, will fit beneath as well. Close, but clear, with perhaps an inch to spare. I pull back into the eddy, and Roy, who will be unable to lie back in his kayak, ponders whether he might still be able to fit beneath, or, if that fails, accept the plunge and swim through.

The bridge is supported by a central pylon that divides the creek into two channels. The current runs faster to the right, and we can see that ten yards beyond the bridge the current erupts into the whitewater of a modest drop of perhaps two feet. The faster we pass beneath the bridge the more momentum we'll have to make it through the whitewater. Roy goes first, uncertain about his prospects. He proceeds with his best option, to maintain the kayak's alignment with the current, stop himself upon reaching the bridge, and then try to wriggle his way below. He sits so much lower in his hull that perhaps he'll be able to fit through after all. I watch as he enters the current, begins back-paddling to slow his approach, and stops the motion of his boat with a steady grasp on the first girder of the bridge, his paddle still in his hands. But now what? He tries to lean back far enough to fit beneath, yet the small cockpit of the kayak prevents him. He is now in no position to push far enough upstream with his arms to then quickly dig in with his paddles and return to the eddy. While acknowledging the inevitable, he makes a second attempt, this time leaning back and to the side. The current quickly catches the bow, swinging the hull broadside to the stream, and sweeps the kayak beneath the bridge— with Roy following in the water.

I resume my position near the bridge, rowing in place, studying the current, checking heights once again. Minutes pass. Roy has managed to find a shallow edge of the stream where he's been emptying the kayak of water and generally reassembling himself. With a final, easy stroke, ending with a slight favoring of the right-hand oar to inch the bow left, I give in and lay back, watching, maintaining the balance of the oarlocks with the feathered blades, holding my breath. The first girder passes and I could touch it with my nose. I reach up with my hands and grasp the second girder, holding the boat in one position. The air is cool and musty, with the smell of bird nests and droppings and damp cement. A car passes overhead and the deep sound of its weight is amplified by this open-ended sound chamber; the water below is black in the shade. I let go of the beam and restore my grip on the oars, and the boat is carried again by the current. The last girder passes and I sit up in daylight the moment I can without slamming my forehead on rusting steel, and quickly position myself for a reverse stroke to speed the hull into the churning whitewater. Time enough for a second stroke, and the stern dives into the froth, collecting enough of the creek to float one of my bags, and I sidle over to the bank to rejoin Roy.

In this way, with variations, we pass beneath and between downed trees, and under bridges, and are twice forced to carry our boats—once when the bridge clearance is too low even for a Styrofoam cup, and once when we come to a half-abandoned factory beneath which the creek drops in several steps over falls. We've covered perhaps several miles in the last four hours, and near dusk pull over where the bank leads into a neighborhood backyard. We negotiate our way carefully through a patch of poison ivy and, five minutes later, having walked around to the front door of the nearest house, we are given permission to pitch our tents near the creek and offered the use of the downstairs shower.

The following day the riddles posed by the creek continue, yet gradually the channel widens and slows as its angle of descent levels. With little notice Chadekoin feeds into Cassadaga Creek, and the Cassadaga joins the Conewango, which leads across the border from New York into Pennsylvania, bound for the Allegheny at the town of Warren. The Conewango wanders between farms, probably through farms, sometimes due north and other times south, and we seem to glide on the slower but notable current through tree-lined tunnels and beneath the blue sky. Turtles slide down banks into the water as we approach, statuesque herons launch into pterodactic flight, and side streams and backwaters, filled by the rain, make me want to lose myself in their deeper green of early summer, still a calendar month away.

We pass an Amish man fishing at the water's edge, dressed in black and white and wearing a smartly woven straw hat. His wife or daughter, in a faded blue dress and bonnet, hair parted down the middle and pulled back, sleeps in the shade of a black carriage, a scene dated only by a fluorescent orange triangle mounted in lieu of taillights to warn speeding, passing cars. My shell is pure white, molded out of man-made materials. Roy follows a hundred yards behind me in his yellow boat. We leave no fumes ourselves, but I am suddenly conscious of our modernity. The fisherman and I acknowledge each other with unobtrusive nods. By dusk Roy and I reach Warren, Pennsylvania, and pitch our tents in a waterfront park located at the T-junction of Conewango Creek and the Allegheny River.

The Allegheny is not as wide as I'd expected and so shallow that a riverbed of polished stones is often so clearly in view that I'm surprised when the hull doesn't scrape. Immediately we descend through broad rapids—nothing to swamp either of the boats, but also the fastest water we've been on, requiring attention. Once again I marvel at the apparent speed of the passing shore. Over the course of the day the riverbanks rise ever more steeply into the ancient, rolling humps of the Allegheny Mountains, giving way occasionally for the placement of such old brick towns as Tidioute, Tionesta, and Oil City, home of the country's first free-flowing oil well, and until the late 1960s the wealthiest town, per capita, in the nation. Other, newer settlements often consist of weekend-retreat cabins lined up like an audience to the passing river. We'd heard mention of twenty-seven bald eagle nests between Warren and Pittsburgh, though I see only turkey vultures gliding on thermals against the perfect sky.

On weekdays the river is quiet, but on weekends the sounds of internal combustion often prevail: chain saws carving river views, jet skis in their usual fifty miles per hour back-and-forth circuits, tractors used for launching the smallest motorboats—like using a wheelbarrow to move a pot of marigolds—and always the ride-on mowers across enormous communal lawns that make one great riverfront fairway. Looking back upon these settlements before rounding the bend into the silence between communities, I see the blue haze of combustion mixed with raised dust, and think less about the oddness of so much work on weekends than about how little of that work we still know how to do without engines. I'm newly aware of the engines I own myself: the chain saw, the motorcycle, my car, as well as an old Mercury kept in storage. I feel just a mite of environmentalist atonement with each stroke of the oars.

At an island in the middle of the river Roy and I come across an armada of fifteen or twenty canoes. Some of their crews are dressed in the white blouses, blue wool overcoats, and tricorner hats of French military commanders, some are dressed more peasant-like as French milice, and still others, less attired in the heat, portray Abenaki Indians; we have overtaken by chance a ninety-mile reenactment of Celoron's expedition to restore French sovereignty over the Ohio River Valley. The French commanders, supposedly to form, keep largely to themselves as their boats are landed and camp is set up, as do the Abenaki, who portray in their natural, scant dress, an ease with the surrounding wilderness. The reenactment does not involve us, however, and after chatting briefly we continue on.

In cycles Roy and I become separated by the differing speeds of our boats, and meet again here and there at towns to relieve ourselves of the repetition of paddling and walk to some pizza parlor. It is then that we catch up on what we each have seen: the bald eagle diving for a fish (I'd missed it), the sounds of songbirds I couldn't name, the canoeists setting up camp on a small island: a woman assembling a folding plastic picnic table suitable for six, while a man amputated dead tree limbs for firewood with a fuming, headache-producing chain saw. A weekend getaway.

On our fourth day together, at Kennerdell, Pennsylvania, Roy and I pull into a campground so tightly packed with trailers and tents there is neither a sense of the natural world nor a shred of privacy, though the edge of utter wilderness lies a hundred yards in any direction. It does not seem to be an escape from the congestion of the home front, but, oddly, a concentrated recapitulation of neighborhood living. Roy has little choice but to end his run here, as we had apparently not been so careful along the banks of Chadekoin Creek after all. He has a spreading case of poison ivy on his ankles, exacerbated by the limited space in the kayak for his legs. He calls his wife from a pay phone, and several hours later she arrives and Roy and I say good-bye.

That night as I pitch my tent by the water's edge I see the lights and hear the high-pitched grind of six or seven all-terrain vehicles across the river, and the lights are dulled by the dust stirred by the machines as they wind back and forth. It is disturbingly aggressive, and I'm glad the river's between us. The next morning I leave before the sun rises and disappear into a fog so dense I can see neither bank, and only the apparent movement of the stones on the river bottom below tells me which way is downstream. I've grown accustomed to Roy's company in these few days, no matter the miles we'd paddled separately. I've searched the riverscape ahead of me, looking for him in his yellow boat, and other times watched behind me, waiting for him to emerge from around the last bend. He has become a reference point for me on the water, and in his company I have found security. Surprised by a felt need to restore my confidence for traveling alone, I hope for the fog to clear.

By the end of the day I reach the uppermost of nine locks on the Allegheny, and over the next few days pass between increasingly industrial shores, planted with gravel operations supplied in part by the dredging of the river itself. Enormous factory buildings line the shore, and empty barges are docked against large, rusting kiosk-like pilings. The barges themselves, typically 195 feet long and 180 tons empty, are unpainted steel and thrown away after patches of several square feet are no longer enough to prevent their sinking. Such derelicts are parked here and there, left to rot, and in some cases filled in, like huge planters, to build the shoreline. Those that are simply left half-sunken along some otherwise undisturbed stretch of shore are at first vaguely scenic, but eventually irksome, like an abandoned car on a highway, left for someone else to remove.

· 9 ·

On the Water

AT PITTSBURGH the Allegheny and the Monongahela Rivers join to become the Ohio River, which runs nearly a thousand miles to Cairo, Illinois, and the Mississippi. Several miles before reaching the Ohio I stop at Three Rivers Rowing Association, which not only serves as a common boathouse for a variety of local high school and collegiate rowing programs, but also vastly expands the typical boundaries of the rowing world, whose stereotype as a white's only, prep school– and college-based sport is a near mirror image of the truth. The association sponsors rowing programs for the blind, provides opportunities for public high schools to form teams, and encourages community members of all ages to learn to row on both recreational as well as competitive bases.

I was expected, as I'd called the director, Mike Lambert, from Chautauqua Lake, anticipating the luxury of companionship with other rowers, or at least a safe place to spend a night in Pittsburgh. Mike has come out in a coach's boat to greet me, as have two rowers in a doubles scull, and I am escorted to the clubhouse dock where my boat looks like a trainer compared to the thoroughbreds around it. I arrive at noon amid a flurry of activity: a group of college women have just hefted a fifty-nine-foot eight-person shell weighing 220 pounds above their heads and begin walking it to the open bays of the boathouse as a group of four middle-aged men—out for a row during their lunch break?—launch a smaller shell. Singles and pairs and four and eights come and go along the dock. Everyone is here to row. Two men in their thirties take special interest in me. One is shorter, and thin, with dark brown hair. He is wearing white socks and canvas shorts, and there's no way to know who's just learning to row and who's teaching. His companion, Alan, is tall with a classic rower's physique, free of any visible ounce of fat, and with long slender muscles built for endurance rather than heft.

Donald, with the white socks, asks if he can take my boat for a spin. Of course, I tell him. And the moment he steps in it he pushes off, still standing with one foot on the beam supporting the seat, the other finding a footing in the cockpit, his hands lightly grasping the oars for balance as he gracefully seats himself. He makes a teardrop circuit with two dozen impeccable strokes and returns to the dock.

"So what do you think?" I ask lightheartedly.

"It only has one speed!" he jokes. He steps out of the scull with equal grace as I comment about its features. I point out the light weight of the wooden oars. It seems a wordless conversation has taken place between Donald and Alan.

"Those are nice oars," says Alan, the blood flowing through his arms clearly mapped by his blue veins. "But hang on, I'll be right back." Two minutes pass, during which Donald comments diplomatically to a man who's just arrived by oar from Brooklyn that, in his opinion, for my height I might benefit from a few slight adjustments to my rig. The adjustable footrests might go aft a bit, for one thing, as this will affect my stroke. He'd be happy to give me some tips on one of the rowing machines in the boathouse. Alan returns with a pair of black oars whose broad, oddly shaped red blades are each emblazoned with a white W.

"Since you're here," says Alan, "you might want to try these oars. They're lighter than the ones you have and they have more efficient blades." He holds them out to me and I take them, one in each hand. They are made of carbon fiber and seem impossibly light, even when both are held in one hand. They're called "Hatchets," he tells me, because of the shape of their blades. "Meat Cleavers" would be more accurate. "People either love them or hate them," he adds, "and if you like them I want you to take them with you."

Donald has proceeded to take my oars out of their sockets, and I hand him the new ones one at a time. He locks them in and says, "You might as well test them out right now." I hop in the boat as adeptly as I can in front of these two. At first the taller blades trip on the water as I reach for the catch, and the two oars seem so light I fear I'll break them if I pull too hard. I'm reassured across the water of their exceptional strength, superior to that of wood. "Hold them lightly with your fingers," Donald coaches as I pass by. "Every so often take a stroke with just one finger on each oar," he calls. "You're just hanging on, not gripping." He's seen the calluses extending from the inside of my middle knuckles well into my palms. "You should only get blisters on the last joint or two of your fingers," he adds. I am suddenly unsure about every aspect of the stroke, and as I force the blades too deeply at the catch Donald calls out for me to "just let them find their depth." He then waves me in to make an adjustment to the rig, and Alan comments, "You'd start looking like Schwarzenegger if you continued the way you've been rowing!" We all laugh, and I know that in the world of rowing this is not a compliment, for the finest stroke involves not only strength but efficient use of the body's and the boat's leverage. Later, on a rowing machine—otherwise rightly named the "ergometer"—Mike, Alan, and Donald give me a lesson on rowing technique, whose main point is that I should pull with the arms only as the legs complete their extension. I'd begun using my arm muscles too early, hence their increasing bulk.

With new wings in the red and black oars, and still amused on one hand by having rowed more than six hundred miles before learning proper sculling technique, and grateful on the other for having learned at the hands of these three—over the thousands of miles to come I will meet a handful of elite competitive rowers, including an Olympian, all of whom know Donald—I leave Pittsburgh on a Sunday morning, escorted to the mouth of the Ohio by a men's eight. Their octonary pattern is mesmerizing, so many bodies in unison in such elegant work. In an eight-man shell each rower has one oar, or sweep, rather than a pair or oars, and the rhythm of eight minds planting eight blades into the water in the same moment, pulling through the stroke with equal timing—as the long slender hull surges ahead—and releasing those blades in one instant for their silent flight forward to the next catch, is exquisite. We wave good-bye, I dip my hat in the new waters of the Ohio, place it on my head, and with river water dripping down my neck continue on.

As I start down the Ohio I am caught up in numbers. I cannot help imagining that I am starting at the mouth of the Hudson or the east end of the Erie Canal. At each of those points I knew the distance ahead of me until the next body of water: 155 miles from New York City to Waterford, 337 miles from Waterford to Tonawanda. Each distance had seemed like a long way to go, and here I am at the beginning of 981 miles, feeling like a kid on the first day of eighth grade, finally past seventh grade, but once again back at the starting gate. This is how I was trained in school to think about time and work, to quantify it and then divide it into weeks and chapters to make its passing seem more manageable. The numbers are a curse when they translate experience into matters of counting up or down, and away. The signage along the Ohio River doesn't help, as its mileage is marked for towboats every five miles, starting at Pittsburgh and counting up.

Having just passed the five-mile sign, the idea of counting strokes pops into mind once again. By the time I've noticed stroke number three I've begun reciting at random a favorite Robert Frost poem:

These pools that, though in forests, still reflect
The total sky almost without defect,

And like the flowers beside them, chill and shiver,
Will like the flowers beside them soon be gone,
And yet not out by any brook or river,
But up by roots to bring dark foliage on.

Within the first several lines I become lost in the rhythm of the poem's imagery and thus distracted from counting the rhythm of the strokes. One more battle within my own mind between counting time and spending time, and for now the distraction lasts. An hour later perhaps I will be teased once again by my need for numbers, and a stroke will be observed and assigned the number one. Noting the second stroke, and the third, seems unavoidable. But then another poem will come to mind or an attempt at focused observation on a point of water or shore, and the numbers will dissolve. I do not allow myself to stop rowing during these small conflicts and have still not counted out so many as ten strokes.

After the break at Pittsburgh, the sculling lesson, and a change of oars, I row forty miles before sunset—still far from immune from numeracy—out of Pennsylvania, the only state to border the Ohio on both sides, and into Ohio to my left, and West Virginia to my right. Days later at a public library I receive an e-mail from Alan, who'd given me the oars. He wishes to provide me with their history.

Hi Nat,

I hope you find the Wisconsin oars to be a bit more efficient as you continue your journey. You'll certainly form an emotional bond with them, which is why I insist that they are now yours.

Just a short history of the oars. They are heavyweight sculling oars with hatchet blades. The original owner was Kurt Borcherding, a fire jumper who also happened to coach the Wisconsin Crew when forest fires weren't raging in the West. Two summers ago, Kurt decided to try for a spot on the U.S. National Team and made it. He's represented the U.S. in the World Championships in 1997 and 1998,

winning a bronze medal in the pair in 1998. Since the U.S. doesn't
financially support our elite athletes—and there is no money in row-
ing, as you have certainly discovered—Kurt was forced to sell his
beloved racing shell to make ends meet. I purchased Kurt's single
scull for the North Allegheny High School Men's Crew, and the
Wisconsin oars came along as part of the deal.

Kurt hated to part with his shell and oars, but he knew they were
going to a good home at North Allegheny where they would be well
cared for and meet with some racing success. He will be ecstatic to
know they are now a part of your incredible undertaking. What you
are trying to accomplish is the kind of thing that Kurt would admire
and appreciate.

I realize this is more than you ever wanted to know about a silly
pair of oars, but we oarsmen take our tools seriously.
Good luck and Godspeed,
Alan

AT TORONTO, OHIO, I am lured to shore by the sight of a marina, a simple set of docks without even a fuel pump, and with an
unassuming restaurant perched on the riverbank. I am soon given permission to tie up the boat, and before long meet Freddy Fisher, a lean,
blue-eyed, bicycle-riding seventy-something who is also a rower. He
is eager to talk with anyone after his own traveling heart, and we sit
down for lunch on a shaded porch overlooking the river. His boat and
my boat are the only two on the docks without engines. Freddy, I soon
learn, had been sent to the Pacific during World War II and had been
happy about going as he wanted to see the world. As with other veterans I've met, Freddy's descriptions of the war are punctuated here
and there with quiet, distant gazes, in this case toward the river, and I
imagine that in these moments his recollections have brought to mind
some darker image, or perhaps an entire physical or emotional landscape that his words alone could not relay to one of another genera-

tion. I feel sure that my own knowledge and imagination of that war will ultimately have been informed as much by these intense silences as by any film or document or lecture.

Freddy loves the river and spends most of his time either by it or on it. "Do you see the white plastic bag tied to the tree?" He points across the Ohio as he leans toward me. I search the far bank and see a grocery bag hung up, I would have guessed, by the wind in a low branch.

"I see it."

"That's my camp," Freddy says. "I tied that bag to the tree so I can tell from here how windy it is over there." I see the bag, but I see no camp, just shaded riverbank. "That's one of my favorite places," he says. "I like to go there and get away from things. Just me and the river. I take my Bible with me."

Freddy reaches the other side of the river by way of his rowboat, a twelve-foot aluminum johnboat painted inside and out a robin's-egg blue, three shades darker than his blue cotton slacks, closer to the color of his summer-weight porkpie hat. The oars are also blue. I study the boat, now docked a short distance from mine, while sitting at the table. A life ring of the variety thrown from the *Queen Mary* is stowed in the stern and two side mirrors purchased at an automotive supply shop, and now affixed at both corners of the stern, tell Freddy what's ahead of him while he rows. A red rag is tied to the top of a white pole that stands ten feet tall in the forward position of a mast, put there to increase the boat's visibility among motorboats and barges on the river. Freddy often rows several miles up the river to a restaurant in the next town and has rowed as far downstream as Wellsburg and back, fifteen miles each way. Amid the company of the other boats in the marina, all either fast runabouts or pontoon boats, Freddy's is out of place, and by far, to my eye, the most interesting.

We talk about traveling, about where he'd been during the war and where he'd still like to go, and at one point he pauses, looks out to the river, then looks directly at me, and says slowly and forcefully,

"You're doing the *right* thing," as if I'd just made some moral decision after torturous internal debate. If I'd had any lingering doubt about this trip myself, he would have put an end to it right there. After lunch we wander through the sleepy neighborhoods of Toronto, following a road by the river. He picks up hickory nuts fallen from trees, offers some to me and eats some himself.

Freddy Fisher, I find, is a gem, a veteran of Pacific battles, a man who prefers his own stride and his rowboat to cars and outboards, and who picks freely from that which is already growing around him. His meteorological instrument is a grocery bag in a tree, and his camp, I've come to understand, is anywhere he finds solace and freedom and shade. I feel now as I'd felt in Michelle's kitchen in Rhinebeck, and when I'd stood in the doorway between two rooms and Mrs. Webb had whispered to me about Patton's army and the hot dog stand at Chautauqua Lake. I wish to be nowhere else in time or place.

That evening Freddy takes me to Yummy's, the local ice-cream stand. He buys the first round, and I buy the second, as well as a third for my seemingly endless appetite. Moths spiral madly in the fluorescent light, a little girl drops her cone, cries, and finds it replaced by a teenaged server with a crewcut (he accepts the thanks from the girl's parents, yet returns to work directly without a glance to see who was watching; I sense his pride in his automatic generosity), and young women lean flirtatiously against powerful cars. The temperature is just right, the picnic table at which we sit is appropriately sticky, and again Freddy is finding pleasure in simple ways, as am I. We say goodbye that night down by the river.

The following day, as I row past Steubenville five miles downstream, where a bridge crosses the river, I happen to look up and see Freddy standing by his white minivan. Once a week, he told me, he drives to the outskirts of Pittsburgh to eat at his favorite buffet restaurant. Smiling, I row toward him as he carefully descends the steep bank, and again we say farewell.

PRIOR TO THE TRIP I was often asked about the the risk of getting run over by a towboat or toppled by their crashing wakes. Now I see them frequently on the Ohio River, perhaps fifteen or twenty in a day. I've come to think of them as the river's equivalent to a steamroller. They move so slowly   perhaps seven miles per hour, only half again my own rate—that I always have time to watch as they approach, particularly when they're overtaking me. At first I kept a wide berth but soon lost my fear and now pass within calling distance to crewmen on their decks.

"Towboat" is a misnomer referring to the combination of a tugboat (equally misleading) and barges cabled together. The tugboat, with few exceptions, is actually a pushboat, and on the Ohio typically pushes a raft of fifteen barges assembled rectangularly, three wide by five long. The tugs are powered by multi-thousand horsepower diesel engines, and each barge is typically 195 feet long by 35 wide. An assembled towboat, or tow, can thus be nearly a quarter-mile long. Nevertheless I soon learn that their wakes are of little threat to me, and I row through them with splashing ease.

The crews are often on board for weeks at a time, not allowed to leave the boat unless, perhaps, assigned by the captain to assist with some errand such as a grocery run. Once underway the work at hand amounts largely to grunt maintenance, particularly the constant work of scraping and painting the tug itself. The prize, of course, is being on the river, which, though its bends and locks must become tediously repetitious, is still an adventure, whether during the spring floods or at the end of a night shift, when the sun rises above a blanket of fog not quite high enough to enshroud the wheelhouse, which seems to float along a river of vapor. I always wave to the crews of towboats and they always wave back. Occasionally I know of a landmark ahead— a bridge, or lock, or riverside town—and feel compelled to see if I can beat an overtaking tow to that finish line. I imagine that the captains notice my effort and guess that I'm trying to stay ahead, yet never have the benefit of knowing where the race ends or whether they've won or lost.

The locks on the Ohio are vast compared to those on the Erie Canal, measuring 1,200 feet long by 110 feet wide. I have yet to buy a handheld VHF radio with which to communicate with the tow captains and call the lockkeepers in advance. An alternative is provided for recreational boaters in the form of a chain that hangs down from a long cement pier extending upstream from the lock. Pull the chain and a moment later a distant electric buzz, like that of a prison gate, can be heard several hundred feet away. I soon learn to quickly row back from the wall into the open after pulling the chain so that the lockkeepers can see me. Several times I've had to pull the chain more than once, only to later be told that the first buzz had been heard but that no one had seen seen me over the wall in my small boat or heard an engine.

When I arrive alone at a lock I am sent right on through, and twenty-five million gallons of river are released from one pool to the next for the lowering of myself and my featherweight craft, which together weigh no more than forty of those gallons. Yet portage, while possible, would be very difficult, as the locks were built primarily for commercial use. In any case, the lockkeepers on the Ohio are as curious about me as those on the Erie Canal, and always wish me good luck. One day my unilateral race with a towboat ends in a dead heat at a lock. The captain opens the door to his wheelhouse and calls down to me to say that he's spoken with the lockkeeper on the radio, and if it's all right with me to lock through at the same time as the barge—a full-size tow—it's all right with both of them. "Fine with me!" I call back, pleased not only by the expediency of locking through now rather than waiting for my own turn, but also by the boyish adventure of being contained in the same lock as the enormous raft.

I am told to enter the lock first and row down to the far end, thus enabling me to leave the lock first as well. If I were to follow the towboat, I would find myself trapped in the maelstrom of its propeller wash if it exited the lock with even the gentlest touch of acceleration. So I paddle through the vast chamber and loop a line around the furthest bollard, designed to float up or down according to the lock's tide. Then the combined bow of the three barges, a 105-foot wall of rusting steel, is slowly maneuvered by the captain, who stands a thousand feet back, into the 110-foot width of the lock with such delicacy that the metal hull never touches cement wall. He is aided by the cushioning effect of the water between his hull and the walls, but his aim into the lock has to be perfect to form the cushion. I have heard from other lockkeepers about greener captains who wiggle and scrape their way in.

As the bow slowly approaches I feel like the troubled heroes in *Star Wars* who find themselves stuck in the trash-compacting bowels of the Death Star, only to be be saved in the final moment by the droids. The open space of the lock shrinks as the towboat inches toward me, until it comes to a stop twenty feet away, and I hear the distant boom of the lock's doors closing. As the water is released the bollards screech and groan as they slide down their metal tracks. I close my eyes and am momentarily absent from this daylight transit between two pools on the Ohio River, and instead surrounded by voices of miserable souls in a dimly lit underworld.

At the opposite end of the spectrum of motorized traffic on the river one finds recreational bass-fishing boats, whose sleek eighteen-foot hulls are powered by massive outboard engines, never less than 150 horsepower and often at least a hundred more than that. I hear the roar of their engines before I see them emerging from around a bend, and I always make sure that they see me in case I should otherwise need to dive like a stuntman out of my boat. Physically they are impressive in the way that sports cars are impressive, whether you like them or not. Their speed and power, and their respective shapes and sounds are difficult to ignore. And yet they seem to corrupt the ego. The bass boats routinely travel at speeds of sixty miles per hour, often more, leaving behind enormous roostertail wakes. Typically one man is at the wheel behind a raked windscreen, and his buddy is in the passenger seat. Both wear sleek robotic helmets. I always wave to them; they rarely wave back.

In the still evening, a day's row below Parkersburg, West Virginia, the river's current is imperceptible, and the water's reflection of the world above is disturbed only by the wake of my boat, which pulses with each stroke of the oars, and by the swirling pools left in pairs as the blades release the silent river. The strokes together are the meter of my life, at a rate of twenty strokes a rowing minute. The pools are the memory; though for several boat lengths they are each distinct, like markings of time, they soon appear to blend, weaken, and fade. Movement forward, time past. Indeed, as I face aft while moving forward I find that rowing corresponds to the passage of time. The water beneath me, like time in the present moment, rushes by, then fades to a near stop much as moments slowly harden into memory. Time sifts experience and the lesser details vanish while memory holds on to the unforgettable. On a long stretch of the broad river I watch as a blue silo on a distant hilltop grows smaller, and the red and green navigation markers slowly vanish, and the intricacies of the riverbanks and the overhanging trees blend away like days and years. Finally the visible length of river is hidden altogether as I round the next bend, and while the navigation markers will be confused in memory with others on the trip, a clear image of the silo, which stands by a barn on an open meadow, will remain.

As I look down to my side again or out to the blades time seems to resume its pace. And though with a glance over my shoulder I might gain a brief view of the riverscape ahead of me, which in the distance still lies in mirage, the details will be revealed only as they emerge to my left and right before they too are sifted away. It had never occurred to me before the trip that the backward-facing position of rowing reflects the experience of passing moments, but I know now that it de-fines the trip by reminding me how much of my life I've spent look-ing ahead. And so I row and watch as my present becomes my past.

There is nothing more than the occasional settlement along this stretch of the Ohio, and with little to eat and just enough water in a gallon jug to wash the sweat from my body, I wish for a town where I might find at least a loaf of bread and a spigot to fill an empty jug. But here between two bends in the river, where the banks are overgrown and leave no spot for even a tent, I am alone. I continue rowing as the sun approaches the closest range of trees to the west, hoping to reach Apple Grove, the merest marking of a town on the map, before dark. There I might ask permission to pitch my tent in someone's field or yard. I've learned to ask a favor while the sun is up.

Then, faintly, I hear the dull drone of an engine and glance over my shoulder to see a small boat heading upriver, at first indistinct, but now coming more clearly into view and toward me. It's a pontoon boat. I wave as they approach, and they wave, a mother and father, and two children. The father slows the boat to an idle and kills the engine.

"You've come all the way from New York?" he asks.

I smile in surprise. "How did you know?"

"I work for a towing company. We heard about you today on the radio from one of the boats."

This morning in the rain I was invited to tie up to one of the barge tows waiting to lock through at Belleville. I'd had to wait myself and was invited into the galley to eat with the crew while rain and time passed.

"They said to watch out for a guy in a rowboat on his way to the Gulf. So when I got off work we decided to take a cruise up the river and see if we could find you. We stopped to buy some chicken, thought you might be hungry."

"I'm always hungry!" I joke truthfully, and with that they hand me a box of fried chicken.

We talk for a few minutes about my trip, and about the river. They tell me Pomeroy isn't far; I'll make it by noon tomorrow. They wish me luck, and say they should be on their way.

"Thanks again!" I call out as he reaches for the ignition. The engine starts and he shifts it into gear. As he peels away he calls out a phrase I would often hear among boatmen on the rivers: "On the water, buddy, on the water."

· 10 ·

In Search of a
Lonesome Bass

THE INCLINE along the course of Chadekoin Creek, an observable angle of the stream's flow that revealed downriver to be clearly downhill, persists from time to time along the Ohio, especially where the river bends. Yet the Ohio is broader, deeper, and in this emerging summer of cloudless drought, ponderously slow. In the still air of a late afternoon the boat drifts, oars idle, at the river's cautious pace, the speed of your hand as it slowly closes in before slapping a mosquito on the forearm. Looking uphill, it seems that the current is too slow for the slope, as if the millions of greenish-brown gallons have been set to a silent, slow motion.

Or is the incline merely the illusion of an optimist eye, a rower's wish that the youthful tumble of the Chadekoin, though clearly diminished, still lives on in the weighted maturity of the Ohio, the way a man approaching middle age convinces himself that he still hasn't reached his physical peak. Indeed, a glance down the river displays a slight angle of descent, so that if this flawless surface were suddenly frozen, a marble placed beside the hull would slowly but steadily roll away and disappear around the next bend. But look again, and say that downriver is upriver, and upriver is down, and the direction of movement seems for a moment to be reversed. I often observed these apparent slopes on the Ohio and was never certain that my sense of up and down was not simply the result of facing aft for hours on end while rowing, paired with the basic fact that rivers flow top to bottom.

A PPROACHING V ANCEBURG, K ENTUCKY, the foliage hardly contains itself, its bloom leaning out beyond the river's edge. The view from the water is of pristine wilderness, though for all I know, a short distance away, a string of cars may be stalled at some shopping district's red light. As predicted by the road map, Vanceburg is revealed beyond a sharp bend as the bushes and trees of the closer shore draw slowly by like a theater curtain. Set on the stage of a forty-foot bluff and guarded by a backdrop of steep, impenetrably verdant hills, the town is seen first as a row of brick and neatly painted homes peering out through the leaves and the white steeple of a church that surely marks the town's center. I remember my first view of Vanceburg for its silence, through the breathless air, across the slow river, amid the evening's summer green, as if I were rowing into the stillness of a photograph.

With the day's rowing behind me I shift my focus to the search for a safe spot along the river to land and pitch my tent. I angle across the current to scout along the small town's embankment, which initially seems to be private property corresponding to the houses above. A quarter-mile downstream, privacy appears to give way to a public riverside park, and there at least I can land the boat without offense. As I study the details of the passing neighborhood, I see a couple standing on a small deck built along the crest of the bluff, and when our eyes meet the woman calls down to me.

"Where'd you come from?"

"New York City," I call back.

"New York City!" she exclaims. "We used to live there! Where're you heading?"

"Back to New York," I volley, realizing mid-reply that I certainly don't appear to be headed back to New York and, anticipating further inquiry at top volume I swing the boat with one oar into a U-turn and closer to shore. With my chin now over my left shoulder, I take a long stroke and, gliding, look back up to them, waiting for them to size me up and speak again.

"You're going back to New York?" she continues, as I fumble with the details of a split-second story of their married lives. I imagine they are not from Vanceburg, but not from New York either, as she'd said only that they'd lived there. I place them walking as a couple along the streets of early seventies Manhattan, neither tourists nor natives, still looking up among the magnificent corporate pillars of the city's skyline, wearing the greatest living city like a new pair of funky shoes, yet bound to return to the easy slippers of the South. Or was one of them actually from New York, having found refuge from urban hype in the arms of rural serenity? With her deep honey hair in a neat Dorothy Hamill, the woman might have transplanted herself from the staid soils of Upper East Side conservativism, while he, with a white shock of hair on each side of his bespectacled head, and the height of a fifties-era basketball player, clad in a loose-fitting T-shirt and dilapidated pants, might have flung paint on the arthouse walls of lower Manhattan. These instant histories, no matter how far off the factual base, are often an accurate gauge of the compatibility of strangers. By the time I've turned the boat and pulled a stroke closer toward talking distance, they've been initiated into my range of trust by the nature of the story I've instinctively created for them. What history they've each invented for me I can only imagine, but her details were probably already in place and favorably assessed by the time she decided to first call out to me.

Was I really rowing back to New York, she'd asked. "Yes," I say, "I'm rowing around the eastern United States, down to the Gulf, around Florida, and up the East Coast."

"How far're you going today?" asks the man.

"Well, actually I was planning to stop here at Vanceburg." That's the truth, for the banks of the Ohio are so overgrown that with few exceptions the most likely clearing for a campsite is found only at the occasional town. Of course I hope that such a neutral response will impose no request while steadying the target for any sort of invitation they might be formulating. I'd aimed, with occasional misfires, to ask for nothing on the trip and to satisfy peoples' curiosity without trapping anyone into assistance. Yet I've learned along the way that my current lifestyle is of interest to people other than myself, that the trip has captured the imagination of many I've met, and that if I'm to be the beneficiary of the hospitality of strangers, I can often trade on the story of my motivations and descriptions about my experiences thus far.

"You're welcome to pull your boat up here if you want," he says, and though I can not take this as a clear invitation to pitch my tent—after all, I have to be a bit ruthless, as the sun would soon set, and much as I would like to talk, my main priority is finding a suitable site before darkness—I optimistically pull a few more strokes to a sandy shore recently cleared of brush and weeds and river drift, as the couple makes their way down the embankment to meet me. We trade questions and answers about the trip, and they follow up this exchange with an offer of a spot for setting up my tent by the deck from which they'd observed me. They tell me that down the road I'll find a pizza parlor and, as they will likely be off to bed by the time of my return—the sun is now setting—they will see me in the morning. Thus I meet Ed and Lois Taylor.

The following day Ed asks me if I'd like to take a day off from rowing and go fishing.

No, I think, I would not like to go fishing. My life spent with baited hook up to this point has amounted to long days in the hot sun, either in some rapacious hunter's shadeless boat, whose schedule for disembarking is beyond my control, or else in my own rare predatory mode, which always seems to coincide with high tide along the coast when it is impossible to dig for bait clams, or with dry fields barren of worms. There were fishing successes from time to time, however, as at the age of four when I caught a lobster on a hook, though in the muted Kodak hues of the early seventies snapshot taken that day, I hold the lobster out at arm's length as if I'd caught a sunken corpse's rotted shoe. The best fishing I ever had was in the middle of Salem Bay, along the North Shore of Massachusetts, where a regional sewer line released an upwelling, continuous mushroom cloud of half-treated human refuse and swirling tissue. Pollack swarmed to this filthy spring and came up four at a time on my multiple lures, to be used as bait, I can now safely admit, for my lobster traps, with which I supplied a small neighborhood clientele at 50 cents off the market price. But aside from that, don't ask me to go fishing.

"Sure, I'd love to go fishing!" I exclaim.

"Okay!" says Ed, with the genuine version of my false enthusiasm. "A friend of mine owns a cabin up in the hills, and a stream pools near his house. There's a red-eye bass we'll catch, and you can see a bit of the countryside while we're at it. Then we'll come back and have a game of chess." Thus far my ideas of fishing along the Ohio have been defined mainly by the bass boats, equipped with every conceivable electronic device for finding what swims below. Here, I am told, Ed has a particular fish in mind, not just any old fish, but one with a history of weakness for his allure.

We would meet Ed's son and granddaughter there. Ed and I climb into his baby-blue truck and weave our way into the Kentucky hills, his two hands on the wheel and my right arm reaching out the window into the warm breeze, blowing by at ten times my normal rowing speed. Despite the twisting of the road I instinctively keep a bearing on my position in relation to the river. It has become the baseline of my life, a confirmation of all that I know about myself. Now my boat is pulled up from the water's edge, and in the nearby tent lies my scant but indispensable gear.

We drive past houses tucked into shaded glens, with neat gardens of vegetables and rows of corn scaled to the needs of each family, and past small farms and open-air barns where tobacco dries on wooden slats. Finally, we turn onto a dirt road along the periphery of an open field, and soon the road disappears into the cool shade of deciduous woods. As it slopes downward I picture a trickling tributary of a creek, mere pennies into the million-dollar account of the Ohio.

Ed parks next to a reclusive brown cabin, and from the back of the truck pulls a collapsible fishing rod with several screw eyes to guide perhaps eight feet of line, and a hook. I follow his nearly worn-out white canvas sneakers down a path to where the trees give way to the light of a clearing and the creek gathers itself in a broad pool before gurgling on.

There we find Ed's son and six-year-old granddaughter already fishing in the hot sun and, after a greeting, Ed follows the edge of the pool to the left and beneath the cover of trees. His granddaughter follows his every footstep, and I follow hers. We suddenly stop when he steps ankle-deep into the pool, reaches slowly down into the water, gently overturns a flat rock, and with the reflex of a mongoose catches a small crawfish with his hand. With a smile to himself he resumes his long, easy stride toward the deeper end of the pool, where its source has been reduced by drought and the end of spring to a slight trickle. I remain behind, however. At less than half Ed's age I feel that I should be able to match the agility of his hand, yet finally manage to catch a miniature crustacean only by herding it with my feet and hands into such shallow water it can do no more than writhe in protest against my disregard for whatever moral code may stand between fisherman and free-range bait. Soured by pyrrhic victory I release the little nipper and rejoin Ed, who shucks the tail of his own crawdad by squeezing it between his index finger and thumb, and baits his hook. As he does so he comments about an enormous crawdad he knows of that we might try catching after the fish.

With his granddaughter by his side Ed steps into the pool, extends the reach of the pole with his long arm, and drops the hook into the cool water beyond the dark form of a submerged log. He plays the rod up and down in slow motion like a maestro with a baton and, failing to achieve the desired response, lifts the hook from the water, takes a single, decisive step further, and drops the hook again. This is not casting into left, right, and center field, hoping to capture the attention of any old luckless finback, but the continuing fixation of a man who'd grown up in the woods of Kentucky—and not, as it turned out, among the postwar urban Beats of Manhattan—on a known fish in a hidden pool, whose predictable bite when properly teased reveals a nerve within the vein of the creek. And then, with a glance of silver muted in the silty water, the fish appears, and with futile caution eyes the hovering ploy.

"I wanted to come see you again, come tempt you," Ed perhaps thinks to himself.

I know, and I can't keep myself away. Every time you do what you do, it's as if my mind goes blank and I forget the times we've met before. I keep forgetting the pain of the hook . . .

"Yes; well—here, come look at this . . . there, no, to your right. Yes, that's it . . ." And the fish strikes, its rebellion against the stinging entrapment portrayed in the pulsing arc of the rod. Ed raises the glimmering fish into the air for us to see. "Isn't it beautiful," he states more than asks, and I study the red ring around its eye. As he bends down to remove the hook and return the fish to water, I smile, not because Ed has caught a fish, but because he's done just what he'd predicted.

"Now let's go see if we can draw that crawdad out," he says, and he reaches down furtively to overturn another rock and outpace the bait below. "They like to eat their own," he notes as we follow him— his son, a granddaughter too young to do anything but follow, and the visitor who'd never even heard of a red-eyed bass—as acolytes to a priest, entirely pleased to simply watch him in his element. We gather around him as he kneels down where the pool rejoins its course to the Ohio in a diminutive waterslide over rock. Ed baits the hook of his rod, which lies on the ground and, holding the line, dangles the lure in the running water beside the shadow of a miniature overhang of rock, a cave two inches tall with a view of the passing stream. "Come on," says Ed, his near whisper almost drowned by the sound of the resuming brook. He drags the bait closer to the opening beneath the rock, and as I began to doubt the full compliancy of Ed's wide world of animals, an ecru claw, three times the size of those we'd caught, reaches out haltingly, as if from Plato's cave, is joined by the opposite claw, and then greedily grasps the bait, tugging failingly with the hubris of a pit bull against Ed's grasp of the line. "See?" Ed looks up as he gives in to the predator's retreat. "They're cannibals too!"

Thirty minutes after Ed and I had arrived in search of a lonesome bass, the four of us start to head out when Ed calls from behind, "First one to skip a stone into the mud across the water, and then we'll go!" Thirty feet across the reflection of trees and sky above, the opposing bank of the pond suddenly drops into the water, exposing two or three feet of mucky earth. This I cannot resist, as skipping is a favorite pastime of mine along any shore with even unsuitable rocks. I could do it well even as a young child, when I was often unable to keep count of the steps of a finely flung weathered disk of granite. Over time, skipping stones acquired metaphoric status in my mind. The teasing of gravity, the suspension of rock over water, the waning beauty of balanced flight, guided and spun by the tip of a whipping finger, all speak of temporal beauty within known limits and defend an ethic of continued effort despite inevitable death. And so I join the others and we skip with abandon until several stones have lodged with dull thwaps in the clay.

As Ed drives back along the winding roads I feel as if I should never need to go fishing again, though all I'd done was watch. Any future venture with even slightly more complex equipment will sully my memory of Ed's efficient simplicity. Later on the trip I would see a group of bass fisherman loading their missile-shaped boats onto trailers drawn by expensive trucks; they were members of a fishing club and their uniform T-shirts were printed with a quote from Hemingway's *The Old Man and the Sea*, a line alluding to the relationship between hunter and prey. Yet I have little doubt that anyone along the Ohio is closer to the angling Hemingway than Ed, who has style no bass fisherman, so long as he's in his bass boat, should ever dare to hope for.

Before I leave, Ed, a former high school art teacher, currently working with inmates at a local prison, gives me a calligraphy lesson, and I give him a sculling lesson. Neither of us excels in the other's strength. And beneath a leafy tree overlooking the river, we each receive a lesson in chess.

With rare exception I never find it easy to leave those I've met. Ensconced in the increasing comfort and familiarity with the life of a household—it doesn't take long before you're in on at least a bit of local gossip, or family drama, or on how to pull the screen door just so to close it properly—the unknowns of the river become quickly imbued with perceived danger. It looks like it might rain today, possibly thunderstorms, I think. Or, If I stay I'll have a chance to visit the museum that was closed, to catch up on the journal. And, more superstitious, Is this the right time to leave?—a question born out of an intangible, unarticulated sense that good things happen in rhythm, that I must have been rowing to a cadence of good fortune thus far, as I've stumbled into no ill fate, and that, like a musician, I should aim to resume the journey on the right beat. And yet, though I might burden or delay departure with such thoughts, I am always happy to be back on the water, and quickly regain confidence that everything I need for my survival and happiness is within the boat, within myself, and close at hand. So I say good-bye again along the banks of the Ohio, and as I row away I watch as Ed and Lois climb the bluff and gaze from their deck as the small boat is carried away and around the next bend.

· II ·

Between Dark Sky
and Dark River

THERE HAS BEEN very little recreational traffic on the river since leaving Vanceburg, and few towns, and daylight is followed by darkness before I can find any spot on the overgrown, muddy banks to pitch my tent. So I resign myself to rowing further into the night, hoping to find a riverfront park near Maysville that Ed had mentioned. Still without navigation lights, I keep an eye out for both passing barges and channel markers.

In the moonless night the boat's speed seems to have increased, as motion is marked only by the sound of broken water and the surge of the hull with each stroke. Whatever the fatigue I feel from the day's pulling is countered by the quiet thrill of rowing on the Ohio River, alone on such a deeply shadowed night, not by plan or by glint of adventurous whim, but simply because I've chosen a lifestyle whose best option, by chance on this summer night, happens to require rowing in darkness along what had once been the main avenue of westward expansion. Had I planned to row at night for the thrill of it, that thrill would have been less. I've sought a life of spontaneity, of quick and competent solutions to unexpected situations, and here in particularly sharp focus is that life. What a pleasantly stupefying shock to at least occasionally marvel at your placement and activity in the world in a given moment, whether in the pet food aisle of the grocery store or while diving into a glacier's lake, and look back fleetingly across your life and wonder how it all led to this point here and now. Was there a single most important moment in my life, I wonder, which, if erased from my history, would also erase my presence here and now on the Ohio River? And what—even more stupefying—could my presence here between dark sky and dark river, alone with a pair of oars in my hands, possibly have to do with any larger purpose?

Over my shoulder I see a faint glow emanating from around a coming bend in the river, not the warmer blush of a town, but something brighter. Gradually the muffled din of machinery becomes clearer—perhaps the Army Corps of Engineers is dredging the shipping channel?—and as I row into the surreal light, as if emerging from the dark side of the moon, I see the void of a stone quarry cut out from a steep hill along the river, and a cloud of white dust from the nonstop mining, lit by a range of argon lights, drifts on a slow breeze across the jet sky. Great trucks and rock crushers and conveyer belts give movement to the scene, and a pair of smaller tugboats maneuvers barges one or two at a time along the quarry's shipping pier and the riverbank. Rows of empty barges, some five deep, are secured to the shoreline awaiting their fill and their conglomeration into full-sized tows ready for long-distance delivery.

Yet while the brilliant glow is emitted by the quarry alone, a larger beast lurks across the river. The Ohio is the oasis of an enormous power plant that drinks through the straws of massive underwater inlet pipes, and from which I'd been warned to stay away unless I wished to mimic a goldfish spiraling down a toilet bowl. This one appears to be like others I've seen on the Ohio, built to be nuclear yet converted to coal. The hefty hourglass figures of the cooling towers, as if echoing the dust of the quarry, breathe their own, grayer clouds into the pitch-black sky. A small swarm of tugs practice their neatness there as well, and as I ponder how to pass among them unnoticed, I see an upstream towboat, just passing through, heading my way. The danger of the tows lies not so much in their size as in their captains' need for a minimum of nighttime navigation lights in order to maximize their own vision. Thus the red and green bow lights, signaling port and starboard, that clip on temporarily to whichever barges happen to be up front, appear to be the same wattage as a cheap flashlight. Moreover, the diesel engines providing their voltage may be as much as a fifth of a mile back, beyond the earshot of the inattentive. And so the bow of a towboat, consisting of the front ends of three barges lashed together and more than a hundred feet wide, makes no sound on a quiet night beyond the gentle lapping of the water it pushes out of the way. If you've heard that clearly, it may well be about the last thing you'll ever hear.

I am closer to the quarry's side of the river, still upstream of the working tugs, and I dart toward the landed barges, thinking to hide within the gaps between their bows and sterns, like a petty thief taking momentary refuge between two parallel-parked cars. I slip into a space not much longer than the length of the scull, careful to keep my bow slightly into the current. If I were to drift sidelong too far beneath the overhanging bow of the downstream barge, which offers nothing to hold on to, I would lose control of one oar, and even this gentle current, were I to lose my balance, might pull me under the broad steel hull. I watch as the towboat labors by, and when it has passed I nose out into the river and edge my way along parked barges, paying attention both to the position of the tugs ahead of me and to the gaps available for retreat. I am close enough to shore that the trees along the riverbank shadow me from the quarry lights, and the barges too, which rise five feet above the water when empty, provide a dark corridor for my white hull.

The tugboat closer to me, still perhaps a hundred yards off, has tied on to one of the empties, and now angles its stern out into the river so as to pull the barge away from shore. I watch to see which direction the captain has in mind, though I suspect he will come toward me, toward the quarry's pier. And so he does; the barge is swung around into the current, though the captain still cannot see me with his dim lights and has no reason to scout the path ahead of him with his spotlight. I duck into the next gap, as deep as the three rows of barges that create it, and sidle my way, crablike, toward the muddy bank and as far out of sight as possible. The slightest strokes of the oars maintain my neutral position against the current. Behind me the rusted steel façade of a barge's transom, once painted freight-train red, rises at ninety degrees from the river, and in front of me and above me the straight angle of another barge's bow, an enormous toothless jaw, appears ready to inhale my minnowish boat. Every sound is amplified and enriched within this echo chamber of water and steel, from the slapping of the smallest waves against the acute angle of the bow, to the creak of my starboard oarlock—an exaggerated reminder of my intention to find some grease to lubricate one of the fittings—to the merest bump of my diminutive bow into the barge transom when I pull too hard on the oars, and the plate steel responds like the distant echo of a Japanese New Year's bell rung with the butt end of a giant beam. It seems as if I've entered a watery cave, as I peer out at the dark form of the passing barge, with two crew members standing at its bow with lines and cables ready for landing at the pier. The brightest light of the tug itself comes not from the pilothouse, whose lights are turned off, but from the engine room below, whose metal door is hinged open to relieve the engineer on a summer's night from the heat of exploding fuel.

I have no choice but to wait for the tug's bulky wake to tumble into the alcove, as the water is still churning from the workboat's huge propeller and I might still be seen. I try to predict the effect of the cornered waves and maintain my balance by feathering the blades. Yet the wake is quickly subdued; after rebounding off the perpendicular transom of the outermost barge, it is smothered by the overreaching bow, and largely deflected, I suppose, downward into the river. The impressive sloshing sound effects soon subside, and I ease myself cautiously back into the open.

I resume my pace toward an inevitable passing of the second tug, and soon take refuge again between barges. Here the gap is wider, with several boat lengths of room, yet I am further from the lights of the quarry and beside a fuller stand of trees. I will still not be seen and need only patience to let the tug pass and regain free reign of the river. I study the power plant on the opposite shore. The svelte curves of the cooling towers are complemented by the towering shoe-box architecture of the control station, whose myriad external white lights give no clue as to the number of floors within—or is there simply one towering room housing enormous needles and coils and humming generators?—and appears to have been inspired by the same page on aesthetics as the skyline of George Lucas's Death Star. Whose electric razors, I wonder, are now charging in towns far away? As I ponder how many toasters powered by the plant will catch fire on bread crumbs the following morning, I realize that the sound of the tug's diesel, while having become more audible, is now idling, and that of all the lonely barges I might have chosen as my foil I've picked the one whose number was up to receive gravel or limestone or whatever is being mined from the earth. At first I remain unseen behind the corner of its stern, yet soon I will be found, and so pull several confessional strokes into the open.

Immediately the spotlight I'd avoided along the S-turn at West Point is on me. As I tilt my head downward and away from the blinding light I gather both oar handles with my left hand, and raise my right hand both in submissive greeting and protest against the beam. The light studies me for another moment and is then extinguished, its orange coil slowly setting to black. I look up to the wheelhouse, expecting communication by bullhorn or to see the captain step out through the pilothouse door to interrogate me. While anyone is free to run the river at any time, the crew of this boat must surely, perhaps nervously, be asking what I could be doing so close to private property in such a boat at such an hour. Maybe they've come for a barge for the power plant, and are wondering whether I'm some sort of ecoterrorist engaged in late-night sabotage. More optimistically, they may have heard of me through the grapevine of towboat radio banter, as had several crews I've encountered.

Yet no one emerges from the pilothouse, and as I pull further out of their way, still expecting a conversation, the deck lights at the tug's bow are lit, the captain eases his vessel with precision toward the barge, and several crew members prepare to secure lines. I row across water gently churned by the tug's propeller, and, realizing that the captain's attention will be restricted to docking alone for the next few minutes at least, I arc into a downriver course, testing departure with a stronger yet still reserved stroke, the way one might back away from a growling dog before turning to run. Then, having maneuvered away from the tug, I pull with full force, once again feeling the exaggeration of speed and the thrill of rowing alone on the Ohio River at night.

Half a mile downstream from the tug, in the center of the river, the air is strangely warm for this time of night, and humid, and steam rises from the water as if from a farm pond on the first cold day of autumn. I pause for a moment, hold the oars in one hand while I glide, and dip a finger into water too hot to swim in, the temperature of tea that's been left to sit for ten minutes after brewing. I glance at the power plant and understand at once that its cooling towers are being used according to their original design, and that a nuclear plant's thirst for the river is tremendous. Beyond surprise, my first thought is to question whether any species native to the river can survive in such temperatures, and if not, what effect has the plant had on those divided by its heat? Then, remembering my escape from the tug, I resume a quick pace, wondering whether flipping the boat here would be preferable to having tumbled into the cold Hudson in April. Ten minutes have passed since I bolted from the tug, and suddenly through the rising steam I see the captain's spotlight once again, aimed downward at the water, searching in slow strokes the area where I was last seen, then glancing to the bank, studiously scanning upriver along the shoreline and among the trees, then back down along beside the barges, along what had been my shadowed corridor. Another look to where I'd been hiding, and the light is extinguished. A mile in the opposite direction, I approach the landing Ed had mentioned. Suddenly weary, I pitch my tent on the end of an empty dock and fall asleep.

· 12 ·

On the Banks of the Ohio

I'VE RARELY HEARD a weather report while rowing down the Ohio and wonder whether the heat along the lower river matches the temperatures of the sultry wave near Pittsburgh, where records had been set, though I'd never seen a thermometer. Here and there I overhear reports of temperatures hovering around a hundred degrees, yet despite having been raised along the cold Atlantic I've learned to tolerate the languid, humid air, and have become accustomed to sweat-drenched shorts and T-shirts by eight o'clock in the morning. The serenest cadence of stroke still dispenses a sprinkling of sweat from my nose and chin as I reach forward for each catch. The drops gloss the black matte of the beam that supports the sliding seat, and I watch as those that land out of pattern soon evaporate from metal too hot to touch. Each hour I stop to eat and drink, half a package or more of saltines with peanut butter, and long swigs of warm water from gallon jugs, often at least three gallons in a day. By six o'clock in the evening, the sun, though still far from setting, has done its withering work, and I treat that hour as an incentive, as the time when I can safely remove my shirt and not be burned. A life of daily improvisation, of material minimums, and of negotiation with the natural elements offers up such a mundane act as the shedding of a soaking shirt as a prize, a moment in which I wish for nothing more than what I feel, the soothing of my long-stifled back and shoulders in flowing air, which, though still warm, contains the subtle essence of cool.

I REACH THE RIVERFRONT at Metropolis, Illinois, toward the end of a day whose welcome dark clouds never let loose with rain yet keep the temperature down. Along the river's edge tugboats are building tows out of empty barges lined two to three deep along the shore, and a short distance downstream a casino boat styled as a nineteenth-century paddle wheeler deals odds to the local sense of luck. Metropolis itself is set back from the river and is thus beyond my view from the boat, but closer to the shore I see what appears to be a cinema, judging by the marquee, and I hope that the day might end with a movie, any movie at all. When I squint to read the listing, however, I think I see

DWIGHT YOAKUM

JULY 9

7:30

Figuring that July 9 was either yesterday or two days from now, I search for my watch amid the clutter by my feet, and find that it is in fact July 9, and 6:45. During this brief interlude the river's current has carried me toward the bow of the casino boat, from which people are watching the river, and now me, from three tiered decks. Hoping to confirm what I've read, I soon find myself in three conversations at once about where I'm coming from and where I am going. The usual confusion about whether I am headed to Brooklyn or from Brooklyn is increased by holding the several discussions at once. As I field the questions I notice one woman leaning over the railing of the second balcony, calling down to an uncertain questioner below, "He's rowing around the United States!" and thus the avenues for misinformation proliferate. An older man with a Henry Fonda fishing cap and a light blue cotton windbreaker snaps a picture and then ambles back into the casino. Perhaps he understood the route, or else didn't need to know. Maybe it was enough to know that someone was going somewhere. I manage to interject a general query about Dwight Yoakum and receive a response from the third balcony. "Yep, you read it right. We've got an extra ticket if you'd like to use it! Park your boat and come on up!" Downstream from the casino boat I come across a cement launching ramp devoid of traffic, a gift to those who wish to land along the banks of the Ohio, whose deep mud makes clean traverses between boat and dry shore almost impossible without a plank to walk on. I hop out of the boat and behind some tall weeds and make myself as presentable as possible without an all-out bath.

I don't dare leave the boat unattended by the ramp, and so paddle back to the casino, whose steel, rectangular hull is held twenty feet out from shore to prevent grounding. I row beneath the heavy cables that secure it to shore, and land so clearly in the public eye, yet so much in the mud, that the boat is now as safe in Metropolis, home of the world's largest sculpture of Superman, as it has ever been on the trip. I manage to disembark cleanly by crawling gently up the scull's fragile bow—I would not indulge the cast of onlookers by slipping into the muck—and taking a few quick and careful steps across the upper reaches of mud, hurry into the casino to meet my benefactors.

While several concert organizers contend with the onslaught of country music fans of all ages at the ticket gate, I take a brief walk into town in search of Superman, which turns out to be a forty-foot rendition in glossy red, yellow, and blue, of truth, justice, and the American way, a nation's imperfect god whose modesty as Clark Kent and token weaknesses for Kryptonite and Lois Lane place him just within the human range of any boy's aspiration. As I wander back toward the concert I wonder whether any town has the world's largest Rubberman or Shazaam. With Superman taken, it's hard to impress, but I guess that Atlanta could take an imprecise stab with Aquaman.

After so many solitary days of humming and singing songs I can't finish, it's a luxury to hear live music, including some of the recent hits I'd heard on country music stations while living in New Mexico. Songs of Dixie, and of rural life and hard living, remind me once again of how far I've come from Brooklyn, and that just this morning, as on the mornings before and those to come, I had no idea what the roughly nine thousand strokes ahead of me would reveal. And this, in place of coming home from work to a lover or domestic routine, or going out to the local café or neighborhood bar, was the day's reward, an extra ticket offered from a third balcony above the river, to an open-air sunset concert in southern Illinois. The music ends with a traditional dirge about a broken heart and the Ohio River, which slowly bleeds through the end of its course en route to becoming, just a day's row ahead of me, the Mississippi. *"Darlin', say that you'll be mine,"* sings Dwight,

In our home we'll happy be,
Down beside where the waters flow,
On the banks of the Ohio.

I took her by her pretty white hand,
I led her down the banks of sand,
I plunged her in
Where she would drown,
An' watched her as she floated down.

Darlin', say that you'll be mine;
In our home we'll happy be,
Down beside where the waters flow,
On the banks of the Ohio.

The concert was sponsored by the casino, and the ticket came in an envelope with a five-dollar coupon to the casino cafeteria and a ten-dollar gambling credit. After proving at the casino entrance that I am old enough to lose and win money, I am given two five-dollar chips, and head upstairs in search of a blackjack table. As I scout for an empty seat I imagine leaving Metropolis with a thousand in crisp bills stashed in the bow of the boat, yet finally appreciate that what I have in my hand is a crisp enough ten-dollar bill and head straight for the cashier. Another flight up to the cafeteria, and I turn in the other coupon for a ham sandwich and potato chips and am invited to share a table with a retired couple from south central Illinois.

I WALK OUT onto the upper balcony of the phony paddle wheeler and into a rising breeze, which blows up an even, tightly spaced pattern of waves that tumble slightly over themselves and are lit on this moonless night by the glow of the casino. Across the river lies the unlit shore of Kentucky, which from Paducah, some twenty miles upriver, to Wickliffe another forty down, rises too little above the river to allow anything more than a scattering of development: a power station, a boat launching ramp, and corn fields hidden beyond the riverside growth of trees. In the distance beyond that darkened shore charges of lightning briefly illuminate the cloudscape above, whose towering heights are bound before long to collapse altogether into gusting wind and rain. Still I have to find a home for what is looking more and more like a wet night. At the last minute before joining the concert crowd that evening I'd eyed both shores for a clearing for the tent and had then noticed the boat ramp directly across the river. Both upriver and downriver from the casino barge fleets are tied to shore, and as I walk downstairs toward the exit, contemplating a safe crossing of the river toward the boat ramp, I feel the pang of separation from scores of people whose mere presence is more comforting than the prospect of finding safe haven in darkened Kentucky, any one of whom might readily offer the safety of a backyard or porch if I only knew how, at this late hour, to ask.

I launch the boat as people stream from the casino to their parked cars, make my way once again beneath the heavy docking lines, and hover close to shore as I study the river up and down for barge traffic. Two of the casino's kitchen staff, dressed in greasy white, smoke cigarettes on a stern deck while on break, and watch as I pull out of their boat's glow and into darkness. I've passed through the last of the locks on the Ohio, and the river's current, though still lazy, is increasing as it succumbs to the pull of the free-flowing lower Mississippi. The shadow of a train bridge, lit dimly for barges at its central span, stretches across the Ohio a hundred yards downstream of me, and I am careful to stay above it, not only because I know the boat ramp to be upstream from the bridge, but because of a mild superstition developed immediately on the trip—and held, not so curiously, by other boaters on the rivers—about not crossing under bridges at night, a cousin perhaps to the taboo against walking beneath upright ladders. With the help of my flashlight I locate the ramp and pull the boat up during a disquieting lull in the breeze, which suggests an imminent shift in wind direction and gears, and I hope I'll have time to get the tent set up before the clutch is engaged.

In a graveled clearing strewn with crushed beer cans, bottle caps, and broken glass, and just large enough for a car to turn around in, I quickly scan with my flashlight for the flattest area to host my tent and shine the beam on mature rows of corn bordered by an undulating dirt road extending inland from the parking lot. I manage to build the tent in the rising wind, and, unable to stake it to the hard, rocky ground, find half a dozen rocks I can use as anchors for the tent's fly. I waste no time as I adjust the rocks, return to the boat to secure anything that might be blown out—I stow the seat pads beneath the aft deck—and with hurried precaution drag the boat, its skeg scraping on cement, another ten feet up the ramp. I look back across the river as the last cars depart from the casino parking lot, the beams of their headlights searching for the way out to Main Street and roads home. The glow of the casino dimly illuminates a river bearded in white as waves of gusting wind race upriver.

There is still no rain, and with the boat secure and the tent cowering in the wind but weighted by the rocks, I stand for a moment at the top of the ramp and wait for shocks of lightning to charge the riverscape with flashes of electric white. Each apocalyptic glimpse reverberates in the darkness that follows, yet is soon replaced with each strike by a new view, a meteorological slide show. Looking upriver I am shown the loneliness of a green channel marker tethered to the river's bottom. Downriver I see the eerily lit girdering of the train bridge. And, gazing skyward, a flash reveals the magnificent ionic vapors above, their vastness greater than that of the widest, bluest sky.

As I turn back to the tent I see in the humid air and the stirred dust the glow of headlights, rising and falling with the uneven track. Who would be out at this hour on such a night, and here of all places? The detritus of past drinking parties crushed and flattened into the ground suggests a late-night spree by the river, and I am now doubly aware of my presence on someone else's turf. Or perhaps a police cruiser making the obligatory rounds, a possibility I prefer. The beams emerge from behind the corn rows, and the glare gives way as the car, an early seventies Chevy Impala, with faded gold paint spotted with rusty lesions and capped by a peeling white vinyl roof, lumbers its way into the clearing, and fails, incredibly, to ground out on the uneven lot.

I walk unthreateningly toward the car as it comes to a stop—waiting by the tent might seem overtly defensive—and greet its solitary occupant through the open window. He seems to greet my left shoulder in return, his stout nose, round chin, and mop of tan hair all tinted by the dim green glow of the instrument panel, and the red hue of a tape player from whose speakers Led Zeppelin gloomily delivers the lyrics to "No Quarter." Empty cans of Milwaukee's Best—*Really?* I joke to myself, now unconcerned about my unexpected company— have clearly been collecting on the seat and floor, and I can easily imagine that all of the bottles and cans on the ground have been delivered by and dispensed from this single vehicle. Our conversation runs neither deep nor long, and after he reaches out over the great wall of his door to shake my hand for the fourth time, he drops the gear shifter into drive, distinguishes the dirt road back into Kentucky from the cement ramp into the river, and the massive thing loafs away. I question the possibility that he might have been more cognizant than I'd realized, that he might return with others, yet the river remains deep in strife with the wind, and in my fatigue I accept the risk and zip myself into the tent.

The following morning, under clear skies, I hear the engine of another vehicle as I am packing my tent into its bag. A dark green late-model pickup eases to a stop and a well-fed older man of Mediterranean descent, with a striking mix of black and silver hair, rests his arm amiably on the truck door. We greet each other, and before he gets around to asking about the boat, which I see him notice through the windshield, he asks, "Did you camp here last night?" I wonder whether I had missed a sign restricting camping.

"Yes," I answer.

"And nobody bothered you?"

"No, not really," and I mention my inebriated guest.

"Well, then consider yourself lucky. If they don't knock 'em off before they get here, this is where they do it. Just throw 'em in the river." And we proceed to talk about more pleasant things like fishing for catfish, in which he is expert, and how to get from Brooklyn to this clearing by a Kentucky corn patch by oar.

· 13 ·

Thrown Out

OF THE THOUSANDS OF JOURNEYS that have preceded mine on the Ohio River, from those of the first Indian colonists and traders, to the traffic of American westward expansion, to the towboat now forging by as I collapse and stow my tent, I'm captured by the story of Anna and Harlan Hubbard, as told and illustrated in Hubbard's own *Shantyboat: A River Way of Life*. *Shantyboat* is a quintessentially American story of departure from life in a cultural center to "the fringe of society," as Harlan subtitled a subsequent book. A librarian and art teacher respectively, Anna and Harlan opted midlife to leave behind the lives they knew in Cincinnati, and drift on an old-school— read *motorless*—shantyboat of their own construction, down the Ohio River, down the Mississippi, downstream to the Gulf of Mexico.

Setting out in the late 1940s, they drifted for several years during the late fall and winter, and each spring managed to find, care of a local farmer, a small riverside plot of land on which they could grow vegetables and from which they ventured by foot and bicycle into the surrounding countryside and culture. The Hubbards were among the last of the shantyboat dwellers on the big rivers and, traveling during the postwar economic and domestic booms, they preceded the coming generation who would go "back to the earth." They were without pretention, had nothing to prove, and for this their life of simplicity and adventure remains all the more appealing. Harlan reveals their original motive on the opening page of *Shantyboat*: "Who can watch the ceaseless lapsing of a river's current without conceiving a desire to set himself adrift, and, like the driftwood which glides past, float with the stream clear to the final ocean?"

The Hubbards' story has largely remained local to their route, and it was only below Cincinnati that I first heard their names and was asked whether I'd read about them. From library to library I've searched for the book, and read chapter by chapter, town by town, until I bought my own copy in a bookstore. Though after a day of rowing I find myself too exhausted to read more than a page, I read each morning of the Hubbards' life as I travel along the same shores.

AT A SMALL VILLAGE on the Ohio River I find a boat ramp at the final edge of daylight. I soon locate a semblance of a park, give myself a gallon-jug bath, and pitch my tent. No two days on the trip blend together. Each one is framed uniquely by sunrise in a new setting—I feel certain that by the end of my life I will have woken up only once in a riverside pasture in Apple Grove, Ohio—and sunset in a destination determined by the chance unraveling of each day. Already I can pick out May 7 or June 12 like books from a shelf, and if I point to the one that began at lock number nine on the Erie Canal, I know that it ended at Brewerton, an inimitable sequence of chance and response between the covers. If a friend had asked me before the trip what I'd done on a given day a week earlier, my memory would have reached for the handhold of routine; if it was Thursday then I must have done whatever it is that I did on Thursdays. Until now my memory has been based on time and the routines that give it shape. While rowing, however, my routine is movement, and if those I encounter along the way want to know what happened ten days or five hundred miles ago, I only need to know where I woke up.

The following morning I roam up a narrow road to a general store, and after waiting for it to open, chat with its owner and once again choose the chocolate bar as the best, most palatable source of calories that I can buy for less than a dollar. Another customer overhears my mention of the trip, and soon I'm sitting in the passenger seat of a high mileage, evenly bruised black Cadillac. He's driven all the way from eastern Pennsylvania for an annual family reunion hosted by his grandfather who, he is sure, will be eager to hear about the trip.

There is no house, but rather a camp scene, with folding tables and folding chairs, and a small trailer home. In any direction other families are gathered likewise across a green field clustered with trees. It is a tract of temporary summer retreats, likely prone to flooding in the late winter and spring. I am soon introduced all around, to cousins who lounge on lawn chairs trading stories of their lives of the previous year, and to children who are stopped from play long enough to meet the man who rowed here from New York City.

"What do you think of *that*?" a mother asks her ten-year-old son. He'd shyly shaken my hand and now answers to the ground, "I don't know." But his mother presses on.

"Is there anything you'd like to ask him?" He repeats his last answer, yet this time looks away with an embarrassed smile, wishing to be released.

"Wouldn't you like to know where he sleeps at night?"

"I guess so," he answers, with no other choice. I tell him that I sleep in a tent each night, sometimes in town parks, or wherever I find a place where no one will mind. I point in the direction of the spot I'd camped in the night before. Finally he finds a polite moment to excuse himself, and immediately recovers his full animation as he returns to play.

I am then introduced to the grandfather, who has been talking with several men in a corner of the lot, which blends into other lots, devoid of houses, each one apparently private but with borders defined more by the recreational sprawl of each family than by hedgerows or fences. He has seen me already, as we'd caught each other's eye upon my arrival. He is tall and strong, perhaps in his late sixties, with short metal-gray hair naturally swept back from his forehead and piercing blue eyes in the weathered face of a lifelong smoker. He is dressed in the blue shirt and pants of a mechanic, with leather boots, and his hands remind me of well-worn tools. When he greets me he looks me straight in the eye, rugged and handsome, and I suspect that he may be part American Indian.

"So I hear you've come all the way from New York," he says with a serrated voice that matches his face. He has obviously been briefed on my arrival.

"Yes," I tell him. "I left in April. I'm on my way to the Gulf, then around Florida and back to Brooklyn." He's visibly curious.

"Well that's a hell of a long way! So what, you've got a canoe?" No one has yet seen the boat.

"No, it's rowing boat, with a sliding seat and long oars. It's faster than a canoe. Then again, I've never really been in a canoe, but I've been in rowboats since I was a kid. I guess you stick with what you know." And in this manner we fill in the details about how and why I've come this far. I learn along the way that he'd fought in Korea, and I tell him that of all the veterans I'd met thus far he is the first of the Korean War. "They call it the 'Forgotten War,'" he tells me, with the subtlest straightening of his posture and a sobering in his already somber eyes. I think back to Freddy Fisher and his distant, veteran's gaze. He takes another swig from the can of beer in his hand.

I ask him, in a conversational shift, whether he's ever heard of the Hubbards. Perhaps he remembers them drifting by on their houseboat. He is suddenly attentive.

"Hubbard?" he asks pointedly. "How do you know that name?" It seems that I've connected more fully than I'd expected.

"Yes, Harlan Hubbard and his wife, Anna. I'm reading a book about them. They built a houseboat back in the late forties and drifted from somewhere around Cincinnati down the Ohio, and then down the Mississippi." He stares at me, and not knowing how to answer his gaze I continue: "They drifted during the winter when the river was up, and then found places to stop for the summer and farmed." I trail off, sensing that something isn't right. If he knows about the Hubbards we should already be talking about houseboats, or perhaps his own childhood by the water, if indeed he grew up on the river.

"So you know Hubbard," he says, and then suggests a different first name than Harlan.

"No," I correct him. "His name was Harlan. He wrote a book about it, published by the University of Kentucky Press." I'd volunteered what I thought was a benign topic for conversation and am thrown by his response. Naming the publisher, I realize, is grasping at straws.

"I don't know how you know about Hubbard," he continues, obviously disturbed. Apparently the Hubbards are not a good name to drop along this stretch of the Ohio. Perhaps they had lived secret lives shrouded in a feel-good story about their American way of life.

The mysterious tension is eased by the arrival of another man. He's heard about the trip and wants to know more. Hot dogs are ready, and during this new conversation I'm led to a table covered with bowls of potato salad, plates of hot dogs and hamburgers, condiments, and utensils. Soon I'm seated in a folding chair answering questions about the trip. A spent fire contained by rocks smoulders on the ground, and from time to time I notice the grandfather, still seated as he was, sometimes looking at me. I'm asked about the remainder of my route, and when I mention Key West, my new company lights up.

"Key West? If you're going to Key West then you'll be going to Islamorada, right?" I tell him I'm not sure, and ask where it is.

"It's one of the Keys. You'll be going right by it! My brother works at a bar there, right on the water. This is their shirt." He sits back and expands his chest so I can see his gray T-shirt, with a pocket screen printed with the bar's name and logo. He then stands up and shows me the back, printed with a lewd play on fishing terms. "It's on the Florida Bay side of Islamorada," he continues, "and you can row right up to their dock. Here, take the shirt." Still standing, he peels the shirt from his back, folds it up, and places it on a folding table by my chair. Sitting down again, his plate neglected on account of his enthusiasm, his plan evolves: "Take it with you, and when you get to Islamorada wear it to the bar. You can't miss it. Everyone knows where it is. Ask for my brother"—he gives me a name—"and tell him where you got this shirt! He'll flip when he finds out that you met me! He'll never believe where you got this."

Everyone in the circle is amused, and I like the idea myself, as the delivery of the shirt to Florida sends forth an additional tendril of expectation that I will make it not only as far as the Gulf, stroke by stroke, but well beyond, to coastlines that still seem so far away as to remain an abstraction.

And then, with one syllable, deep and singular like a crack of lightning from a fuming cloud, the easy banter of the picnic is silenced. "OUT!" We all look to the grandfather, who's now on his feet, standing by his chair.

"GET OUT!" He walks slowly toward us, utterly in control of everyone before him, but to my dismay his eyes are locked on me. I look back at him blankly, speechless, resigned to my obvious conviction without indictment—but for what? His judgment is so solid I feel I *must* have done something wrong, but remain visibly at a loss. His voice, up to the last word I will hear from him, never eases, is never lowered. Those around me look at him, and at each other, and at me, searching for an explanation. I return the glances, defending myself with my mystified look, yet sensing the doubt already seeded in some eyes. "What," they might be wondering, "does the old man know about our visitor that we don't know?"

"GET OFF THIS PROPERTY. NOW!" I've stood up.

"What did I do?" I ask feebly, not professing any claim to stay, but simply wishing to know as I leave which toe I'd unwittingly stomped on. In response he threateningly points beyond the black Cadillac to the road returning to the general store. I look to him, and to those around me, who are stunned themselves and in no position to defend me even if they wish to. If this scene were suddenly transposed to that of my imminent death, say on a sinking ship, and he were the only soul present to hear my last request for a farewell to my family, I wouldn't bother asking. He'd just say "GO! OFF THIS SHIP!" And, like Spencer Tracy as Manuel in the old black-and-white film *Captains Courageous*, I'd slip silently away, as I do now, feeling unpermitted even to say good-bye to the man who'd given me the shirt, which is left where he'd placed it on a table by my chair.

I'm flustered as I walk back to the boat, at first unable even to analyze the details of my visit in a search for what went wrong. I feel both innocent of any wrongdoing and guilty by the force of his judgment. What had I said? Do some prisoners wrongly convicted come to believe that they did in fact commit the crime? How will I resolve this on my own, the possibility that I'm capable of so offending someone without even realizing it? And he is a war veteran, too. I'm not a pacifist, but nor have I served in the military, and I consider it an honor to meet anyone who has, particularly those who've served during wartime. No matter how you cut it, there's a clear connection between those who've chosen or been conscripted to join the military and my freedom to spend months roaming down American rivers. It would be one thing to have ticked off a plain jerk, but I was pleased to have met this man and grandfather, and touched by his manner as he'd mentioned the Forgotten War.

As I am distracted by the process of getting back on the water, the only place I now want to be, the dust begins to settle in my mind and our discussion about the Hubbards emerges into view. Had we been talking about two different—very different—Hubbards? But how could that have set him off? Just then the massive Cadillac floats down a hill to the top of the launching ramp, driven by its owner who's accompanied by several of his younger nephews. It's a friendly visit, I can see, for which I'm grateful. I walk to the car as it comes to a stop.

"Oh man!" says the driver as he opens the door and gets out. "I'm glad we caught you before you left. We just wanted to come apologize for our grandfather." I smile inwardly, knowing this certainly wasn't their grandfather's idea, and smile outwardly too.

"I was sorry," I tell them, "that I couldn't say good-bye on my way out."

"Well, I don't know what got into him," he goes on. "Sometimes he just gets like that. But you hit the button today!" I tell them about the Hubbards, that I can only imagine that my Hubbard and his Hubbard are two different people, and suppose that his, with whom I perhaps became associated, was not a good egg. They again profess their bafflement, yet are soon more interested in the details of the boat, which lies by our feet at the river's edge.

"Oh," says one, turning back to the car, "we brought the T-shirt!" While parting I ask them to sign my address book, which they each do. One inscribes in large capital letters below his address and phone number a summary of my visit: "THROWN OUT!"

Several weeks later I receive an e-mail from one of those who'd wished me luck at the river's edge. He tells me that despite their enthusiastic descriptions of the boat for their grandfather, he still has not changed his mind about me. "When he saw you take the T-shirt he thought you were a con! We keep trying to tell him, but he won't change his mind!" I hadn't thought of the shirt, and now my best explanation takes on depth. I contemplate sending a copy of *Shantyboat*, but think twice about it, realizing that his mind is so fully set that any attempt on my part to change it, short of resurrecting and delivering Harlan Hubbard himself, on his houseboat down by the water's edge, would be construed as one more piece of a river-running scam.

———

THE FOLLOWING DAY—and 981 miles since I'd waved good-bye to the crews of Three Rivers Rowing Association in Pittsburgh—I reach the junction of the Ohio and Mississippi Rivers at Cairo (pronounced K-row), Illinois. Early the next morning I row beneath the last bridge across the Ohio, and shortly after sunrise the Mississippi appears a reddish shade of coffee in the early light. While some of the silt of the Ohio is carried from as far away as Chautauqua Lake, the silt in the Mississippi is carried from Alberta and Montana. Evidently there's more of it in those western reaches, as the colors of the two rivers contrast sharply, and the Mississippi soil reaches into the clearer water of the Ohio like drops of food coloring in a glass of water.

· 14 ·

The River Melts the Land
and Carries It

WHEN I CLOSE MY EYES at night I see the Mississippi River. No shore, no boat, no sand bars. Only water, silty brown and swirling, so close in my mind it seems I could reach into it with my hand and watch my fingers disappear into alluvial opaqueness. The river melts the land and carries it. It is a river of water and soil, Ol' Muddy, running southward through the continent, starting so far to the north you'd have to drive through Pennington, Minnesota, on the Leech Lake Indian Reservation, hardly seventy miles from the Canadian border, to cross the country without bridging it. Yet it is not a still frame of water I see with closed eyes, but an endless shifting of myriad sub-currents, of whirlpools the size of saucers, smoothly flowing mushroom domes of upwelling water thirty feet wide, and countless other zephyrs of liquid movement, constantly morphing and eddying, an ever-changing puzzle of water. Looking down from a bridge one sees the river as a single, steady whole. But its flow is in fact incalculably complex, and it is this motion that puts me to sleep.

I sleep lightly on the trip, rarely for more than a couple of hours at a time when in my tent. Any change in my surroundings might be a threat. I wake up when the wind rises, and when it dies. I wake up when I hear engines, when I hear waves breaking on the shore, and when the sky begins to lighten. I've woken up now to the sudden light of a towboat's sweeping beam, which filters briefly through the tent as it searches a mile or two beyond me for a guiding beacon. I love the way the light precedes the sound of the engine. The actual passage of the boat is an event still to come.

The last town visible from the river was Helena, Arkansas, thirty miles upriver. The next river town is Greenville, Mississippi, ninety miles down. For all I know there are towns three miles or five miles to either side of the river. But I can't see them or hear even the distant acceleration of a car or truck. I could get to them if I had to by traipsing through thickets and swamps reportedly full of poison ivy, and hiking up and back down the slopes of levees thirty feet high, which run clear to New Orleans and beyond to help control the river during floods. But so far these towns might as well be in Nebraska for all they've meant to me. It's not that I'm lonely here; in fact I'm fascinated that such a remote world remains in the heart of the country in 1999. But the towboat's beam, now extinguished, is welcome, as is the growing drone of the engines. They provide their own sort of reassurance, and I am reminded of the way I'd sometimes gone to sleep as a child, with the bedroom door open to the distant sound of talk and laughter in the living room among my parents and their friends.

I can see the night sky through the fine mesh of my tent. Even once the sun sets the humid air still holds the heat of day, and after I've taken a gallon-jug bath I zip the tent door closed and sit as still as I can, watching the river, slowing my pulse, and attempting to stop the beads of sweat forming on my clean, naked self. The river is almost as quiet as the sky. Occasionally a whirlpool gathers momentum and size until its hubris is put in check by other currents and audibly disrupted. The steadiest sound comes from the nearest channel marker as it slices the current, like the sound of a small distant wave breaking on a beach. It neither crescendos nor dissipates, but just holds. As for the sky, the stars pass in their usual silence, though an occasional jet flies below them, chased by its own wavering, thunderous wake. And if I look long enough in one place a shooting star, the size of a pebble yet as bright as Capella, streaks silently earthward like a belated ray of sunlight.

Aided by the current I have been rowing about sixty miles a day on the Mississippi, sometimes more, rarely less. Before long, and with so few towns along the way, the bends and straight avenues of the river begin to look alike, and in the heat and solitude I sometimes lose track of whether I've already rowed around the bend I'd seen coming—or is that the one still ahead of me?—and of how long I've been at the oars. Time dissolves in the heated repetition. I rarely talk to myself, and never yell just to hear my own voice where no one else will hear me. It's not that I feel I'm being watched—though on more populated stretches of the trip I haven't always been so sure—but that calling attention to myself would somehow invite bad luck, and I feel I have temerity enough just to be here, let alone further announcing myself to the river. Ultimately, I feel safer when I'm quiet.

Every so often while rowing I see a towboat. If it's heading upriver we will meet before long. It might be making three or four miles per hour upstream, though sometimes less depending on the size of its engines and load. Where the river narrows a bit and the current is thus increased, towboats have been known to fight for hours, making no headway upriver. Occasionally, as I've been told, a captain will go off duty with his boat in such a position, only to return hours later to find that his replacement had made no more progress himself. Eventually something gives. Either the barge is beached along the sandy bank with some expectation that the current will change, or the captain manages foot by foot to play back eddies in the current to climb the river. I have watched as upbound tows remain nearly stationary, their progress observable only from a long gaze at the shore beyond.

Heading downriver, however, the goal is not to make up for lost time and take full advantage of combustion and gravity, but to prevent the mammoth tows from getting out of control, particularly along some bend where another tow might be encountered and currents can become chaotic. Often the captains push their engines just enough to maintain steerageway through swirling currents, while economizing on fuel for engines which, even two alone, can produce 10,000 horsepower, and consume 250 gallons of diesel fuel per hour. Though they might make eight or nine miles per hour on top of the river's rate, they instead make six or seven, slightly faster than me.

At Memphis I finally acquired a handheld VHF two-way radio, having often wished I'd been able to communicate with the towboat captains to allay any concerns they might have had about whether I would stay out of their way. I turn it on when I see a barge approaching, and particularly when two barges approach or overtake one another the radio provides a window on the captains' lives within the wheelhouses. There are few professions in which colleagues are so genuinely polite with each other. Miss Manners herself would be impressed if she sat on a blanket on the riverbank at a bend or by a bridge and tuned a handheld marine-band radio to a working channel—13 if on the Mississippi above Baton Rouge, or 9 if below. Sooner or later a southbound barge will approach one heading north. Often the cut of the river will be such that the two wish to cross paths at the bend in order to take respective advantage of the currents, the upriver barge looking for back eddies along the inside of a bend, the downriver barge looking for the fastest, outer track. Or perhaps even three tows, say the *Enterprise* heading upstream and about to overtake *MacMahan* below the bend, and the third, *Theriot*, heading downstream at the top of the bend.

"This is *MacMahan* calling upbound barge . . ."

"Mornin' Cap, *Enterprise* here, I was just about to give you a call."

"Mornin'. We've got *Theriot* coming down and I can pull over to let you two pass, if you want."

"If it suits you, and I'll see if *Theriot* wants me to hold off to let him cross . . ."

"This is *Theriot*, mornin' there, *Enterprise*. I'm makin' about seven miles an hour, and I can swing wide long enough for you shoot right on through."

"Sounds good, Skip, sounds good . . . anything behind you?"

"Clear's as far as I can see, and nothing heading upriver since Vicksburg—you got clear sailing all day."

"Sounds real fine. You have a good one now."

All of this in the most pleasant, chatty tones—as it needs to be, for the Mississippi and captains' wheelhouses above the river can be lonely places. Each passing barge represents, in addition to a navigational hazard, a brief social encounter for crews that, though they may be traveling through the heart of the country, are not allowed to leave the boats for weeks at a time.

Tows on the Mississippi are typically built of thirty, thirty-five, or thirty-six barges, each five or six wide, almost always a number resulting in a perfect rectangle. I occasionally see one with forty-two and once even forty-nine, and I've been told that during the height of harvest season a southbound tow was once built with eighty barges. According to a brochure published by the Iowa Department of Transportation, a single barge is the equivalent in its weight capacity to fifteen hopper cars of a freight train, or fifty-eight large semi trucks. A mere fifteen-barge tow, a quarter-mile long, carries the equivalent of 225 hopper cars or 870 large semis, which, bumper to bumper on the interstate, would stretch eleven and a half miles. The larger tows on the Mississippi are measureable in acres.

It has become an unavoidable pastime of mine to keep an overtaking tow behind me as long as possible. The closer they get the harder I pull on the oars. Just this evening, when the sun had fallen so low that I'd already taken my shirt off, I had watched obsessively as the broad bow of a tow gained on me, feeling like John Henry as he hammered rock in a race against the automatic tunnel borer, my brown arms glowing in the deepening light and raining sweat with every stroke. Every so often I manage to pass a slower towboat, albeit briefly, but this evening I could feel the scull reaching hull speed with the completion of each stroke, and still I lost ground. As the steel bow caught up to me, not a hundred feet to my left, I locked my gaze on its position, watched as I matched its speed while driving the oars through the water, but ceded a foot during each recovery. Still I was driven, beyond driven, my mind oblivious to the passage of time, and immune to the tedium of repetition.

The tow was five barges wide and seven long, each one 195 feet in length, and it passed me one foot at a time over a half dozen miles. I relented when the stern of the tug finally edged ahead of me, and surfed its wake until it too had passed, then pulled out my radio to greet the captain. "You must be the one comin' from New York!" he exclaimed, and our conversation, each of us in plain sight of the other, ended with waves farewell.

THE BARGE whose beam had swept through the tent has now hiked its way abreast of my campsite. Its engines will now begin to fade, though the sound of its trailing wake crumbling on both shores will continue to rise. I wonder whether my presence on the sandbar has been noted.

Thus far each night on the Mississippi an upriver breeze, hardly enough to quiver the tent, has carried through sunset, and I've camped on the northern reaches of sandbars that form on the north sides of the islands and that are exposed by the falling river. If the island itself, thickly grown with trees and thickets, is ten acres in size, the sandbar is perhaps fifty acres of pristine, wind-patterned beach. The mosquitoes never detect me here. It is now the middle of July and, having been blessed in part by the summer's drought, and now by campsites so far downwind of whatever hordes of insects may dwell in the island's green, I've rarely had to contend with more than a few bloodsuckers. My bottle of insect repellent, purchased three years before and already half empty when I'd started the trip, is still half full.

Tonight I am camped on Island 64, where the river now runs through the Jackson Cut-Off, a shortening of its previous course that both lessens shipping distances and increases the rate of current so as to create in the river a self-dredging effect. Imagine that you are drawing a large S in sand with your finger, that it is filled with water, and that the curves in the S are two bends in the Mississippi. Now place your finger where you began the S, and dredge a channel straight down to the beginning of the lower bend. You've added the Jackson Cut-off. Now imagine that water is flowing from top to bottom. It will, as in all physics, take the path of least resistance, and the upper bend of your S is now abandoned by the flow, perhaps eventually to dry up or become an isolated oxbow lake. During the 1930s and 1940s the river was shortened by 150 miles through a combination of such cut-offs.

Looking at a road map of the region one can see the difference between the river's course prior to the cut-offs, marked by the coloring of state boundaries, and the river's present route, marked in blue. It seems, looking at the state lines, as if the river were a coil of wire and, looking at the river's current route, that the coil has been stretched. The existing state boundaries were all determined prior to the program of cut-offs. My Island 64, lying on the west side of the river, is part of Phillips County, Arkansas. Yet Island 65, the next island south and also on the west side of the river, is formed in part by the oxbow lake created by the dredging of Jackson Cut-Off. It, however, lies not in Arkansas, but in Coahoma County, Mississippi. So if the $64,000 dollar question asks whether the state of Mississippi—or Kentucky or Tennessee, for that matter—lies to the east or the west of the Mississippi River, the correct answer is both east *and* west.

My timing with the sandbars, by chance, is perfect, as I will later be told that they can be among the greatest treacheries of the river. They grow more stable as the river falls and ebbs away from them, yet when the river rises it may carve away the sand from below, leaving little indication underfoot that a great mass of sand is about to simply collapse, the air between its grains suddenly replaced by water, and its grip upon limb and body unyielding. At Natchez I will soon be told by an oil prospector that a fear of the river is pervasive among locals, and few who live along it consider it a recreational opportunity. Of those who'd been more brazen he knew of four who'd instantly drowned as the river inhaled sections of sandbars from below.

If there is one name to know along the Mississippi it is perhaps James Buchanan Eads, an engineer and a businessman who knew the river to its literal depths. In 1846, at the age of twenty-six, Eads had made a small fortune in the salvage business on the river, at first using a forty-gallon whiskey barrel converted into a diving bell to plumb the black depths while raising sunken cargo and even sunken ships. He might as well have kept his eyes shut for all the light that reaches even a few feet below the river's surface. It was this work that both fueled his lifelong affair with the Mississippi and revealed to him its hydrologic nature, knowledge that would serve him for the rest of his life and whose application would give us the river as we now know it. The river below, as Eads described, is a dark world of tidal wind and sandstorm:

> *The sand was drifting like a dense snowstorm at the bottom. . . . At sixty-five feet below the surface I found the bed of the river, for at least three feet in depth, a moving mass and so unstable that, in endeavoring to find footing on it beneath my bell, my feet penetrated through it until I could feel, although standing erect, the sand rushing past my hands, driven by a current apparently as rapid as that on the surface. I could discover the sand in motion at least two feet below the surface of the bottom, and moving with a velocity diminishing in proportion to its depth.*

Not surprisingly, with the invention of scuba diving still more than a century away, Eads became well-known along the Mississippi for his underwater salvage work, and three decades later he applied his understanding of the ways in which the river scours and carves its course to the problem of the sandbars that tend to form at the mouths of rivers. Commercial shipping between other coastal ports and New Orleans had been plagued by these bars, and no amount of dredging had managed to maintain channels of sufficient depth where the river gives way to the Gulf of Mexico. After heated lobbying of Congress in competition with rival engineer Andrew Humphreys, chief of the Army Corps of Engineers, who wished to solve the problem with an escalated dredging program, Eads was given a government contract to achieve what many thought could not be done: he would build two parallel jetties that would extend the reach of South Pass, one of three main channels leading through a fan of marshland from the end of the Mississippi to the open gulf. Rather than allowing the river to simply end immediately in the beachside shallows of the gulf, Eads would force it to continue hundreds of yards farther into deeper water, where the silt would become more broadly dispersed. The jetties would so constrain the channel's current that its rate would not only continue into deeper water, but also carve its way through existing sandbars. In short order, upon completion of the jetties, a typical depth of eight feet above the sandbars was scoured to thirty feet. In 1875, the year Eads began the jetties project, the port of St. Louis had shipped 6,857 tons of cargo via New Orleans to Europe. A year after he finished, in 1880, 453,681 tons were shipped by the same route. Before long New Orleans, having been the ninth largest port in the country, ranked second only to New York City.[4]

This same principle was later applied on a much larger scale to the Mississippi itself. In the five-mile stretch of Jackson Cut-Off alone, ten stone jetties of various lengths project at ninety degree angles from the riverbanks into the channel. Large eddies swirl slowly beneath each jetty, while the current in the main channel is focused more narrowly, as if through a funnel, and thus sped along. As with Eads's channel at South Pass, the river dredges itself. I think of Eads when I see these jetties. I think of him too when I wonder how deep the river is below me, when I watch the blades nearly disappear in the water during their catch. When I think of him he is at the bottom of the river, breathing in the space of a forty-gallon whiskey barrel pumped with air from above.

But more often I think of Anna and Harlan Hubbard, who drifted on their houseboat a route I'm now retracing. I always take notice when I pass the places that they mentioned: Wolf Island Bar, Morrison Towhead, Island 21, Mhoon Bend—remote, uninhabited places whose names create a common language for those on the river. Of the journeys of all of the explorers I've read about, from Joshua Slocum's single-handed circumnavigation of the world, to John Muir's "Thousand Mile Walk to the Gulf," to Wilfred Thesiger's desert venture across the Empty Quarter of Saudi Arabia, none has so captured my imagination as the Hubbards'. I imagine them on their houseboat in a shaded cove out of the river's current, their oil lantern casting a faint glow on the surrounding woods, their two dogs running through the brush, the wood-burning cookstove heating the cabin on a fall evening. Such a mixture of high adventure and domesticity, with no less use for a straw-bristled broom than for the long sweep oars used to lever their boat out of the way of barges.

I finished reading *Shantyboat* yesterday morning. The Hubbards ended their trip some five hundred miles ahead of me, near New Orleans (and then continued their wanderings along the Louisiana bayous), still to me a world away. Yet I could not have finished the book on a more appropriate day. I reached Helena, Arkansas, at noon and, not anticipating another true river town for more than a hundred miles, expected to get out of the boat and wander through a cultural oasis that had to have at least a convenience store with ice-cream sandwiches, if not a laundromat too. Yet still a mile upstream from Helena I was approached by one of the handful of recreational boats I would see on the 950 miles of the lower Mississippi. It was a couple on an aluminum pontoon boat hooded with a red canvas canopy. I felt their inquisitive aim the moment they motored toward me, and in short order

I was invited to tie the scull up to their boat and join them. As it happened the scull fit neatly between the two pontoons and under the deck, with the stern protruding slightly like a torpedo ready to be launched backward. They introduced themselves as James and Debbie, and told me that they were out enjoying the water. The remains of a picnic were in the ice chest. I should feel free to help myself, I was told, to make a sandwich and have something cold to drink. They were both in their late fifties, perhaps, and I soon learned that she had grown up on a houseboat on the river. She talked about the water, which her family drank after letting the silt settle in fifty-five-gallon drums. She wouldn't have traded the lifestyle for anything, she said, though she'd often wondered what it was like for kids her age to live in one place. Her father's boat had had an engine, and thus they'd managed to run up and down both the Ohio and the Mississippi. I asked whether she'd ever heard of the Hubbards and described the book that I'd just finished.

"Hubbard!" she half-exclaimed, in pleasing contrast to the last response to that name. "My parents knew the Hubbards! I was just a girl then, but they tied up next to us for several nights. I've heard that my family was mentioned in that book but I've never seen it." I put down a half-eaten sandwich and reached from the pontoon deck down to the bag in the scull that contained the book.

"What is your last name?" I asked as I retrieved it.

"Story," she said. "Debbie Story." I remembered roughly where Hubbard described her family and handed her the book.

"I just finished it this morning," I told her. "You can have it."

Debbie sat down and began flipping through the pages, but before becoming immersed she mentioned that she'd kept a collection of old letters to her parents, including some of the Christmas cards the Hubbards had made and sent to those they'd met. After finding Hubbard's mention of her family, she perused the book slowly, stopping to study each of Harlan's simple, evocative sketches of the rivers and river life. She sometimes smiled, sometimes seemed lost in memory, and several times said half aloud, "That's just the way it was." As she drifted through time and James and I talked about the trip, the river carried us past the city of Helena, which I never did visit.

Lying now in the tent I hear the fading groan of the towboat, which has now passed, and can just make out the sound of its wake against the banks upriver. I absentmindedly massage one hand with the other, as their tendons, stressed from the days of rowing and given a rest at night, tighten and pull my fingers into half fists that cannot open on their own. I will again massage them open in the morning. For now it is this slight effort, as well as images of water, that draw me back into sleep.

· 15 ·

"Hey, Matt!"

BATON ROUGE is announced as I head downstream by a several mile stretch of river whose banks are layered with barges often seven or eight deep. Past these barges and around a bend the capital city comes into view beyond the girdered span of a highway bridge. In the foreground along the far bank the skyline is dominated by manufacturing plants and refineries, whose tall narrow stacks exhale violently steady flames. Further down the embankment the capital building itself rises as a modest, slender skyscraper above the vast canopy of the delta's forest, its upper levels providing politicians with broad views of their electoral domain. Yet it's the ships that hold a rower's eye, oceangoing freighters with looming bows and heights measurable in stories. The smaller of these are six hundred feet in length, less than the average towboat, yet more imposing and, at full speed, perhaps three times as fast.

At 230 miles from the open gulf, Baton Rouge is the uppermost terminus for such vessels. Thus, from a commercial point of view, the bridge represents perhaps the most significant boundary along the entire river, above which towboats monopolize all inland, domestic shipping and below which the tows are smaller and play second fiddle to the international freighters. Indeed, while I'd passed occasional gravel quarries and grain docks farther up the river, the scale of material and chemical industry at Baton Rouge is unprecedented and begins immediately below the bridge.

Some ships are docked at loading platforms along the shore, and others are rafted together and anchored on the open river. By and large they are foreign, from predominantly Asian, Mediterranean, and South American ports. With few exceptions they are imperfectly kept, with rust-streaked paint and diesel-sooted exhaust stacks, and in such relief the typical river tug is notably immaculate.

As I pass beneath the bridge and eye the ships—none happens to be in transit at the moment—I recall warnings about their wakes, estimated in one recreational boaters' guide to reach six feet, and while two or three shipping facilities between Baton Rouge and New Orleans will sell basic provisions such as ice and fuel, no recreational boats are allowed to actually tie up because of the risk of their being pummeled against wharves by the aftermath of a passing freighter. My only solace lies in the hope that these wakes are of the rolling rather than breaking sort, and the knowledge that estimations of wave height are frequently though unintentionally exaggerated, often by a factor of two.

In the early afternoon heat I pull up along the city's riverbank by the dock of a tugboat company, two stone throws from the capital tower, and walk into town in search of water at least, if not some food. There are no stores in immediate view but I find the air conditioning of the city library, which is preparing to close. At the information desk I ask two attendants where I might find a market or convenience store nearby, a question I immediately regret.

"Well . . . no, not around here," the one begins, then turns to her friend, "do you know of any stores nearby?"

"No, I can't think of one." A pause. "Now wait a minute"—and it seems that a full minute does pass—"if you drive down that road right there and turn right at the T—"

"Actually," I interject, "I'm walking."

"Oh! You're walking! Well, you'll have to walk a long way. Where would you send him?"

The debate seems to go on and on and nowhere all at once, as possibly the most interesting topic they've had all day. Still sweaty and sun-tired and leaning with my back against a cement pillar, I wonder whether they'd notice if I leaned a little deeper into this pillar and took a quick nap, but am aroused by a sudden exclamation.

"Wait a minute! Now hang on! Isn't there a store just the other side of the park?"

"Well yes," comes the unimpressed response, as if that had been an option all along, "he could go there." I return to the heat outside imagining their response to a request for the nearest library.

The store beyond the park is well-supplied in the ice-cream sandwich department but has no bottled water, and with my sugar level up I leave with confusing directions to what sounds like a lot of pavement and food chains. Hot, tired, heading inland, and imagining carrying even just two instead of four or five gallons of water several miles back to the river, I find the practice of foraging in a new town for basic needs to be suddenly and distinctly unattractive. At a post office I wait for two people in a passing conversation to say good-bye, and then ask one for clarity on directions I'd been given. I hope by some miracle she'll say something like "Say, you look hot and tired—have you been *rowing*? Wouldn't you like a ride?" Instead she points me in the direction most directly away from the river. I continue my trek thinking I really ought to turn back and find some faucet on the side of a building where I can fill my empty jugs, and then hear from behind me the double blast of a car horn that I believe just might be for me.

There, stopped in traffic for me is the woman who just updated my directions. She calls through the open window of her white sedan that it's too hot for someone who doesn't know where he's going to walk there. I jump in and introduce myself, and soon we're talking about karma and taking risks, and the need for parents to take more responsibility for the raising of children, and we agree, despite some of her experiences as a former Baton Rouge police officer, that people are generally pretty good. She quotes Khalil Gibran on the limited ability of parents to influence and appreciate their children's aspirations and allows me to buy her French fries at the drive-thru before returning me, five gallons of water in hand, to the river.

Below Baton Rouge the Mississippi begins to narrow and deepen, an engineered evolution that created and maintains the accessibility of the river to freighters. The sandbar islands I've been camping on have diminished in size, and just upriver from Plaquemine I find my final private refuge for the tent on the slightest island beach, a mere sliver of land compared to the vast plains of sand found upriver.

The following day I find the Mississippi marked at mile 173 by a beacon perched high on a beach on the inside of a bend. This, my last night of camping on the river, is the first night I've pitched my tent on the banks and not on an island. The way the sand has been built and steeply carved, it is only after I've dragged the boat out of the water and scaled the beach's slope that I notice two men by a pickup truck preparing multiple rods for fishing. Otherwise the four or five acres of the beach's plateau are empty, though it seems likely that such an expanse of accessible sand is a site of late-night riverside revelry. I approach the truck as the younger of two men, one in his early fifties, the other in his late seventies, is rummaging through a tackle box set on the open tailgate. He eyes me casually as if I'd been expected, as if I were a neighbor who'd borrowed his hedge clippers earlier that afternoon. His greeting is in his warm glance, through glasses that reflect the last flush of daylight held in the ghost-clouds of late afternoon thunderstorms, the mature light no longer warm, but not yet cold, a Mona Lisa moment in the spectrum between summer day and summer night.

His companion is his father, and they've driven an hour and a half from Lafayette to try their hand at catfish. This spot is normally worth the drive, he says, but the lures they've already got in the river have yielded nothing. When I ask whether camping is safe he assures me that they'll be up all night, and after a few pleasantries, not even including the exchange of our names, I return to the boat feeling not only safe, but guarded.

In the remaining light as I make sure the boat is secure, a man in a well-worn twelve-foot aluminum skiff comes across the river toward me, his bow headed slightly upstream to compensate for the slipping current. He could be thirty-five, or perhaps ten years older, with a weathered face and piercing cerulean eyes, dressed in a white T-shirt and old jeans. The plastic bait barrels and a tool box and lengths of tough line reveal this to be a working boat, and he tells me that he fishes for catfish. He's come to find out about the scull, which reminds him of a pirogue, a flat-bottomed, low-freeboard, double-ended skiff, a local featherweight jack-of-all-trades along the bayous, capable, if used carefully, of floating back from the swamp a hunted alligator or deer. After talking briefly across the water he motors the bow of his boat into the sand, kills the ancient outboard, and moves nimbly to the forward thwart while drawing from a rear pocket a box of thin cigars. He pulls one out, puts it in his mouth, and lights it, protecting the flame from a light breeze by hands that are large for his medium build. One look at those hands and you'd have to guess that they've been working hands from the start and that whatever calluses he has are the same ones he'd developed by the age of eight. He holds his head close to mine and looks straight at me as we talk—he with a soft Cajun lilt—looking only occasionally aside to comment about his 1950s-era outboard, the gear in his boat, and the mechanics of my scull. We talk for less time than he takes to finish his smoke, but the experience is disarming, as if his piercing eyes have gleaned something about me I don't know myself. We say good-bye and as he opens the throttle of the engine I am left with a final breath of cigar smoke as he makes his way upriver into the near darkness.

Here along the bank, no longer afforded the isolation of island encampments, I am given hints of the culture that lies beyond the river's edge, beyond the standardized industry and uniform codes of river traffic. To the south and the west of the river are the bayous, the mingling of water and land inhabited by the Cajuns. Yet like the Kansas interstate, from which white farmhouses and gleaming silos are seen like castles across green seas of tasseled corn, the river will continue to rule me along its course, allowing few chances to step out of the boat and into the accent of the world beyond.

The next day I am to meet Bob Schmidt in New Orleans. He is only the fourth person on the trip that I've known before, an acquaintance made in Maine the previous summer. When I'd heard he was from Louisiana I mentioned my anticipated trip, and he'd said to call if I ever made it as far as New Orleans. Several days ago I called from the office telephone of a remote chemical station farther up the river. I reintroduced myself and reminded him of my trip. He is a cousin of friends of my family and readily offered me a place to stay for the night. He'd been in the business of rebuilding Detroit diesel engines for work in the oil and shipping industries and knew many of the facilities along the river at New Orleans. Call back in a couple of days, he'd told me, and by then he'd have made arrangements in New Orleans for a place to store such a recreational boat along such a purely industrial riverfront. I'd thanked him and said I'd call. "Well I'll look forward to seeing you, Matt!"

I didn't think twice about the rhyme of my name. Having introduced myself as either Nat or Nathaniel throughout my life, I've become accustomed to immediate translations into Ned, Matt, Tad, Daniel, and Nate. But Matt is the most popular twist. I see it on the dentist's calendar when I check in for an appointment, on Post-it notes when I've left a message—"Matt called. He'll be late"—and once even on a wedding invitation. Occasionally I spell it out for a receptionist, N-A-T and watch as the receptionist's script records M-A-T. M and N are so close to each other in the alphabet, it often seems they've acquired each other's phonetic flavor by mere proximity, and to distinguish the *N* you have to bare your teeth, which doesn't make much difference over the telephone. In any case, it's all close enough for me, and I've learned that when it does matter it usually sorts itself out.

I'd spoken to Bob again by telephone and he'd given me the river location of Bollinger's Shipyard on Algiers Point, across from the Vieux Carre, or Old Quarter, of New Orleans, known popularly as the French Quarter. Bollinger's lies at mile 95, and I've got my work cut out to make it 78 miles down the river in time to meet Bob at the end of the following day, and so I resolve to be on the water well before the sun is up with hopes of reaching New Orleans and getting off the busy river before sunset, as I still have no navigation lights.

I awake to find that the father and son team had given in to sleep themselves and am soon on my way, drenched in sweat, as usual, shortly after sunrise. Though still more than a hundred miles from the river's mouth, the Mississippi's elevation has already reached sea level and is now coaxed forward by its upper self rather than drawn by gravity. Although the river narrows below Baton Rouge, and is more obviously defined by the levees, which further upriver are hidden within forest, it is also deeper here, which may explain the slackening current, now not much more than three miles per hour. The river traffic increases with the passing miles, and for long stretches I row while looking over either shoulder, giving only an occasional glance astern. Small tugs ply the river back and forth with single barges like a fleet of forklifts in a vast warehouse. Medium-sized tows of rarely more than fifteen barges assert their hometown rights to the main channel along with the more imposing foreign freighters, which kindly slow in passing so as not to snap the cables webbing the barges together with their rolling wakes.

The first freighter I see running on the river moves at a rate that focuses all of my attention. Unlike the plodding tows that emerge slowly around bends, this ship has suddenly appeared and I will soon find out what a freighter's wake could mean to me. Looking to my left I see a line of six barges tied to shore and sprint toward them, hoping

I might be able to use them as a shield. I follow the line to its end, all the while keeping an eye on the freighter, soon to pass me. It's red hull is six-hundred-feet long, and its white superstructure, topped by the captain's bridge, would be the tallest point in sight if not for the smokestack of a distant chemical plant. I am relieved to find behind the last barge a narrow alley of water between it and the riverbank, and pull in to safety. The ship has now passed—I can see on the broad stern that it is registered in Norway—and its wake is now beginning to surge into shore, with little effect on the heavy barges. As I'd hoped it is a rolling wake, no more than four feet in height, and after it washes ahead of me down the banks I return to the river unconcerned about the wakes of the ships to follow.

Above New Orleans, above the Huey Long Bridge, the industry along the river is almost constant and the view is dominated by a shipyard with a contract for massive navy transport vessels. The river turns almost 180 degrees below the bridge, and as I follow the bend I am met by a late afternoon wind that, against the flow of the current, builds the heaviest wave conditions I've rowed through thus far, enhanced and complicated by the wakes of steady barge and ship traffic. With two miles to go until the next turn, where I might expect the wind to fall in my favor, I have little choice but to row and not stop rowing as I follow a line of barges tied to shore. The bow of the scull slams down into successive waves, which repeatedly bury it and send gallons at a time over the deck coaming and into my back, which does a reasonable job of deflecting much of the water back into the river. If I allow the bow to drift even slightly at an angle to the oncoming wind and waves I might easily be forced by their strength into a broadside position that would certainly result in swamping, if not capsizing. I fear losing the grip of an oar, and several times larger waves, in slapping an oar blade on its way to the catch, shock one handle out of my grasp, yet I am able each time to trap it between my forearm and leg and regain control in time for the stroke. I am hell-bent for New

Orleans, on its very doorstep, and welcome as its entry-toll the drenched chaos in the boat.

I make it around the bend and thus ease myself into the wind's favor. I stop to pump ten or twelve gallons of warm water out of the bilge before searching for Bollinger's, which I fear I will miss in the waning light, in which case I would have to continue the search by turning upstream, without lights, on the still buoy waterfront. I call with the radio to the captain of a passing tug. He can hear me, but spots me only at the end of our exchange. He points the way, and I see Bollinger's between dusk and dark across from the lights of the French Quarter.

Bob had said he would meet me at the shipyard, and although I am late and concerned he will worry about me, I stop rowing as I pass beneath a highway bridge and let the river carry me. I've been using food all day as an incentive to keep rowing, and now pull out a plum, a rare prize in the boat, and try to savor it. Here I am afloat on the Mississippi River, in a rowboat, sliding on this grand current through New Orleans. Bourbon Street, the destination I'd proclaimed to the jogger on 110th Street along the East River, runs parallel to the Mississippi several streets back from the levee. New York City is not the far end of a straight line away from me, or a marathon twenty-four-hour drive, or a three-hour flight, but worlds away, back the way I've come, around every river bend, through every lock, up rural streams and back along the shoulder of Portage Road to Lake Erie, eastward through the canals of upstate New York, and down with the tide on the Hudson. I know now that the early pioneers, when they said good-bye, said good-bye for good, for no matter how wondrous their treks into new territory, they would never revisit the tedium of their routes.

Now the evening glow of New Orleans, my floating presence before that city, and the current's quiet flow past the French Quarter— all had seemed in advance to be mathematically inevitable, the final sum of a precise number of strokes measured by the calluses on my hands. And a side of me is only gently struck by the logic of these city lights, as a math student is relieved, but not stunned by the expected results of a cleanly worked solution. Yet when I think back to the miles behind me, and the equivalent of a working week of hours spent in locks, and the countless beads of sweat and hundreds of thousands of strokes—a million?—the tedium of which is generally forgotten, I sense again the distance I've come, and New Orleans at nighttime is then a prize. "Remember this," I whisper to myself.

Having acknowledged my own arrival and tossed the plum pit in the river, I start pulling toward Bollinger's and almost hear my name, loud and clear: "Hey, Matt!"

· 16 ·

The Taste of Salt Water

I AM DIRECTED by yard crewmen in hard hats to pull in between a floating drydock and the looming bow of a ship under repair and I land at the slightest hint of a beach strewn with flotsam and jetsam. I step into a knee-deep mixture of mud and sand, and secure the boat to one of the pilings that supports the wharf above, and also to an enormous log of driftwood well beyond the reach, for now, of the river. I gather my gear and climb up through a barrier of riverweeds— "Watch out for rats!" cries one of the crew—and thus arrive at Algiers Point, across the river from the French Quarter, where I am warmly greeted by Bob and the nightshift of the yard, a tough looking crew in their helmets, boots, and soiled shirts, whose curiosity about the trip and accommodating offers of a shower and food open a window upon the rich landscape of Cajun hospitality.

I am thankful for Bob's assistance, for I realize that without it there is truly no safe place to leave the boat along the river, let alone pitch a tent. Moreover I am exhausted and grateful for the opportunity to submit myself to the passenger seat while someone else drives. In this state I listen passively as I am introduced all around as Matt.

During the hour drive to Houma, a hub of Louisiana's oil-drilling industry set in the heart of the bayous, I am revived by a breeze of conversation as Bob inquires about the details of my experiences since Brooklyn. Meanwhile, as the sweltering daily heat is held well into the night by the ever-present humidity supplied by the Gulf, the windows are rolled up to retain the cooling blast of the air conditioner, and I clench my arms and legs in a vain attempt to reduce my odiferous emissions, reminiscent of the deepest bowels of a men's gym. An hour later I meet Bob's wife and son—"Nice to meet you, Matt!"—and make my way via the shower to bed.

The following day Bob takes me on a driving tour of the surrounding bayous, a veinous network of narrow channels. Though the front yards of houses might be divided from the canals by paved streets, the waterfront is private property and it is the rare homeowner who has not developed at least makeshift access to the water. Broadbeamed shrimp boats ranging in size from twenty to fifty feet, their nets hanging from raised booms like an osprey's drying wings, are tied up to ever-rotting piers, along with flat-bottomed skiffs of all varieties. "There're still a lot of coonasses in the fishing industry," Bob informs me, "though they're getting a lot of competition these days from the Vietnamese." He goes on to describe the effects a fluctuating oil economy has had on the region, but I am still working on his use of the term "coonass," which I take as a reference to Cajuns. I know Bob is not of Cajun descent himself, and am surprised to hear him use such a derogatory term considering his eagerness to show me around his adopted hometown. I catch up with him as he points down a side channel off one of the bayous, wide enough for a rowboat and arcing away into humid green swamp.

"It's a real labyrinth out there," he says, turning his eyes from the road for a moment of eye contact. "I even know some coonasses who've gotten lost out there." It is then that he must have seen something in my eye, for he stops himself and with a wide-eyed recollection of a neglected step, says "You must think I'm putting down the Cajuns when I call them coonasses! That's the name everyone uses around here—especially the Cajuns!" And so it is, as I would find out over the following days and the coming months while wandering through the bayous and among Cajuns themselves, whose jocular self-deprecation reveals not insecurity, but that rare combination of cultural pride and modest ego that I've found elsewhere only among the American Indians of the southwest.

In all ways I am treated like family by the Schmidts, a luxury that only compounds the severity of my continuing crime of hesitance about fine tuning their pronunciation of my name. Having offered their house as a base camp for the end of the trip, Bob returns me the following day to Bollinger's and the final hundred odd miles of the river. Yard staff of all positions, from welders to the yard's general manager, help me load the boat, and as I prepare to climb in, one of the crew comes up to me and says he and his partners thought I might like to have something cold for the river, and is Coke okay? With this he hands me a small, lunch-sized cooler with the Bollinger logo printed on the side. I can see that it belonged to one of them, as it is labeled on one side with with a French surname in black marker. It is filled with ice and six red cans out of the soda machine.

Is Coke okay? *Anything* is okay. That they had decided to do something in a group, that they dug quarters for the machine out of their pockets, that they are as tough looking in their hard hats and uniforms as any men could hope to be, yet concerned about my welfare on their river, nearly breaks my heart. They could have all gotten together and pooled thirty-five cents for the next time I wanted to call my mother. They could have just waved good-bye as they'd waved hello. Anything at all or nothing would be just fine. I know the cooler will join my collection of other simple good luck gifts given along the route, and suspect that out of all of the gold and loot acquired by the early explorers, it must have been the smallest, unexpected keepsakes, simply given or traded by those they met, which meant the most as they sat as old men in chairs looking back upon their world-expanding days.

I'd been told that in certain seasons and in certain weather conditions, salt water has been known to reach as far up the channel of the Mississippi as New Orleans, and from time to time I dip a finger in the water to taste for the Gulf. By Pointe a la Hache, the southernmost point on the river to be crossed by car and ferry, and with some sixty-five miles still to open gulf, there is no salt despite the fact that the river's delta is by now blooming into the Gulf, and a mile beyond either side of the levees are open bays of salt water.

Mile 0 of the Mississippi lies at the "Head of Passes," whose three options each lead to the open gulf. Southwest Pass is used by the shipping fleet, and South Pass and Pass a Loutre are these days used only by commercial and recreational fishermen. Southwest Pass is the longest of the three, and yet my obsessive instinct to row the longest possible way to open water is easily checked by the rationale that there's always a longer way to do anything. Besides, any nagging questions about my resolve with a pair of oars have long since been answered. Also, in avoiding Southwest Pass I can row the last miles to the gulf free of commercial traffic for the first time since the upper Allegheny.

These hundreds of square miles of the outer delta, having been drilled for oil, are now nature preserve, veined with bayous generally free from human encroachment except for the sounds of the outboards of recreational fisherman and helicopters that fly drilling crews between the mainland and offshore oil rigs. Otherwise it appears as pristine wilderness, home to alligators and water moccasins and a full roster of shorebirds. On either side of the pass a seemingly endless maze of bayou is lushly shaped by fields of marsh grasses eight feet tall, and Bob's comment that even locals can get lost in the intricacies of south Louisiana waterways seems credible.

Still at ten miles, eight miles, and less, no taste of salt water. With three or four miles to go I can see the lighthouse at Port Eads rising above the marsh grass, its tapering white tower capped by a black housing for its Freznel lens so as to stand out against the sky for mariners as a reassuring symbol of the channel's mouth. And then, as

I'd absentmindedly followed so many bends before, I curve through a subtle turn in the channel's course that proves to be the final bend of my row to the gulf. The first had come as I'd rounded the east end of Grand Street and rowed beneath the Williamsburg Bridge, with the skyline of Manhattan to my right. How many bends had followed? Hundreds anyway, perhaps thousands. Each one had led to another, and only in mirage on the longest straight avenues of the Mississippi had the route ever seemed to vanish in the distance. Yet now I look down a final stretch of river, and there is no mistaking the end of embankment and the unchannelled, oceanic horizon beyond.

Two miles later I've passed the lighthouse and arrive at what appears to be the end of South Pass—and in my mind, the end of the Mississippi—with a view toward shrimping boats on the open gulf. The western bank continues as an outer shore of a delta peninsula, and the east bank is extended by Eads's jetty, barely breaking the water's surface, nearly drowned after decades by its own weight. Yet with only a hundred yards to go there is still no salt. I row parallel to the jetty, with greener salt water on its outer side, and beneath me the brown river, its exhaling current nearly spent, some volumes of which started their descent toward the gulf as far away as Saskatchewan and Alberta, or, like me, in Mayville, New York, where they fell as rain into the creeks that feed Chautauqua Lake.

A quarter mile beyond the end of the jetty I see the spars and rigging of a partially sunken shrimp boat and row toward it, sure that there I will have met all my own criteria for being not only at the gulf, but in it. And then I notice a change, only barely perceptible at first, like the slow dimming of theater lights, slight enough that you ask yourself whether anything has *really* changed (and eventually one learns to trust the question itself as evidence). Here is a shift in the movement of the water, from the minor windblown chop of rivers to a deeper groundswell, which develops over hundreds and thousands of ocean miles and continues even after wind has died. I am now beyond Eads's jetty. I dip my hand in the water and taste salt.

Once arrived I feel no need to linger. Each day of the trip has justified itself, and I am able now to name from memory every stopping point since Brooklyn. I take a few photographs, casually round the shrimp boat—an oar blade catches for a moment on the submerged rigging—and head back up the pass. Before long, within a mile, a group of recreational fishermen pulls alongside, and the driver, who's heard about me on the radio, asks whether I'd like a ride. I'd been offered rides many times before, from Budda as I approached the portage, riverboat captains who'd offered to tote me over the next stretch of river, and from other recreational boaters. It always felt right, but lonely too, to say thank you, but no. I can remember the first stroke of the oars in Brooklyn, which was followed by thousands more, and have wondered where the last would be. Here it is, by the lighthouse at Port Eads. I take one last look at the port oar blade, painted red with a white W for Wisconsin, as it floats easily on the surface near the outboard engine, and reach for a handhold on the powerboat and the first free miles of the trip.

WITHIN A DAY I and the boat have been ferried by car back to Houma. I am out of money, and indebted to my credit card, that drug of legal tender. Moreover, I need a new boat for the row home. While the scull has been ideal for the route thus far—for one thing, I would have been utterly unable to pull anything much heavier over the hills to Chautauqua Lake—it is built for relatively protected waters and would inevitably be swamped along the coastal route. Furthermore, the coastlines I've already had experience with over the years, namely those of southeastern Florida and New England, are more rigidly private than the riverbanks, and, where private, more developed. It is one thing to ask to camp along someone's muddy riverbank, which in some cases is also the edge of a cow pasture or cornfield, and quite another to seek haven in someone's manicured waterfront yard, complete with palm trees or weeping willows and a swimming pool. After a hundred days, most of which have included the routine of establishing trust in the quest for encampment, I now require a boat in which I can sleep at anchor, which would be not just my vessel, but my home.

Thus, with the need to pay off the bank, acquire a new boat, and build at least a modest reserve in my savings account, I have resigned myself to a hiatus in the trip. Certain that the ideal boat will most likely be found in the Northeast, which is rivaled for small boat building only by the coastal northwest, I will hop a plane to New England, and return to Louisiana for the second leg of the trip as soon as I can.

I spend several days with Bob and his family in Houma and, availed of the use of Bob's pickup truck and tools, I set about building an eighteen-foot crate to ship the boat home. On the morning of the day of my flight, I come downstairs to sit with Bob and his wife, Alice, for a casual breakfast before heading to the airport. The previous night they'd invited guests for dinner, and as Bob poured drinks for the three of us while waiting for the company to arrive I saw my savior in a bottle of gin, thinking that loosened laughter would help resolve the name fiasco with an inebriated touch of grace. Yet as I sought that moment of silence between topics I became lost in the current of conversation, and before I knew it the doorbell had rung. In a final act of corruption, I stepped right up, reached out my hand, and said, "Hi, I'm Matt!"

Now at breakfast I watch with increasing angst as the doughnuts and orange juice slowly vanish, as if I'm absolved of my responsibility for the task at hand so long as they last. I am faltering again. My bags are packed by the door and within three hours I will be rolling down a runway headed away from Louisiana. What then? I will surely see the Schmidts again, indeed hope that I'll have the chance to show them around the next time they are in Maine. They are cousins of people I've known all my life. And I hope to visit them again while rowing through the bayous on the second leg of the trip. Whom will I say is calling then? Alice reaches for the car keys on the kitchen counter and says, "Well Matt, are you just about ready to go?" My name is up.

"I have to apologize to you," I begin, clutching the edge of the kitchen counter behind me for support. Bob has turned from the opened refrigerator, and they nearly crush me with their jointly mystified expressions, which insist that I can't possibly have anything to apologize for.

"I should have said something right from the start," I continue, "but one thing led to another and it just got out of control." I am searching for an angle, trying to butter the bread before putting it in the toaster, and delaying the delivery feels good. Not to mention futile. The cluster of keys is silent in Alice's hand. Bob's deep brown eyes probe for an explanation. I continue to maneuver, fearing the silence between my words: "I've put you both in an embarrassing position. It's so ridiculous. I kept wanting to say something but kept missing the moment." I hesitate, my pleading gaze shifting from Alice to Bob to the tiled floor, whose gray grout offers no escape. Bob has taken a seat at the kitchen table. What sins have I given them time to imagine during this excruciating preface to a confession? What offense, they must be wondering, has this guy even had time for? Did he jam the VCR? Has anyone seen the dog? Worst of all, is he not who he said he was? I check the floor, glance at Alice, and then look Bob straight in the eye, ready to enunciate as I've never enunciated before. "My name," I say, with no choice but to bare my teeth, "is Nnnat."

The silence that follows is broken only by a deep chuckle from the ice maker. Alice looks to Bob, and Bob looks to the floor, which provides no more help to him than it had given me. "And all this time," he finally says, "I've been introducing you to my friends as Matt." Alice, having let a diplomatic moment pass, says "Well that's okay! Now we know!" Bob rebounds, stands up, and with a generous smile adds, "Oh don't worry about it. You'll just have to understand if we keep calling you Matt!" I smile as Alice opens the door, grab my bags, and walk idiotically into the morning heat.

A short time later I step aboard an airplane—checking, as I always do, the rivets on the fuselage by the door—and am whisked from New

Orleans to Manchester, New Hampshire, in the same time it had taken me to row the length of Manhattan or South Pass. I've requested a window seat in case we fly over the rivers I now know, and though I sleep most of the way, I happen to wake up as we fly over Manhattan, an island metropolis five miles below. I avert my eyes from the Brooklyn Bridge, which I want to see again only as it appears over my shoulders while rowing into New York Harbor. Yet I follow the course of the East River past Roosevelt Island and into Hell Gate, out of which I'd only barely pulled myself up into the current of the Harlem River. I see the Harlem bend to the west to cap Manhattan and meet the Hudson, which on a windy April day had seemed like a freeway to a first-time driver who pauses at the on-ramp, uncertain whether to accelerate. By that point the blisters on my hands had opened to reveal the deepest layers of skin, wounds now thickly healed as the plane slowly veers away from the course of the Hudson, which disappears from view beneath clouds.

· Leg Two ·

· 17 ·

The Journey Resumes

TRAVELING THE MISSISSIPPI ALONE gave me no particular claim to having been to southern Louisiana, at least not among southern Louisianans. For one thing, there's hardly the equivalent of a freeway exit for a small boat on the Mississippi south of Baton Rouge. An occasional cement boat ramp offers a chance to get off the water but no guarantee of your boat's safety while you head into town for a fresh jar of peanut butter, a box of saltines, and a gallon of water. Otherwise, several locks provide exits from the river, the two above New Orleans leading into subsequent downstream currents that are essentially one-way tickets into the bayous, and the two at New Orleans leading immediately to industrial waterfronts that offer no invitation to captains with only paddles for locomotion. Indeed, in the final 173 miles of the river from where I'd camped in the company of the father and son team of catfishermen, I'd stopped only three times, and even then only where special permission had been granted by way of Bob's connection with Bollinger's. Thus I'd rowed along the vena cava of Louisiana, yet had missed the outer veins of the bayous, where the extremities of the Mississippi Delta blossom into the Gulf of Mexico.

What little I'd seen in Houma the summer before had piqued my interest, and given the chance to start the second leg of the trip anywhere I please, I've chosen to row down the Atchafalaya River, which leads by any variation of back eddies and sidelong glances into the Cajun bayous. But the two months I'd thought I would need to get back on the water stretched into six, as the bills of even cautious spending exacted their toll on my date of departure. As the weeks accumulated into months, and a departure planned for October retreated into November and beyond, it seemed at times that the resumption of the trip was just a dream becoming engulfed in the current of my working life and other aspirations. Back in a world defined by business hours, social outings, and a list of petty projects, I often found myself drifting off into memory of the trip, most often to the Mississippi and its desolate sandbars. At first, perhaps while stuck in traffic, or awaiting change at the supermarket checkout counter, or walking my dogs through the woods of midcoast Maine, a glance to my leathered palms gave proof of the memory. Yet within weeks even the calluses, prized symbols of physical work, softened from disuse and fell away.

References to rowing and to the trip continued, however. In September I took a walk down to the basin of the Charles River in Boston. Here the river broadens before passing through a dam into Boston Harbor. On a fine late-summer evening, single scullers and crews were training on the river, as there is hardly a college or university within reach of the Charles that does not have a rowing team. Near the boathouse of a private rowing club I watched as several scullers returned to the club dock. Soon they were chatting among themselves and stepping out of their boats. As two of them then hoisted their light shells in the air and started walking to the storage racks, a third, with broad shoulders and cropped reddish-blond hair, no doubt a former college varsity rower, remained on his knees, leaning over his floating shell, fiddling with adjustments to his rig. He glanced at me as I approached casually on the dock, and I greeted him. I asked him how the club works, and whether it owns some shells for common use by its members. He glanced at me again, sizing me up in a fleeting moment. Was it the way I was dressed, in the slip-on black canvas shoes of an old Cuban musician, with blue jeans and a plain white T-shirt? Has my hair grown too long? Maybe my questions were too naïve. He turned back to his shell and was looking into its bilge when he said with conclusive condescension, "First of all you have to know how to *row*." I paused for a moment, looking out to sailboats beating and reaching across the Charles. He kept fiddling as I then turned and walked away, suddenly yearning to be back on the Mississippi River.

Whenever I could I drove to the local marine store or camping outfitter to acquire equipment I'd been lacking on the first leg, including such items as clip-on, battery-powered navigation lights, a small anchor, several feet of chain, and a hundred feet of anchor line, or rode. I added a second sleeping pad and a full-sized pillow to replace the travel pillow of the first leg, which had been one step up from a pin cushion. I bought a vest life-preserver to replace the cumbersome five-dollar special I'd had before, and to this attached a waterproof flashlight and a rigging knife. All of this and more accumulated in a pile on the cement floor of my brother's basement, which I sometimes visited just to confirm, in sifting through the gear, that the trip was really only half completed.

The crowning acquisition, of course, was the boat, which, like a plane ticket once purchased, made departure inevitable. The search for the right hull had been a long one. Various builders tried to convince me that their designs were perfectly suited for the conditions I would encounter. One was unmatched in elegance, and fast to boot, yet its beam seemed too narrow for sleeping in any comfort, and I worried too that it might broach, that is, yaw dangerously to one side and perhaps then capsize on the face of following, imperfectly shaped waves. Another company offered me the use of one of its boats in exchange for publicity. Though I never actually saw the hull, its beam also seemed too narrow, and in the picture its freeboard seemed too low for its length. True, I was going by feel alone. I studied the canoe beside my brother's garage, and fishermen's skiffs tied up to public docks. While eating breakfast I even studied the width of the kitchen table with my arms out as if describing the size of a fish, and imagined the ends as gunwales; it seemed just about right. I was certain on a length range of sixteen to eighteen feet, and few of the boats available in that range—most of them built in one man shops—offered beams of more than forty inches. I settled upon forty-eight inches as my ideal.

A forty-eight-inch beam, however, raised the weight. I soon found that most of the boats that met my beam criterion were built out of wood, and were either too expensive or too heavy, or both. One hundred and fifty pounds seemed like a reasonable limit. Thus, with weight, beam, and length—not to mention price—held strictly in mind, I would have known my boat just by its dimensions, without seeing so much as a picture. My only other hope was that its stern would be like a canoe's, rather than a flat transom, so that any following waves that might surge from behind would ease rather than slam the boat forward. Finally I found it, displayed in a grainy black-and-white photograph half the size of a business card. It was built by a small shop in Ontario. The measurements sold me: 17 feet, 130 pounds, and a beam of 45 inches. I ordered it as cheaply as I could, which meant no blue stripe, for a savings of $60 Canadian.

In November I rent a truck and drive to Ontario to pick up my new boat. Including a couple of hours of sleep by the side of the road, stops for gas and the border patrol, it takes me eighteen hours to drive from Portland, Maine, to the boat shop, located down a long dirt road through the woods. The nearest town, a hamlet really, is far enough away that when I stop to ask for directions no one in the local grocery knows the builder's name. When I arrive the boat is quickly loaded on top of the truck, and I say I shouldn't stay long as I'm anxious to pay for the truck for only two days, and I know I'll have to sleep more than a couple of hours on the way back. Yet I am convinced to stay at least for a quick lunch, as another rower, from Alberta, is due to arrive any minute. I'm told that I'd be interested in his story, for he'd once tried to row a boat from Coney Island to the mouth of the Yukon.

Hardly a minute passes before the sound of an engine enlarges down the driveway, and the unlikely, unfinished story told to me by lockkeepers on the Erie Canal is about to be completed. An early nineties silver Thunderbird, looking more utilitarian and less athletic than its designers might have hoped, shifts into park, and Mark Robbins, in his late forties, perhaps even fifty, dressed unassumingly in jeans and a crewneck sweatshirt, steps out of the car. Ours is a meeting of pure coincidence. He is visiting only briefly to consider the purchase of a piece of land.

I tell him what I was told along the canal, and over lunch Mark tells the story himself of his 1990 venture. His motive, in part, was the unmet challenge of a solo voyage by paddle from the open coast of the Atlantic Ocean to that of the Bering Sea, a journey of 7,300 miles. Yet the mileage was perhaps not even half of the challenge, which was to connect the two dots, very nearly seven times zones apart, within one paddling season. The fastest route requires transit through the Erie Canal, which is closed until spring. Meanwhile the deadline for arrival at the mouth of the Yukon is determined by that river itself, which normally freezes by the first of October. Going by the statistics of ice one would have to average better than forty miles per day—including 120 miles in portage—for 180 days. The route has already been completed once by a pair of canoeists. But Mark would be the first to complete the trip alone, in a lightweight canoe set up for rowing rather than paddling.

The details relayed to me along the canal were correct. Mark was on schedule to complete the route by the time he reached Fort Chipewyan in northern Alberta. He'd averaged forty miles per day for 5,500 miles since leaving Coney Island. A relatively short distance later he would cross the continental divide and, with the current of the Yukon, easily make its icy deadline. At Fort Chipewyan, however, Mark diagnosed himself with giardiasis, an intestinal infection caused by a flagellate protozoan common in rural and wilderness waters. But local medical staff concluded he had some other infection and refused him the medication necessary for giardia. Over the following days Mark rowed onward to Fort Simpson, losing thirty pounds of muscle mass along the way. Stripped of his physique and psychological fine tuning he was unable to continue, and his recovery time prevented any further attempt at completing the route before the Yukon froze.

His decision to try again, in 1996, is the most remarkable aspect of an astonishing story. It is impressive enough to focus so comprehensively on such a singular and gargantuan task, but to respond to such disappointment with a return to Coney Island for a second visit to every mile of the first attempt leaves me speechless. The table is silent, waiting for him to continue. He pauses himself, as the story gets only more difficult to tell. Mark rowed the Hudson again, and followed the Erie Canal. He rowed his canoe forty miles across Lake Ontario to Toronto in the calm of night. Sadly, Toronto became both the end of his second attempt and the end of a dream, for once again the invisibilities of water took him to task, and he was infected with a virus that attacked his heart. He is a gentle, stoic man, with a reclusive streak. Yet his emotions now, though kept in partial check, are expressed in a lasting silence, until he tells us that he hasn't been able to row more than a mile since.

That Mark never reached the Bering Sea by oar has no diminishing effect on my esteem for him. The route was clearly within his physical and psychological range, judging only by his first pursuit, and I suspect that I think even more highly of him for the fact that he turned around and tried again than I would have had he made it the first time. A half-hour lunch is easily extended into an hour, during which I'm continually amazed that I'm sitting across the table from the man who rowed from Coney Island, and that this table is not at a rowing regatta but in a house in the woods of Canada. What was the likelihood of my brief visit here coinciding with his brief visit? I can only smile and shake my head from time to time as I think about it while driving back to Maine with a new boat for my own trip. With the luxuries of the scores if not hundreds of towns to come and no pressure of deadlines, my own route now seems like an easy walk through a lovely, timeless park.

THE NEW BOAT is built out of fiberglass, white on the outside and gray on the inside. It is molded in the lapstrake style of wooden construction, and if not for this one could accurately imagine it as a broad canoe. Fiberglass seats in the bow and stern are molded to fit, and two wooden bench seats allow the boat to be rowed by one person or two.

I opted to adapt the sliding seat from the scull to this boat, even though I'd heard arguments that fixed-seat rowing, while less efficient in short distance racing, is more efficient for day after day hauls. This reasoning assumes an efficiently designed hull for a given length, and then relies on the theoretical maximum speed, or hull speed, of a non-planing, or displacement hull, which has to literally displace water rather than skim across it to achieve speed. For a sense of the difference between a planing hull and a displacement hull, imagine standing in the shallow end of a swimming pool with a frisbee. With its face lying on the water's surface it can be skimmed across the water with ease. Yet with the frisbee floating vertically, even the strongest efforts to push it by hand face-first through the water meet with resistance that cannot be overcome without extraordinary additional power. Hull speed is generally determined in nautical miles per hour—one knot equals 1.15 statute miles per hour—by multiplying the square of the waterline length of a hull by 1.34. In short, the longer the boat the greater the hull speed. My boat is 17 feet long, and thus its theoretical maximum hull speed, when not planing down the face of a wave, is 5.5 nautical miles per hour, or 6.3 statute miles per hour.

The argument for fixed-seat long distance rowing continues by pointing out that a fixed-seat rower can easily approach the boat's hull speed for short distances and can remain within reasonable range, say four to five miles per hour in my boat, for long distances. And in so doing he is using his arm and back muscles almost exclusively, with little contribution needed from the calorie-burning legs. The sliding seat rower, by comparison, can come even closer to kissing hull speed over the short distance, but over the course of a day of rowing is unlikely to greatly exceed the fixed-seat rower's progress, though he will have burned far more calories with his legs. Put differently, one might compare the sliding-seat rower and the fixed-seat rower as a twenty-five horsepower outboard engine compared to a fifteen, where hull speed is nearly achieved by both engines, yet with a notable variance in fuel consumption.

It was a convincing argument, which I agreed with and then chose to ignore. For one thing, the stroke of the sliding seat had become second nature to me. I'd come to row as I breathed, one stroke to a breath, and was often jolted out of some distracting reverie—perhaps by a shift in the wind or by the sudden instinct to glance over my shoulder to check for barges on the Mississippi—to realize that hundreds of strokes had passed without notice. My sculling stroke, though imperfect in form, had become my possession. I preferred its fuller, mesmerizing motion, the wider span and longer reach of the blades, and the expansion of the body from the horizontal crouch to the opening, powering extension. Furthermore, I had reached the Gulf in the best physical shape of my life, and I could not accept the idea of making so little use of my legs over the several thousand miles still to come. One proponent of fixed-seat rowing suggested that without the sculling stroke I wouldn't have to carry so much food. But I don't care how many calories I burn. I love to eat.

In making final preparations, I removed the forward thwart to provide room for sleeping at night. The aft thwart was left in place, as it provides lateral structure to the hull, and the beam of the sliding seat, once secured to the bottom of the cockpit, cleared that thwart perpendicularly by a quarter inch. The outriggers were lashed with hose clamps to a set of bronze oarlock sockets, and the boat was thus converted to a heavy water scull.

As for a tent to fit over the boat, a stop at the local plumbing supply shop yielded a variety of PVC piping and joints for about fifteen dollars, and several hours with a hacksaw and a tape measure—I finally chose my height sitting cross-legged as the defining height for the tent—yielded a simple tent frame, with a central spine running fore and aft, and three sets of legs that were footed in three more sets of oarlock sockets mounted on the gunwales. A local sail maker cut a heavy grade of spinnaker cloth—the weight, ounce for ounce, of regular tent material—that fits tautly over the frame and snaps beneath the gunwales. With two windows netted against gnats and mosquitoes, and waterproofing on both sides, the boat was given a roof and made a home. I will carry my pop-up tent for the variety of occasionally sleeping ashore, yet am grateful I will no longer have to ask permission to sleep on private property.

FREEPORT, MAINE. Two o'clock in the morning, Christmas day, 1999. The dim bulbs of the garage lights reach faintly into the cold night. Through the still trees neighbors' windows are warmly lit with electric candles, and I can still taste the spiced cider served hours before at the red house across the road. The boat rests on pads on the garage floor. The sliding seat is tied in place, and the oars are lashed snugly within. Parked just outside of the garage door is my 1985 Pontiac Firebird, a low-slung, wide-tired, V8-powered rolling amplifier for belting out Bruce Springsteen's *Born in the USA* while laying tracks from a standing start across the intersection of Main Street and Elm. This particular example, however, has not been worshipped with hand wax by a high school senior as was intended, but relegated to the dirt roads of New Mexico, where the paint slowly faded and peeled and is now callused with lesions of hard rust. The muffler hangs a bit low, and one of the flip-up headlights is stuck in the upright position.

Fittingly, the last three letters of its yellow and red New Mexico license plate read "JNK." Whenever I feel like I should own something with four cylinders, or better yet drive no car at all, which is most of the time, I recall what my cousin, the previous owner pointed out: "It's not really about going fast. As often as not your safest move is not to hit the brakes, but to hit the pedal and get ahead of a dangerous situation. It's all about safety, Nat." To which he added, "But I'll tell you what, when people see this mother in their rearview mirror I can *promise* you they'll get out of the way!" So far he's been proven right.

And now the combination of perhaps the two least congruous vehicles ever lashed together, one an emblem of brute strength, a substitute for the male ego, powered by nonrenewable, polluting fossil fuels; the other a quiet ambassador of traditional elegance, fueled by any old heap of calories. Four foam blocks designed to slip over the gunwales of a canoe are put in place on the boat, and my brother and I, breathing out mist in the cold air, heft the awkward boat slowly to our chests, quake for a treacherous moment beneath the weight, and then slowly rotate the boat upside-down and lower it to the top of the car, careful to adjust the blocks so that the boat's weight rests on the metal part of the roof, not the glass T-top.

The boat is longer than the car, and the windshield is now nearly obscured like a ballplayer's face beneath the bill of his cap. The windows of the doors flare out half an inch from their rubber gaskets as the frame of the roof sags. It's unconventional. I wonder whether we'll even make it out of town before getting pulled over, but finally say, "Well, this ought to work." After lashing the boat both fore and aft and to each of the wheel wells, we head off for several hours of sleep before making a predawn Christmas morning departure.

Nearly twenty-four hours later, after spending much of the day making the holiday rounds on our way out of New England, we have learned that the boat will tolerate the speed limit. We plan to deliver me and the boat to the lower Mississippi by way of a wedding in St. Louis and have headed west across New York State on Interstate 90 and into a late-night Christmas blizzard blowing in from Canada and the Great Lakes. The Erie Canal, by now probably frozen, runs parallel just a mile or so away. The roads have not yet been plowed or sanded, and the car occasionally drifts on wide tires from its increasingly icy course and is barely brought back in line. It would never have occurred to my brother or me to listen to a weather report before setting out in a car, and if the storm doesn't pass then we'll just have to pass through it. Sidelong gusts of wind, building upon the hurricane-strength apparent breeze of the 65 miles per hour speed limit, have stretched the lines and straps holding the boat down, and the hull has suddenly slipped laterally across the roof, so that looking out through the window of the driver's door, now blocked shut, I can see the inside of the hull. Moments later, pulled over to the shoulder, my brother and I have crawled out through the passenger door and alternately wriggle free our frozen knots, blow warmth into our numbed hands, and wrestle the boat, just as wide as the car's roof, back into its narrow margin of safety. This is not cartopping at its model best, but at least we've picked our day well, for aside from a mild tide of last-minute travelers en route to family reunions, we've had the road almost exclusively to ourselves. We even had a roadside fast-food joint to ourselves, where we ate a modern American Christmas feast for five dollars, sitting in molded plastic chairs, listening to holiday Muzak, while employees standardized in uniform rayon leaned idly against the stainless serving counters.

Back on the side of the road as we resecure the boat, the red lights of the dashboard and the blast of the heater from beneath the rumbling hood promise warmth and protection from the vast, unsurvivable cold night. A semitrailer rolls by pulling a cloud of snow behind it. We tumble back within the car and can't help spinning the wheels as we regain our speed. I am struck by our proximity to the canal, by the reminder that in traveling you can never predict when you'll again cross a point on a former path, which, though perhaps given little notice the first time is subsequently given renewed and deepened meaning. No door, once opened, is ever fully closed, and therein lies a wistfulness, where past experience echoes, time dissolves, and our former selves—as my own self rowing along the nearby canal nine months before—seem so unreachable. We continue on and pass through a thousand miles of northern winter, whose shades of dormant black trees and brown farmland are dusted now and then in white.

S E V E R A L   W E E K S   L A T E R , toward the end of January 2000, I stand on a bluff at Natchez, Mississippi, 150 feet above the Mississippi River, looking upstream. I've been here nearly a week waiting for a vast, plodding cell of drizzling cold to pass before setting out. Looking north, the raw, diluted brown of the river below fades into the gray of the sky and a southbound towboat, a quarter-mile long and measureable in acres, is dwarfed in size by the great river. Behind me the inhabitants of the small city of Natchez, no longer a port of river commerce even in the summer, have retreated to its inner warmth, and it now seems that the river has a daily audience of only one.

Aside from once rowing a dinghy a couple hundred yards I have not pulled on a pair of oars since I reached the Gulf last August. It is not a deeper confidence that I've lost, but the sense of rhythm with the river and rowing. My hands are soft and the river is cold, and to depart on anything but a sunny day would seem to tempt treacherous fate with hubris. As it is, once again, I'll be stepping into a boat I've never rowed.

As I picture the completion of the circuit in my mind I am nagged by the thought that I've rowed so little of the New England coast on which I grew up, and that the combined routes of two previous rowing ventures had taken me only half way up the Maine coast. While I'm at it, I decide, I will continue after reaching the Brooklyn Bridge and row on to Eastport, Maine, at the Canadian border.

Finally, one morning the sun lights up an empty blue sky. The waterfront, though virtually devoid of traffic during the previous week, has become a center of attention, as both the *Mississippi Queen*, a replica paddle wheeler that ferries tourists up and down the river, and the *Explorer*, a floating hotel on two enormous linked barges, have landed their guests for a day's tour of the manicured antiquity of the city's antebellum neighborhoods. Their aluminum gangways reach out across the water to a long launching ramp and throngs of visitors, cameras and purses in hand, hike up the cement slope to the road, restaurants, and shops. My boat, a mere beetle between the two hulking beasts, is floating gamely at the river's edge, and I stow my gear haphazardly, uncertain where it will all go, anxious to be on my way. The obsessive ethic acquired during the first leg of the trip of paring my gear to the barest minimum must have atrophied during the months ashore, for once again I've brought along a full complement of cooking equipment, as well as a ship's library, an enlarged pod of cameras, two pairs of shoes in addition to my rubber sandals, and an extra duffel containing cold weather clothes. The boat is so much larger than the scull, I'd thought, and I would be spending so much more time in it, that I might as well feel at home. That ethic, I would soon realize, works only so long as your mission in life doesn't involve pulling your own weight.

I am sent off from Natchez by Jimmy and Britton Gammill, friends from the summer before and who'd welcomed me to stay with them while I waited for the weather to clear. Several of their friends are present too, including an orthopedic surgeon who is providing the favor of narrating the departure into a tape recorder. Heard faintly in the background is the music of a radio played by idle stewards of the *Mississippi Queen*.

"This is James here; I'm a retired orthopedic surgeon helping get, ah, Matt's? Oh, Nat's boat in the water. We also have Pedro Castillo from Venezuela with us. It's a cold day. We had a heavy frost here in Natchez this morning. Nat's been staying with Jimmy and Britton Gammill, and Jimmy's down here helping Nat get his boat in the water for this voyage around the tip of Florida to Maine! Very exciting.

The *Explorer* is here, the *Mississippi Queen* is here. It's a bright sun-shiny day down here at Natchez-Under-the-Hill, and nobody's been shot or stabbed in the last two hours. How'm I doing? Okay. They're now loading up Nat's supplies. Plenty of fresh water. Also one six-pack of beer. That may not last very long! The river is quite low. We've had a drought the last ten months, and it's well below its normal level. Pedro's helping to bring down some more supplies now. Pedro, would you like to say a few words?"

"Yes," says Pedro in his Venezuelan acccent, "I like to say a word. I want to wish him good luck and I hope a warm weather meets you down the south area, and let me tell you, we're here loading two hundred pounds of stuff in a hundred-pound boat! Mr.—what his name again?—Mr. Stone, yes, so wish him good luck and a healthy and a safe trip!"

The doctor resumes: "This is becoming rather precarious here. Nat's having to load everything at the front end of the boat, and he's not in the boat yet, having to protect this gentle, fragile shell against the rocky shoreline we have here"—the banks are layered with a carpet of rock to prevent erosion—"and Nat's trying to position the boat to where he can get in the boat and the underneath side won't be damaged on the rocks. Nat has just successfully entered the boat without harming it on the rocks. Jimmy's now handing the oars over onto the boat, and the final few supplies. Nat's going to have to spend some time balancing out the boat . . ."

In the foreground the tape records the sound of something splashing in the river, like hands in a full kitchen sink, and a wooden pallet used to slide the boat over the embankment of crushed granite, which the doctor reports as having nearly floated away, is dragged ashore. I blithely comment that this is the first time I've ever been in the boat.

"Yeah," says Pedro, as if I'd pointed out that the river is wet.

"The first time?" exclaims James.

"Yeah," says Pedro, "you'll get to know it soon!"

"Don't tell me that!" says James. "Nat's just informed us that this is the first time—this is an alpha trip in this boat." Britton has just arrived on the scene and her voice emerges over the activity.

"It looks mighty small!" she calls out. "Well, the weather seems pretty good, don't you think?"

"A rather cool breeze on the river today," James reports, "and Nat, I would like to add, is in shorts. So hopefully he'll get pumped up and burning some calories here soon!"

"All right bud. Be careful!" Jimmy calls.

"Good luck!" adds Pedro.

"Wear your life jacket!" chimes Jimmy.

"And remember," James hollers, "to call Mom!"

"If you get lost," Pedro advises, "if you see this bridge again, you know you're coming back!" Everybody laughs.

I pull out from the shore, stop to clear baggage from the path of the sliding seat, and pull a few strokes into the current. I drift down to the outer beam of the *Queen*, as James has been given permission by a crew member to board the boat so as to hand me the tape recorder rather than risk knocking the hull on the rocky shore. Before leaving I take a photograph of the group.

Months later when I recall this departure, the stillness in the photo mutes the voices of the tape, the splashing of the pallet in the river, and the background music from the *Mississippi Queen*. The energy is missing from the image. And yet it seems to tell more: Jimmy, in blue jeans and a blue Oxford shirt, is caught looking down at his own camera. Pedro peers out from the hood of his sweatshirt, his right, gloved hand poised in an open-palmed wave. Britton stands by herself farther up the boat ramp, also waving, her brown glove blending into the arc of a trunk of driftwood deposited by some earlier rise in the river. Where is James? Still on the *Queen*, perhaps. The photograph distills from sound and from movement the gut-wrenching innocence of being, and the very taking of the picture is at once a futile attempt to stop time and, as an act of memory, a statement of love. Even among friends and new acquaintances the refusal with a camera to let a moment in time pass unrecorded is one of the most intimate expressions imaginable. So there they were, by the cold coffee of the river, wind-quivering in the bright light, which cast a warming doubt over winter's grasp on Natchez.

As I put the picture down a voice from the tape echoes. It is Britton, looking beyond the clamor of men launching and balancing the boat and beyond the calls for good luck, who says in soft Southern to no one in particular, or to the river, "He'll do just fine."

Like a Moth in
Its Chrysalis

"THE BOAT." The boat has no name, at least not officially, nothing painted at the bow or stern. I'm ambivalent about the naming of boats, particularly those picked out of a catalog or off a showroom floor. It's one thing to build a boat oneself, and somewhere in that process of carving and planing and sitting pondering, to stumble across a fitting name, one tuned to both the contours of the hull and the passions of the builder. It seems less genuine to me to try to name and thus personalize someone else's creation, particularly an assembly-line product like so many of the modern generations of fiberglass petroleum-powered runabouts.

Of course, there's the question of what a boat's been through. The farther it's been, the longer it's evaded the treacheries of weather, the more a boat acquires its name, and the more the name exudes meaning. Some names are even retired, like the playing numbers of extraordinary athletes, due to the greatness of their adventures. No one would dare name their sailboat *Spray*, as Joshua Slocum, the first man to circumnavigate the planet alone, has already taken that transom plate fully around the world. So too with the U.S. Navy's *Constitution*, Ted Turner's *Courageous*, and the great Nova Scotian fishing schooner *Bluenose*, beaten only once in a race by the *Gertrude*

L. Thebaud. Even the *Naughty Bowline*, if there's ever such a vessel, will draw respect if it's probed the ice floes of Baffin Bay.

In the best cases a boat's architecture is so exquisitely beautiful, so perfectly balanced, and such a tease to the frictional laws of hydrodynamics, that naming is unavoidable—the architecture commands the best from language, and the boat and the name enlarge one another. Look up the black-and-white images of such sailboat photographers as Morris Rosenfeld, and dwell upon the masterpieces: *Ticonderoga*, *Cotton Blossom*, *Shenandoah*.

Maybe, as by tradition in many American Indian communities, boats shouldn't be named until after they've proved themselves, until they've demonstrated their tendencies, both weak and strong. By this method I might have emblazoned *Little Don't Stand Up* along the prow of the tippy scull. Yet this new boat of mine will remain *the boat*. I didn't build it and it isn't built of wood, and so I've shrugged off the pressure to name it aptly. "Hello Boat!" I will say after returning from some excursion through a town.

The river, which is now lower than it had been last summer, is still vast. It whirls and eddies and upwells in a near silence that seems only to increase its strength, as the calm before a storm breeds the fear of anticipation. Occasionally two small whirlpools collide, and the river is audibly tickled by itself as it hints of much larger pools in both its past and its future, liquid funnels that, by many accounts, have spun towboats on their heels and inhaled full-sized trees harvested from shore by floods, trunks first and leaves last. The summer before at a riverside park in Greenville, Mississippi, I'd heard from a retired husband and wife relaxed in folding lawn chairs their account of a Mississippi whirlpool that engorged such a tree. "We stood there for twenty minutes, and I'm telling you that tree, as big as these ones right above us"—he'd held tightly to the plastic handles of his chair while pointing fully upward with his chin to the heights of mature trees— "well, that tree never did come back up."

What mathematical formula, I wonder, would explain the result of a single whirlpool, its size, its placement in the river, its moment in time? How much space, in twelve-point font, would such a formula take? Would a football field be big enough? What moment in history could be erased without minutely altering the pool's occurrence? The invention of the light bulb? Elvis's last trip to Vegas? What if the wall of Genghis Khan had never been built, or if Bud Cort had refused to play his Harold beside Maude, or the heart rate of a buff bellied hummingbird was 1,360 beats per minute instead of 1,260? And could such an equation even be isolated from the larger equation between the Original Cause and all of its effects, including the moment and manner with which you turned the last page? Time and the river and solitude amount to such musings.

Thus distracted I retrace a fraction of my previous summer's affair with the Mississippi, follow its S-curves and broad avenues, and feel the boat as it cuts across aimless, feuding subcurrents and is nudged left or right, sometimes slowed and sometimes accelerated by the manic whims of the river. I am aiming for an island that I camped on last summer, yet realize now that the scale and distances of the river have been reduced in my memory during the months I spent working in Maine. As the day wears on and I approach the channel's drift to the left or right around a bend, I think I recognize a detail along the river's edge and am sure I will find the island around the next turn, only to then recall, or not quite recall, the new stretch in front of me. The second time through a once-practiced routine is supposed to seem easier or faster, the way a three-hour drive to a family reunion seems like two and half on the way back.

NOW THE SUN IS SETTING, the temperature is quickly falling, and I am anchored in a mild eddy in the narrower channel between the island and shore, away from the shipping channel. Though I might simply wash up on a sandbar if the anchor were to slip, I've paid out an extra length of anchor rode, for the smaller the angle of rode to the river bottom the better the anchor's grip. I then take to the oars and push hard in reverse to dig the anchor more surely into the sand below. I've also doubled the knot around a bronze fitting at the bow, which serves as both a handle for pulling the boat up on beaches and as a bow ring for lines. The alternative to drifting ashore if the anchor fails is drifting down the river, which tends to eventually pull all that floats upon it into its main channel, which is also the shipping channel.

It is cold enough—I am expecting frost—that I can do without a bath of any sort. I hardly broke a sweat during even the warmest hours of the early afternoon. So I set myself to the task of establishing a procedure for converting the fifty-odd square feet of the boat from traveling mode to living and sleeping mode. My first lesson is that I have too much gear to achieve this transformation with any sense of order. Imagine traveling in a station wagon packed with luggage in the back, and shifting the luggage forward and out of the way, without getting out of the car, so as to create a nest in which you could sleep for the night at a highway rest area.

I try to predict what gear I won't need for the night, and ferry it toward the stern. I then pull out the pipe-frames of the tent and the tent itself, which is still furled. Reaching my upper body aft over the newly piled gear, and mindful of the effect of my weight upon the boat's stability—I may be within several hundred miles of the balmy Gulf of Mexico, but I am afloat on winter water, all draining from the north—I fasten the first two snaps of the tent beneath the wooden gunwales toward the stern, continue with the next set of snaps a foot forward, and then, before snapping any further, proceed to assemble the tent's frame.

The upright legs of the frame are similar enough in length that I'd left one set factory gray, painted another set black, and the third red. I know that the gray frames, the longest, sit in the center set of oarlock sockets. Yet I cannot remember whether the black set goes forward or aft. The two sets, red and black, vary only an inch or so in length. I study them, try to picture the tent's assembled shape, and decide that black goes aft.

Looking from the bow toward the stern the three sets of supports resemble the legs of three capital A's without their crosses. I then draw out the one-inch white pipes, four to form the central spine of the frame, each of clearly different lengths, and set them in their obvious places. With the tent's skeleton up, like the simplest frame of Mongolia's first prototype yurt, I continue to unfurl the tent up and over its form, and fasten the rest of the snaps, stern to midships, then bow to midships—ends to center—by reaching my hand outside of the tent and working my way along. Two reinforced slits on each side of the tent create small flaps that correspond to the outriggers reaching out beyond the gunwales. They also allow me to reach my hand outside to secure the last snaps. Then the flaps are secured with Velcro so as to form an imperfect seal against the inevitability of mosquitoes later on the trip. I'll stuff a shirt or towel in these gaps when I reach warmer, more insect-laden climates. Naturally, I reach a point on my first attempt to raise the tent that the cloth assumes an awkward shape and fails to reach fully around the gunwales. So I start over nearly from the beginning. This time the black poles go forward.

Fifteen minutes later I reside in the boat like a moth in its chrysalis. I am now left with the longer task of organizing my existence amid the heaping clutter of gear. I've stowed the oars aboard as well, for though I cannot imagine how they could jump from their locks, I know that if I were to lose them I'd be more than three hundred miles up the country's largest creek. Somehow, during this process, I've managed to open virtually every plastic container I have for one reason or another. Once tightly packed, it now seems they've all exploded. I've pulled a flashlight out of one, and a weather radio out of another. I mine for a wool sweater that I'd thoughtfully placed at the bottom of one duffel bag, and I find long underwear tangled in a second duffel. A supply of peanut butter and crackers is found in a carryall bag, which had become a cornerstone of the aft heap, and, naturally, once I've fished those out and inched my way back to the bow, fearing all along the possibility of flipping the boat while trapped within it (and it occurs to me then that I should attach an extra knife, like a fire ax, somewhere easily within reach in case I ever have to cut a quick way out through the tent), I realize that I might have fetched the knife on the same trip. To save my flashlight batteries and add ambience to my first evening back on the water I pull out a small oil lantern, a rustic, cozy touch for any river setting. With appropriate caution I had stored the bottle of lamp oil in the safest, least accessible place, beyond the aft heap, through a miniature plastic manhole cover that, when unscrewed, gives way to the space beneath the stern seat. Minutes later, with the bottle finally in hand, I carefully top off the reservoir and hang the lantern from the tent frame. But where are the matches?

In this manner I bang out the first few notes of my new lifestyle. I finally reward myself with saltines buried in peanut butter, lay back into my nest of two bed rolls—one is made of foam and the other inflates with five deep, dizzying breaths—as well as a sleeping bag and feather-filled pillow, and describe in my journal the first day of the second leg of the trip.

> *January 31. A day of transition from creature comforts to austere*
> *pulling and living. I feel virtually none of the apprehensions of*
> *leaving Brooklyn, but instead the held breath that comes with diving*
> *in no matter how many times you've dived before. . . . I made it as*
> *far as last summer's island, a few more bends in the river than I'd*
> *recalled. The river has fallen six to ten feet, and there are enormous*
> *sandbars now where there were none, a long low tide. The barges are*
> *as frequent and as polite with one another as last summer, and I*
> *overheard on the radio one captain say to another, "Check this dude*
> *out! He's got it goin' on!" The other replied, "I'd have a square*
> *transom to put a motor on, or at least a sail!"*

How do I feel about being back on the water? Driven, for one,
to complete the circuit, happy to have put it all together again
logistically, and there's nowhere I'd rather be. I have longer to row
than I've admitted, but Freddy Fisher's words, "You're doing the
right thing," still ring true. My only apprehension is about the
performance of the tent in rain.

A towboat labors up the river. A coyote howls.

ATCHAFALAYA. Did you rhyme it with "Patch-a-duh-tiyah"?
Nope. I tried that too, trying so hard to get it right the first time. It's a
gift when you can, whether you're referring to the Atchafalaya, or to
Xujiazhai, or to Tóhajíílee. Pronounce it wrong as if you think you've
got it right, and you might get corrected if you're lucky. Work it out
slowly and politely, and you're an earnest outsider with possibilities
for inclusion. But nail the timing and the beat and the silent syllables
the first time, and the locals wonder where you've been all these years,
because you must have a little bit of them in you. Atchafalaya. The
rules of the language blend and fade. The *A* and the *t* are for looks
only, and the remaining syllables melt across one easy breath, "Chaff-
uh-lye." But whisper it first to hear how the breath, from the depth of
the stomach, blends the river's pronunciation like watercolors across
thick paper. *De Chaffuhlye Riv'uh.* And there you are, headed down
through a Cajun filter to the sea.

The Atchafalaya roughly parallels the Mississippi to the west,
though where the Mississippi, with its big bends, shoves its way left
and right to the Gulf like an ornery old king elbowing his way
through the masses, the Atchafalaya, belying the easy drawl of its
name, runs nearly straight, deep and fast. At first there is only the
channel, half the width of the Mississippi, nearly devoid of sandbars,
and once along its course I envision the bayous leading off of the
main channel like branches from the straight trunk of a cypress tree.

I reach the town of Simmesport at the end of the second day. I've resolved—it's early in the trip—to protect the thin fiberglass hull, which flexes under the mild pressure of a hand like the trunk of a car, at all costs. I will only pull it up on sand, if at all, where I can be sure no passing boat or ship will send its waves to grind the hull further, for the grains of a typical river beach, though moist and forgiving under foot, are equivalent to those of a sheet of 80-grit sandpaper. Before long, due to bad habits, the bow would be worn through and require patching. At Simmesport the banks of the river are so steep and continue so steeply below water that none of the riverfront homes has so much as the simplest pier. Even if I found a place to tie the boat gently to shore, I couldn't be certain a towboat wouldn't flip the hull with the sharp rebound of its waves off the bank. And yet I fear that anchoring at the river's edge is not much safer than sleeping in a car parked on the shoulder of a highway. Tows will come sooner or later and rock the boat. And worst—well, I hope they'll see me.

I pass beneath a train bridge after sunset, turn the boat into the current, and drop the anchor just outside of the shipping channel, defined at this point by the two pilings of the bridge. I reason that an upriver barge would be making slow enough progress that if by some chance it strayed from the current I would have time to hear its droning engines echoing off the banks. If a downriver tow were to get out of control, hopefully the bridge supports would protect me.

I drop the anchor into the dark water and wait for the rode, which is slipping quickly out of its canvas carryall bag, through my left hand, and into the water, to go limp. And yet the anchor continues to dive. I shift my sight from the line's entry into water to its frantic departure from the bag. I'd bought a hundred feet, plus several feet of chain, never thinking I would need this much, but just as the bottom of the bag begins to appear from beneath the fleeing coil, the blur of the line in my hand freezes for a moment as the anchor hits bottom, then slowly begins to pay again as the anchor grips and the current continues to carry the boat downstream. I quickly belay the line through the bronze fitting and tightly grasp its remaining length—the canvas bag is now empty—and the boat seems to suddenly accelerate upstream. As I tie my knot a glance to shore confirms that I am stationary. The anchor, despite the rode's apparent plumb-line descent, has held. I take to the oars and paddle fiercely against the grip, and check the shoreline. The boat is hooked. To test once more I row several strokes into the current to slacken the rode, then back the boat down again. The anchor's hold suddenly snaps the boat to a stop, and the wake of the hull's apparent movement resumes.

As I fall asleep, with my ear to the pillow and the pillow to the hull, I listen to the Atchafalaya as it whispers beneath me, like the day's airy breeze compacted by darkness into a current of water. I feel the boat shift ever so slightly, like a weather vane whose upwind is upstream, and as I slip into sleep, the river's trickling murmur is not the sound of the hull being dragged against the anchor downriver, but of its release from gravity. It seems as if the boat has acquired its own motive and its own power, that the river is not running past it, but that it is gliding effortlessly up the river. And so I am released into that other world of untethered possibilities, the mind's free range.

The next day, at Melville, I manage to land the boat gently along a shallow embankment and behind the length of a utility barge held ten feet offshore and involved in the construction of a gravel loading facility. I hike over the levee and into town, a sleepy outfit riding out a trough between heydays. On almost every one of the town's neighborhood blocks sagging wooden homes are "For Sale by Owner." The sign remains in place for one that is now simply missing, as if the buyer wanted a house, but not a house in Melville. Not all of its roots have been plucked; short pillars of brick that had supported it and a variety of other underhome detritus remain. Something sapped this place. Other than the style of a few late-model cars—few enough that I walk idly down the middle of Main Street—there is little evidence that the year is any closer to 2000 than the year I was born.

With a blind eye to my feeble and dwindling bank account, I step into a diner, empty but for the driver of a delivery truck parked outside, and a waitress, who glances through the kitchen's serving window and emerges to take my lunch order. I've become adept during the first leg of the trip at ordering the largest amount of food possible from a menu for the least amount of money. This normally calls up the age-old diner team of a chef's salad—iceberg lettuce, carrot shavings, two cherry tomatoes, and, if I'm lucky, blue cheese dressing—and the soup of the day, often accompanied by crackers, if not bread and butter. Add the tip, and you're still out no less than four dollars at best. With the aim of rowing my way back to Brooklyn on five dollars a day, trips to even the most modest restaurants have to be infrequent.

As I eat I listen as the waitress—a twenty-something belle whose tight-fitting jeans and shining chocolate-colored coiffure suggest that while her work is in Melville, her play is somewhere else—explains the observable listlessness of the town with a story about Huey Long, the populist Depression-era governor and senator of Louisiana, and his unforgotten campaign stop here. On his first gubernatorial campaign Long planned a stop at Melville, the proposed site for the State Route 90 highway bridge across the Atchafalaya. Yet the citizens of Melville, thinking Long didn't stand a penguin's chance in the bayous of winning the race, decided to spare the cost for a proper candidate's bandstand and made Long stump at ground level. But Long did win and he didn't forget, and the more faithful residents of nearby Krotz Springs gained a bridge and the commerce of Route 90.

I have no specific plan in mind for carving my way through the bayous. My only glimpse of them had been at Houma the summer before, and I recall Bob Schmidt's report that even Cajuns take a wrong turn in the maze every so often. Yet in Melville I can find no fishing maps of the area and wander aimlessly back to the boat, studying the houses and streets along the way. Sagging and bereft though Melville is, it is my kind of town, like an old hand tool found in an abandoned barn: With a wire brush, a sharpening stone, and oil for the wooden handle, its luster may be restored and its usefulness, which, though perhaps not superior to its modern hardware store descendants, is still preferred because you saw it for what it was, style so rare you may make it your own.

At Krotz Springs, a step up in liveliness from Melville, I inquire at the town offices about maps for the Atchafalaya Basin, and while explaining my need am overheard by Karen Johnfroe, in line behind me, and who extends an insistent welcome for me to come home to meet her husband, Ulysses, a tugboat captain. "We've lost a lot of our own boys in that river," she tells me, "so you might as well talk to someone who knows it before you go any farther." Her warnings match with those I'd heard about the Atchafalaya in advance. Its relatively straight course and current, fueled at times by both the Red River and outflow from the Mississippi, make it one of the fastest rivers navigated by commercial boats. Once again, on her warnings, I imagine enormous whirlpools that could swallow me and the boat like an hors d'oeuvre of two-legged shrimp on a fiberglass cracker. And though the Atchafalaya thus far has been tame compared to the Mississippi, I keep my mouth shut and allow prudence, in the form of Karen, to sit me down.

Ulysses Johnfroe sits at the end of a long kitchen table, a tell-tale symbol of family life that relies not only on the rituals of eating, but of welcoming guests, whoever they may be, to eat and drink with them. I am reminded of my stop at Kanatsiohareke, the Mohawk community on the Erie Canal, and of Zuni, where only the most basic greetings are uttered to old friends and new acquaintances alike before the standard invitation to eat is issued, for invariably the cooking is done not just for those who are present, but also for those who might show up, and there's still food on the table.

"It sounds like you're on a journey," says Ulysses, reaching out his hand after hearing Karen's brief explanation of whom she'd brought in the door. "I thought you could talk to him about the river," she adds. "He hasn't been able to find any maps on the Atchafalaya or the bayous." I shake his hand, perceiving that his towboat days had been many and are now mostly behind him. His hands are thick and strong, and weathered, yet it's clear that they had once been stronger. They are veteran river hands.

"I'm afraid I don't have any of those charts now. I think Johnfroe's got 'em all." That is, Johnfroe Johnfroe, Ulysses's son. "But pull up a chair and we'll see what we can do for you." He turns back to Karen. "We've still got some soup on the stove, don't we?"

I describe the boat at his request. More so than I've yet realized I have entered true boating country, a waterside culture as dependent on and interested in boats as any in the country, from Puget Sound to Chesapeake Bay to the coast of New England. Hoping to squelch any imminent suggestions that I not go further on the Atchafalaya but launch again somewhere safer, I make special points about the boat's seaworthiness, omitting the fact that I've now spent only my third day in it, and mention the exceptional balance provided by the oars, particularly when feathered. "I don't even look at barge wakes when I cross them," I brag. I add that the river's current seems no more than three to four miles per hour, about the same as the Mississippi. In the end we agree that the river is low and running idly, and that if I made it this far I should fare well enough through anything likely to come my way.

We talk on about the Cajuns' roots in the eastern provinces of Canada. The Cajuns, or Acadians, before they inhabited and adapted to the swamplands of south Louisiana, occupied portions of what are now the Eastern maritime provinces of Canada, especially Nova Scotia. But territorial claims and control of these lands shifted hands between the English and French for more than a century and a half until 1755 when, under English control, the vast majority of the Acadian population was deported as war loomed with France.

Some of the Acadians were sent to prisoner camps in England while others were sent to England's thirteen colonies to the south, where the Acadians were reviled not only for their new destitution but for their Catholicism in a fundamentally Protestant land. Many of those Acadians who survived deportation and persecution eventually migrated to the south and west, and made their new home in the lands I've now entered.

But, as I soon learn, while Cajun geography is now secure, the language and thus culture are threatened by the diluting effects of American culture. Ulysses notes the gradual loss of Cajun French in schools. "It's just Parisian French they're teaching now," he says, looking across the table to a ten-year-old grandchild who's quietly joined us, "but no one talks Parisian here. It's a different language. And if I speak Cajun in Paris, they won't understand a thing I say!"

Karen, who disappeared half an hour ago now returns with a daughter and a box full of canned meats, bread, potato chips, and cookies. "Here!" she says. "This is for you to take in your boat. You can't live on just peanut butter and crackers! I guess if you're rowing it won't last long, but it'll take care of you for a while."

Touched by their easy generosity and feeling helpless once again about how to fully express my gratitude—for their welcome and their trust, of which the parting box of calories is an extending symbol—I am returned to the river's edge by Ulysses and his grandson, who are both eager to see the boat.

By afternoon the river, whose main channel continues clearly on, begins also to branch out into simple, quainter detours. I am now well within the swamp of the Atchafalaya Basin, twenty miles wide between the levees that contain it, and seventy miles long, with the river as its central artery. I follow a sharp and simple turn to the east and enter a world of narrow paths filled with water. I am in the bayous.

· 19 ·

Like Carter Got Oats

I FOLLOW A ROUTE vaguely eastward through the maze of bayous. I row along Bayou Indigo, twenty-five feet wide, which twists beneath overhanging trees and steep, muddy banks six feet tall, a quiet and remote world. Turtles warm themselves in patches of sunlight on sodden logs and slide into the water as I approach. A blue heron thrusts itself into flight and disappears around the coming bend, only to alight and be disturbed again as I catch up to it, a cycle repeated half a dozen times. Occasionally the channel is narrowed by fallen trees, and I slip beneath their spans or work my way around them, catching the oar blades in the banks, the branches, and the bottom below. I think back to Chadekoin Creek and to Cassadaga, northern cousins to this intimate world so far removed from the architect's rule and carpenter's level.

I reach Pigeon, along the eastern edge of the swamp, in the late afternoon, and after wandering down the main road of the settlement, which stretches along a fingerlike peninsula between two channels of water and whose main establishments consist of Hebert's (pronounced "A-bears") Grill, a gas station, and a bar, I return to the boat. It is tied up to a dock that complements the town launching ramp, a major point of entry into the Atchafalaya Basin for commercial and sport fishermen, all of whom trailer their boats. A large dirt parking lot is half filled with late-model pickups, each one partnered to an aluminum trailer, and as the sun descends on this Saturday afternoon the ramp is the busiest place in town. Bass boaters returning from a day spent fishing hop onto the dock to retrieve vehicles, and one by one the slipstreamed, monstrously powered boats—their throaty engines cut, and the motors impressively tilted upward by the flick of a switch—are winched onto trailers and, still shedding water, whisked away.

My boat attracts little attention as it lies tied up at the far end of the dock, out of the way. I watch this scene with interest, and soon notice a constant among the transient crowd, an older man with white hair combed back and away like early Elvis. He chats with those in trucks who wait their turn and walks with a long-since acquired limp. Dressed in a khaki uniform, badges on the sleeves, I guess that he collects launching fees for the local Department of Fish and Wildlife, or perhaps makes sure that everyone has fished within their permit quotas. He has seen the boat and noticed me as well, and as the driver he's been chatting with shifts into gear for his turn at the ramp, I meet Albert "Scoober" Williams, a watchman hired by the local police department to prevent vandalism to vehicles in the lot. He tells me that I'm free to spend the night in the boat tied up to the dock, that he'll be on duty until the early hours of the morning to watch over the trucks of those spending the night at camp in the swamp. He warns me that it's supposed to be cold tonight, in the low twenties, and says I'm welcome to join him awhile in his pickup, which he'll have running to stay warm. He'd like to hear about the trip.

His truck is a two-tone brown and beige 1976 Ford with aftermarket wheels, wide tires, and a chrome CB antenna. As we sit on the bench seat later that evening the engine hums deeply to the tune of dual exhaust pipes and warm air blows through the vents. The truck is parked near the ramp and faces out across a northern branch of the intracoastal waterway, whose channel forms the eastern border of the

Basin. The trees of the swamp, leafless in winter, are gloomily lit by the yellow glow of street lamps above the parking lot. Occasionally a stand of trees is brilliantly lit by a stark beam from up- or downriver. The light holds for a few moments, then quickly scans along the shoreline, and is extinguished. Several minutes later a tug labors past, guided by an occasional marking of the banks with its powerful lamps, and pushing no more than two or three barges on this smaller commercial channel. The lights in the captain's wheelhouse are turned off, but the door is open to the engine room below, whose flourescent light reflects off the water.

Scoober, now in his mid-seventies and a resident of nearby Plaquemine, tells me that he was raised in the Basin, and in a rambling way proceeds to describe a once vibrant, now vanished way of life among the most remote of Louisiana bayous. As he talks—and when there's silence—he gazes across the river to the swamp. I am struck by the idea of an older man sitting for hours on end as audience to his own memories playing across the screen of dimly lit trees—the literal edge of the world of his childhood—or perhaps leading his eye back into Little Bayou Pigeon and through the decades to his youth. What does he see?

Scoober tells of a nearly self-contained world of small settlements scattered throughout the thousand square miles of the swamp, each community typically consisting of several families, while some of the larger settlements included churches as well as schools, serviced by a painted yellow schoolboat. It was a world of improvisation and neighborly codependence, he says, and as he adds a more personal history to the maze that I've been rowing through, I willingly cast aside my standard skepticism toward descriptions of an idyllic past.

He stops to light a cigarette—the smell of acrid menthol fills the cab—and then continues in his heavy Southern accent. "Life was so common then, I mean so pleasant. You got along good, you know? If you had something, I had it. If I had something, you had it. If you got ready to do something, like change the propeller on your boat, you had more help than Carter got oats! Like killin' a pig. Everybody get together an' do it. Some had smokehouses and some didn't. Well the ones that had it would cure meat for the ones that didn't have it. An' you didn't have no iceboxes. You had to get rid of it right away. The way we used to keep meat—I bet you're gonna laugh if I tell you! Like pork? You kill a big fat hog, man, you run the fat out, the grease, and you precook your meat and bury it in that, in that grease! That's how you preserve it, save it."

He reports matter of factly and yet with pride about the ways in which basic living was managed without modern appliances, and often speaks in the present tense about retired solutions for getting by. "We salt eggs! Ever hear o' that? You take a box, and you put a layer of salt in there, and then you take the eggs and stand 'em on end in the salt. And then you put another layer of salt, an' you get it in between each one of them eggs, and then another layer of eggs, and another layer of salt. They'd keep for months like that! We always had a bunch o' chickens, and I seen my Momma saltin' eggs about three or four months before Easter, and when it come Easter time she'd supply the whole settlement. Nobody didn't have nothin,' but everybody had somethin'." The momentum of Scoober's reminiscence carries him from topic to topic despite the occasional arrival of another bass boat, which only briefly asserts the present until trailered away in our side-view mirrors.

"We didn't have no laws as such. You had to make your own laws. Somebody was the head, in other words the chief of two or three settlements around there. And then somebody'd come and fool with us, somebody'd come in an' do somethin' wrong. The chief'd tell 'im, you know, 'Get your stuff together, don't be here when the sun comes up tomorrow. You'd better be gone.' They had to leave. They might go ten mile farther down the road, and get in another settlement, but if that settlement find that he got runned outta ours, they'd keep boosting him on down, until somebody'd kill 'im." Scoober kills the truck's engine as the cab is now warm. "There was just no law," he adds. "Nothin' else to be done about it."

"An' them tradin' boats would come through. There was about three or four of 'em in the Atchafalaya Basin, from Catahoula, Morgan City, Butte La Rose. What it was, they'd come by with fish, and there was a little grocery store on 'em, and we'd buy all our groceries from them, buy all our clothes from them. We was lucky if we got to town once a year. Plaquemine was the closest town. St. Martinville [along the western boundary of the swamp] on that side, Plaquemine on this side."

I envy Scoober for having had a life so devoid of products and thus, by necessity, so improvisational. I ask him what, if he could go back to the world he's described, he would take with him from the present day. "Not too much o' nothin' we got. We don't have nothin'. Would I give what they had then for what they got now? No I wouldn't. I'd rather what I had then than what they got. Because everybody was happy then. It didn't cost you much to live, you live out in the swamp, no 'lectricty, no air conditionin', no fan, no nothin'." This talk of nothing resonates with me. Though I've only just set out on the second leg of the trip I've already begun the process of purging the boat of what I don't truly need, ridding myself of clutter. The more your possessions and the greater your luxuries—the more you've got somethin', Scoober is telling me—the less you appreciate, the less you live, the more you've got nothin'. But the more nothin' you've got, if you're lucky to live so wholly within the natural world, the better.

"People was more healthy," he continues. "People live to be eighty, ninety years old. A hundred years old. They talk about tobacco and snuff! Everybody on that river smoked, chewed, dipped snuff, or somethin'. And drank whiskey, that ol' homemade whiskey, that rotgut stuff. You didn't have no money to go to the store and buy it, but they'd make it out of corn or anything they could git. And they lived to be a hundred years old! What's killin' you now is the dope they put in anything they makin' now. The food you eat? It's all got dope in it! Look at the fertilizer and stuff, what all they got in there. You can raise a cucumber on a vine and a certain amount of that stuff you put in the ground to raise it is gonna be in that cucumber. You can say what you want, but if anybody want to stop and think, you got any common sense, it's got to be in there."

Scoober reaches for the ignition and starts the engine again, and I welcome the blast of the heater as I anticipate setting up my bed in the cold boat. I ask him how many people lived in the basin when he was growing up. He repositions himself on the seat, then looks back to the swamp. "I'd say by the time I got my leg shot off, at that time, there's probably at least two thousand people livin' out there. That's out in the bayous, away from the levees. I'm talkin' about out in the swamp. All the way to Morgan City, where you could see the Morgan City bridge." He looks at me with the faintest hint of a smile, probing my surprise. "Did you know I've only got one leg?" I tell him I'd noticed his limp.

"I was just a kid. I got it shot off about nine o'clock one morning. It was five o'clock in the evening before I got to a doctor. That's how far out in the swamp. My Daddy had to pack me on his back over three miles at least, and it was just hanging on a piece of skin, just flopping, you know? When it hit a bush, or a limb or something, it would be like a shock. I didn't bleed a teacup full of blood. It was shot so bad there was nothing left anyway. We had this little boat, had a little horse-and-a-half Detroit engine. We had to come back to the house, for which was an hour's ride, or better, and then we had an eight-horse out-board, but it had no gas. We had to go two miles in the little boat to get gas for the big boat, which wasn't much faster, but it did about seven or eight miles an hour. My Daddy bring me to Catahoula, then he had to walk from Catahoula levee, and I just laid in the boat all that time until somebody come get me. I didn't have no pain. I didn't have no pain until I got to St. Martinville, when the doctor started digging in and trying to clean it up and then it got to hurtin' and I passed out. My Daddy shot his own leg off when he was eighteen years old." Wisps of menthol smoke once again curl and expand throughout the cab.

Scoober spent most of his working life as a towboat captain, moving cargo along the major commercial waterways from the Gulf Coast to the Mississippi, Ohio, and Missouri. I am curious to know his opinions about the Army Corps of Engineers' efforts to control the relationship between the Mississippi River and the Atchafalaya, once a natural spillway of the Mississippi and consensually understood by engineers and fishermen alike as "the way the Mississippi wants to go." In an effort designed largely to protect the economic interests along the Mississippi from Baton Rouge down to the Gulf, the control station at Old River, whose lock I'd passed through, opens its floodgates when too much water in the Mississippi threatens to overwhelm the dam structure and finally claim the Atchafalaya as its new route to the sea. Alternately, when the Mississippi falls in times of drought, the floodgates can restrict flow to the Atchafalaya in deference to the need for both adequate shipping depths along the Mississippi and sufficient current to prevent the Mississippi from excessive silting.

Such management has comprehensively altered and in some cases eliminated the human and ecological landscape of the swamp. Generally the region is said to be filling in because its reduced currents are unable to carry sediment through to the Gulf. The swamp is being literally suffocated by sand and soils carried from even the furthest Pennsylvanian, Albertan, and Montanan reaches of the Mississippi drainage basin. Other developments have contributed to the demise of life in the Basin as well, including the acquisition of much of the region by private companies, including those hopeful about the petroleum reserves below. But Scoober latches on to the work of the Army Corps of Engineers. He talks about the variety of canals, or cuts, carved by the Corps over the years throughout the Basin in efforts to compensate for the Atchafalaya's isolation from the Mississippi. Each one, as Scoober tells it, seems to solve one problem while creating three more. "When they first started dredging out there, they screwed up the Atchafalaya Basin. It's unbelievable how deep that water used to be in them places. Like Jake's Bayou. Jake's Bayou man, I remember when Jake's Bayou had a hundred foot of water in it, dead low water. And current? Even in low water that current'd be boilin'. That kept it open, see? But they dredged oo many difforont prongo, and diked off the main ones, to where they got the current screwed up.

"Big Tensas Bayou"—pronounced "Ten-saw"—"Little Tensas, both of 'em. They diked Grand River off, and it changed the current's direction, and run the current backward on the Little Tensas, and what used to be downstream, it went upstream. The Big Tensas, it just completely sanded up. They diked Big Tensas off so it just filled in. Big Tensas is where I used to live, and they had a hundred foot of water there when I was a kid, and now they got trees bigger than you can reach around. So let's say I was eleven, see if I can see how many years ago it was"—his lips whisper through the math—"that was sixty-one years ago. That's how much it's changed in sixty-one years. And I could also go show you where I was livin' there in the house on the bank there, where I got my leg shot off, where I had a swing on a tree, and it was over a hundred foot, that limb, and I had that rope tied to that swing, and now, that limb, maybe it's that high from the ground." Scoober levels his hand at the center of the steering wheel. "Same tree! That sand just filled in that much. See, years ago you used to have all clay bank out there, now you got just sand. You can't find no clay out there unless you dig down deep.

"There's too much water to farm the land, but you ain't got enough water to fish and crawfish, not like we used to. A young guy, I guess about half my age, he was asking, what if he went out and get him some nets, and do some fishing, could he make any money at it? And I told him, I says son, I said, fishing is a thing of the past. You ain't got no water to fish no more. You ain't got no market to fish no more. If you catch 'em you can't sell 'em. The market split out on 'em.

It got so bad where all the fish businesses went out of business and they got them fish ponds now, them farms. See you didn't have that when I was a kid, you didn't have no fish ponds, no crawfish ponds, no turtle ponds, none of that. Now it's so easy to get it out of them ponds, they got it any time they want it. And you just got seasonal fishing in the spillway and stuff, and you ain't got much of that, you ain't got much of a season 'cause you ain't got no water. Last two years crawfishin' ain't done nothin', and that was one of their main last sorts of makin' a living within the Atchafalaya Basin. Last two years they went in the hole. Now another friend of mine, he got a few crawfish traps, he got an old boat, the motor and everything is paid for already. Now he can sit down and just wait, and if the water gets happenin', he might get a week's or two fishin'. That'd be all right, seein' as he's already got stuff. But to go buy that stuff? He'd be crazy to buy it. It just ain't worth it.

"Sand is killing this Atchafalaya Basin. They don't know what to dredge no more to do any good. They done screwed it up so much they just ain't much they can do. That was the Corps of Engineers doin' that, reroutin', tryin' to control the current, tryin' to—in other words tryin' to outsmart the Good Lord. You can't control mother nature." He lights another cigarette, pausing until he's exhaled a first breath. "Nowadays, the truth, if it was just me I'd be livin' out in that swamp right now. You got some that stay out there. It depends, you know. They call it camps. It's not like it used to be, though. I mean you didn't have all that convenience. They got air condition', they got freezers, they got iceboxes, they got everythin' out there now. But nobody raises no families out there, no." He pauses again. Each take on the cigarette seems to elicit a new thought. "I don't know," he laments. "Maybe someday that Basin'll just be all filled in and they'll start buildin' houses out there." On this cue I picture vast developments of catalog architecture and look-alike front lawns and paved driveways. And a contrived nature trail raised above the ground so as to not disturb the native ecology. Somewhere a sign will tell the brief history of a long-since ceded world of deep water, yellow school boats, and salted eggs—a good deal o' nothin' replaced by a whole lot o' somethin', which somebody will have called progress. Yet what we look across to now is simply another moment in the slow ecological disaster of the taming of a great swamp.

Another tug passes by, this one without a barge, perhaps returning from a one way delivery. Scoober's mood lightens as he is reminded of times on the big rivers. He tells me of the days when the city of Chicago managed to sell its human sewage as fertilizer, which was shipped by barge down the Illinois River to the Mississippi and beyond. We both laugh. "We used to call it the 'Honey Run!' " he exclaims. "I always said it was the luckiest city in the world!" Meanwhile I am still stuck on a phrase he'd used earlier, whose meaning I thought might emerge on its own. I look at him inquiringly.

"Like Carter got oats?" I ask. He laughs. "Oh, that's just an old sayin' people used to have. I don't know where it come from exactly. Like you might say someone's got a load o' fish or whatnot. Like Carter got oats."

I feel sorry to leave him before his shift is over, but soon it will be Sunday morning, and I wish to be on my way before the inevitable hordes of bass fishermen show up with their high-speed craft, which will race along the narrow bayous like Indy cars through a quiet neighborhood.

· 20 ·

Thibodeaux and Boudreaux

AN UNWRITTEN COMMANDMENT of the bayous dictates that if your boat even vaguely smacks of either unusual design or a distant home port, you are obligated to stop and discuss its purpose, its construction, its mechanization, as well as your route, with every crawfisherman, shrimpfisherman, tugboat crewman, catfisherman, bayou-side pedestrian, bridge tender, construction foreman, oysterman, recreational fisherman, and fish cleaner who might ask.

One ten-hour day, governed by this rule, I manage to row a total of only eight miles along Bayou Lafourche—that's right, "Lafoosh." At one point I row past a group of older men sitting in a semicircle beneath an enormous oak tree, as older men have a god-given right to do at three in the afternoon. They are dressed in combinations of plaid shirts and jeans and white rubber calf-high fishermen's boots, and presiding over every movement of automotive and marine traffic that passes them by. An abandoned, tilted gas pump now functions as a scenic prop, and thick beards of Spanish moss drape from the branches above. I realize that waving is enough for neither them nor me, spin the boat around, and tie up to the bank. I soon recognize that I've stumbled into a local institution. The circle of chairs clearly remains in place when they go home at night, and men come and go casually in their pickups from this waterside court. They speak mainly in a Cajun patois of French and test me, but rusty high school Parisian is of virtually no use here, for the Acadians have come a long way since they last lived anywhere near the Seine. Discussion about the boat and my trip is followed by comments about the gradual loss of Cajun French, as well as standup performances of "Thibodeaux and Boudreaux" jokes, self stereotyping Cajun humor based on two characters known to all, and available to any who wish to create new jokes around them. One of the more jocular of the men stands up and asks earnestly whether anyone had heard about the day last week when Thibodeaux and Boudreaux went fishing.

> One day Thibodeaux and Boudreaux found the perfect fishing spot. No hook came up empty, and after awhile the two noticed they didn't even need bait. Hours went by as the boat filled up, and the two hardly had time for words as they reeled in fish after fish. Finally, when the sun started to set Thibodeaux said to Boudreaux,
> "Boudreaux, we should mark this spot so we can find it again."
> "That's a good idea," said Boudreaux.
> So Boudreaux found a screwdriver, pushed some fish out of the way with his feet, and marked an X on the bottom of the boat.
> "Come on, man!" exclaimed Thibodeaux, "are you that stupid?"
> "But you said we should mark where we are!"
> "I did, I did," said an exasperated Thibodeaux, "but what happens if next time we come out in a different boat?"

Others are prompted in turn to stand up and deliver. Over the weeks that follow I will hear dozens of such jokes, rarely the same one twice. I wonder whether any social science has come up with a better single measure of cultural confidence than a people's pleasure in teasing themselves.

Throughout southern Louisiana, from the Atchafalaya Basin

down to Lake Verret, to Bayou Terrebonne and Bayou Lafourche, Cajun life remains a culture on the water. It is the rare side yard that does not house on a trailer some homebuilt skiff—these days built mostly of welded aluminum—though often the boat and trailer are parked in the driveway next to the family truck. The bayous themselves, in towns such as Pierre Part and Cut Off, are lined with makeshift wharves and small piers, and it's often hard to tell whether those houses located along the narrow strip of land separating the bayou from Main Street face the road or face the water.

Shrimp boats with names like *Captain V*, *Addie Inez*, *Night Moves*, and *Captain Paw Paw* are tied to some of these wharves when they are not out for days or weeks at a time in the Gulf of Mexico. It is now February, and boys in skiffs with small outboards race up and down the watery boulevard after school. A small barge, perhaps sixty feet long, has been hauled out of the water and rests on three stout stilts as men below repair leaks with sheets of metal and welding torches. For those who like the water, and who like people who like the water, this is heaven on earth.

One of the shrimp boats is named *T-Maroo*, perhaps after its owner, who would be the first son of a Mr. Maroo. "T" is shorthand along the bayous, its etymology evolving from Junior to Petit, to Tiny, to T. It is a common construction, so if you ask for T-John or T-Mike in a bar, you probably have to be a T-bit more specific. A man named T-Black, who served me a dinner of fresh whiting and mustard greens picked from the vacant lot next door, tells me that "a Cajun is rich when he lives by the water."

WHILE I ORIGINALLY HAD NO INTENTION of stopping in New Orleans I have now spent enough time here to have learned the bus system, from Chef Menteur in New Orleans East, to Tchoupitoulas. I've ridden from the Museum of Art in the center of the city to Manhattan Boulevard on the other side of the Mississippi,

and from that bus stop walked thirty minutes to the caterering business that hired me for two days of flaking lettuce and flipping hamburgers during Mardi Gras. I've been to such local hangouts as the
Dragon's Den, the Funky Butt, and Snake 'N Jake's, watched horse
racing for a buck but no bets, and eaten at the counter at Liuzza's, run
by a woman who, if you mention you're from the Northeast, will inform you that she once taught at Harvard, and if you express even remote interest in that, she'll mention the more distracting fact that she
abandoned that tweedy academic hillside to become a Playboy Bunny.

During the weeks that lead up to Mardi Gras—"Fat Tuesday," the
last day for purging the baser spiritualities before engaging piously in
Lent—the whole of south Louisiana, clear over the border to Mobile,
Alabama, the birthplace of Mardi Gras, becomes increasingly preoc-
cupied with its annual, crazy, rhythmic, and magnificent cultural
bloom. Miles-long parades—including one no less than nine hours in
passing—of outlandish floats honoring the historical and the mythical
are musically punctuated by an astonishing supply of marching bands.
I've watched small-town parades and found the passing of drums and
tubas to be an exercise in tedium. But this is different, like an un-
laughable gesture made funny by its repetition. The entire procession,
from French horn players to flag-waving horsemen, to torchbear-
ers—or "flambeaux"—to the floats themselves, pulses along human
arteries formed by throngs of people on both sides of the city's long
avenues. The give-and-take relationship between performance and
audience is as intimate on this grand scale as that between a jazz quin-
tet and its listeners in a brick-walled, smoke-filled closet of a dive.
Hordes of plebeians on the ground yell and jump and reach, with arms
outstretched, trying to garner the attention of the variously masked
and painted lords and ladies, phantoms and deities of the floats, who
reward the adoration of the crowd by casting into the sea of faces a
seemingly endless supply of plastic beaded necklaces, while some pick
and choose, tease and deny, with more treasured baubles. It's fright-
ening, the unified, mass, public worship, and the roles, en masse, that

we willingly adopt. And yet the thrill when, from a distance, from the middle of a crowd, I attract the attention of a certain goddess, and she looks at me, and coyly hesitates, then looks away, then looks back again, smiles, and hurls in my direction a string of heavy, plastic pearls.

Elsewhere on narrower streets, below crowded wrought-iron balconies, groups of friends and strangers spontaneously join in primitive stomping dance around anyone with even the most makeshift of instruments. Two hours before midnight and the beginning of Lent I am one among a circle of thirty people dancing around two men beating out wild rhythms on five-gallon plastic pails and a third with two heavy sticks whose dense wood clacks loudly. Other music with deep basses and steel strings emanates in the background from the open doors of packed bars, and everyone is moving to the nearest rhythm. With eyes half closed my normal composure is overcome by the beating of the drums and the unified chaos of movement around me, and my body and mind are released into free interpretation of what I hear and feel. Several men dressed as king's jesters join in, each holding a long trailing flag of a castle tower attached to a wooden pole, and the flags are waved around to the music's time, their tails lapping across shoulders and heads as if in blessing. The energy throughout the circle repeatedly rises and wanes according to that of the drummers, whose buckets are now cracking beneath their frenzied blows. Next to me, a man in his late thirties with long disheveled red hair held loosely in a ponytail and dressed in a Hawaiian print shirt, filthy blue jeans, and running shoes, catches my eye for a moment and sums up Mardi Gras with a question and an answer.

"Do you know why we're doing this?" he asks with exclamation.

"Why?" I call back through the din.

"Because we *can!*" he yells, a claim of freedom that releases from within him an adrenal boost, and with closed eyes he pounds the pavement even harder with his dancing feet, arms flying, and is lost again in the music.

And because this is who we are, I think to myself, released by the tradition of carnival, and by the laws of New Orleans, to plumb the deeper, animalistic depths of ourselves.

By midnight the crowds disperse, and an army of city workers and machines hose down and sweep away the muck and detritus accumulated over several days, and groups of sobering people walk by with crosses of ash, symbols of both mourning and penance, on their foreheads. Lent has begun.

Yesterday I attended a home show at a convention center on the south shore of Lake Ponchartrain, the small inland sea to the north of New Orleans that, with the Mississippi, reminds the city that its final mayoral report will someday probably be about a great and final flood. I watched a demonstration of nonstick pans, temporarily helped hand out brochures about a most comfortable cedar swing, and was asked by an above-ground swimming pool saleswoman, who thought she might have hooked her prey, whether I knew the intersection where her showroom is located. I almost did. As I walked away with a brochure in hand (a twenty-year guarantee is illustrated by photos of an elephant entering and exiting the flexible pool), I was reminded that I haven't rowed an inch in ten days.

Over this period one invitation had led to another, beginning with that from a man my age along Bayou Lafourche to join him and his friends for the upcoming Mardi Gras celebrations. I rowed for several more days, and at Barataria met Henry and Corinne Burlette, a retired couple, by their waterfront home. Their neighbor Rose had asked if I'd like to make some money working for a catering company. Henry and Corinne said I could leave my boat with them during the festivities. With Mardi Gras now behind, I myself have been in their care—Corinne, by chance, had been a nurse—as my stomach has been rebelling against the quantities of oysters I consumed while in New Orleans.

SOMEWHERE ALONG THE SPECTRUM of control of this trip, between that which I have influence over—the boat, my navigation, my abilities to supply my needs, including the need to connect with people—and that which is beyond my reach, is luck. Luck has been assigned to me by someone on virtually every day since Brooklyn, in various forms and phrasings, the most common, of course, being "Good luck!" This was said from the dock on the East River as I put the oars in the water for the first time, and I heard it perhaps a dozen times before the end of that day from people fishing along the eastern shore of Manhattan. There are many variations on the theme of luck, not all of them spoken. There had been the jogger at 110th Street who'd punched his fist into the air. Not just "Good Luck," I'd guessed, but also "Be Strong." Others have honked their horns, from cars and semitrailers crossing bridges to tugboat captains, and this I imagine translates into "Hey! We see you! And wherever you're going, we hope you make it!" I have also been given tokens of good luck. I have in the boat a freshly minted Georgia Peach quarter given to me in Pierre Part, Louisiana, and a Sacajawea dollar put in my hand by a shipyard chandler several days later in Morgan City.

As many believe, luck blends with fate. The "luck of the draw" was "meant to be." If you're thought to be lucky often enough, you're then a lucky person, which is more than a matter of twice rolling double sixes when you really need them. It had seemed like fate when I'd met Marcina in her daughter's kitchen, and Mark Robbins during the slimmest window of rural opportunity when picking up this boat. And luck and fate are often tempered with faith. A husband and wife, who'd picked me up along the Hudson in their restored '39 Plymouth when I was hitchhiking to town, returned me to the river after a good luck—or good fate—recitation of the Lord's Prayer. I was given a Bible in New Martinsville, West Virginia. In Golden Meadow, Louisiana, where I'd explained to an older couple that my destination was the Canadian border with Maine, I was given a much smaller Bible, the width of a business card and not as long. In their minds I was rowing not only to the Canadian border, but also to the beloved Acadian homeland from which their ancestors had been evicted. Yet I myself lean uncertainly toward fate, that "all the world's a stage" and we are, though perhaps with growing insight, merely living out a lucky and luckless script.

Before setting out on this second leg of the trip, a close friend gave me her necklace with a pendant of St. Christopher, the patron saint of travelers. Two weeks ago, as my neck is now covered with sunscreen each sunny day, I opted to hang the necklace instead around the bracket that holds the two support stays of the outrigger. If either one of these breaks it is then possible to take only the most gentle strokes without breaking an outrigger as well.

In leaving New Orleans I will retrace several miles on the Mississippi River, entering from the intracoastal waterway through Harvey Lock, upstream and across the river from the French Quarter. I will round the sharp bend between the French Quarter and Algiers Point, where I'd stopped at Bollinger's Shipyard the summer before, and soon thereafter I will duck out of the river's current and into a narrow channel where the intracoastal waterway continues east. A deckhand on a towboat had once asked me whether I'd rowed around Algiers Point on my way to the Gulf. I said I had. "Well that's the most dangerous bend on the whole river!" he'd exclaimed, not only because of the current and sharpness of the turn, but because of the never-ending traffic of freighters and barges.

And so I pass through Harvey Lock and once again enter the Mississippi, a river with which any captain will unavoidably develop an everlasting affair that will include, among fear, respect, frustration, and solitude, at least a little bit of true love. I choose to cross the river, toward the city and the French Quarter, so as to benefit around Algiers Point from the swifter current along the outer bend. I wait for a mammoth red freighter to pass on its way upstream, and also for a towboat heading down, and then start pulling while watching as two other tows approach from each direction at greater distances. I should be able to cross both of their paths in time.

The tows are now a hundred yards or so to either side of me and closing in, yet by my eye I have already reached safely beyond their courses. I've left my radio on in case I suddenly need to contact a towboat, and now hear the captain of one commenting to the other, neither one guessing I can hear them, "That's a small fish playing with the big fish!" And the other one says "You got that right!" I pass by the *Delta Queen*, an ornate paddle wheeler built in 1927 and still in the business of carrying passengers, now all tourists. She's a working relic of the past, lying docked to a wharf by the French Quarter, whose old brick buildings and gabled roofs seem to be herded by the more modern towers of the city's skyline.

The river bends from north to southeast, and I am increasingly exposed to a headwind that had been largely blocked by Algiers Point, and now riles the countering current. I row with my head turned over my left shoulder, scouting the chaotic mix of wakes, swirling currents, and windblown waves. Some strokes of the oars require pressure on only a single blade to compensate for an eddy of current, and some waves call for a loose shifting of my weight to prevent a gallon of the river from sloshing over the gunwales. I approach two enormous navy transport ships docked to a long wharf, amazed as always that such large vessels float as high as they do, and pass so closely that I can look directly up and see nothing but flaring bow in battle gray. A hundred yards out into the river the waves are strong enough that they snap the cables securing a raft of laden barges to a tugboat heading downriver, and I watch as the captain speeds ahead of his errant cargo before it barrels at the current's three miles per hour—that is, thousands of tons at three miles per hour—into some pier or ship.

The lock that leads to the continuation of the intracoastal canal lies shortly beyond the navy ships. If I were to miss it I wouldn't find another eastbound cut from the river for more than eighty miles. I spot the turn into the calm channel, yet near the entrance I feel the snap of breaking metal as I pull on the oars. One of the stays for the outrigger has broken. I waste no time studying the damage, as I will soon be drawn beyond the turnoff by the tide. Alternating my gaze between my placid destination and the flexing of the unsupported beam holding one oarlock, I pull as hard as I dare without inflicting more damage and only barely, by a handful of timid strokes, nose the bow into safety.

Such a failure a mere minute later would have rendered the boat, with me in it, one more piece of flotsam on a windy, trafficked, intensely industrial stretch of river. Still hanging from the bracket in front of me is St. Christopher. Lady Luck, or fate, or divinity, I don't know, but I decide then and there I will keep the miniature Bible and the two freshly minted coins, and continue to say "Thank You" when people wish me "Good Luck!" Only an hour later, as there happened to be a Coast Guard station adjacent to the lock, and an officer on duty with access to a workshop beyond any one man's wildest dreams, I am back on the water and leaving New Orleans, six weeks after I'd descended through the Old River Lock near the head of the Atchafalaya River.

· 2I ·

A Breathing,
Observing Presence

THE INTRACOASTAL WATERWAY leads in a nearly straight and lonely course east from New Orleans toward the Louisiana state line with Mississippi and the Gulf of Mexico. Aside from a brief glimpse of open ocean when I'd reached the end of South Pass last summer, the route has been channeled since I first set out from Brooklyn, and I welcome a return to the vast horizon of the open coast on which I was raised. I have been fascinated by the rivers, whose tides depend on precipitation and not the sun and moon, whose waters hold no salt, whose currents eddy and swirl rather than ebb and flow, and whose boats and people and ways of life were so different as to be a new world to me. But I feel at home on salt water, and indeed safer on the open ocean, despite its currents and weather, than on a small lake with the eerie silence and stillness of its depths.

As I leave the channel of the intracoastal, which empties lazily into the Gulf, I am met by several dolphins attracted by the rhythm of the blades, and which, not quite leaping, playfully break the water long enough to eye me. I've speculated for months about what it would be like to row on this open coast and whether the boat would be sufficiently seaworthy, but for now this welcome by the dolphins and a gentle following breeze on a sunny day all seem auspicious.

Having meandered so aimlessly through the bayous for weeks on end I now feel the urge to simply row, and while I have no particular schedule but to reach Eastport, Maine, before cold weather sets in in the late fall, I suspect that the urge will last.

SEVERAL DAYS LATER, after having waited out a storm at Biloxi, Mississippi, I head east despite continuing winds and storm clouds from the south. The boat proves stable enough to travel broadside to occasionally breaking waves, and I remain close enough to shore that within minutes I would be able to surf onto a beach. East of Ocean Springs, Mississippi, however, the coast arcs inland to form a bay, and I choose to row directly across it, from Belle Fontaine Point six miles or so to Pascagoula.

The wind direction begins inching from south to southwest —to my favor as I head east—and maintains its speed of fifteen miles per hour with occasional gusts to twenty, yet a brooding cloud the shape of an enormous scythe blackens northwest of me as I try to convince myself it isn't edging in my direction. But a mile offshore the wind suddenly stutters to a halt like a car run out of gas. I eye the cloud and know that this calm before the storm will not last long, and I also eye the shore left behind, knowing that an imminent wind will prevent me from returning to that safety. I drop the oars and quickly set about stowing gear—stopping to take a picture along the way—and tightly snug the tent down over my bags to keep it from billowing in the wind.

I see and hear the wind before I feel it as it sweeps across the water like a great, invisible broom from the west. The waves that were built all day by the south wind still heave the boat, but the new wind blows their crests into hairy spray and a new pattern of waves starts building across the old. A decommissioned lighthouse at Belle Fontaine Point seems to look on with cool detachment, and with no other boats in view I am on my own. I take to the oars as the wind continues to rise and shift toward the northwest, and while I aim due east for the distant shore of Pascagoula, I make a mental note of the fact that Horn Island and Petit Bois Island lie ten miles southward in the Gulf, should the wind swing farther north and blow me offshore.

The new waves grow and soon match the size of those still rolling in from the south, and every so often two waves cross each other to form a much larger wave. I take gentle strokes for fear that if I build too much speed the boat might start surfing down a wave and broach, dumping me and all my gear into the strife. Even without me pulling on the oars the wind and waves carry me as fast as I would row in calm conditions, and a gust of wind blows my well-fitted canvas hat off my head and into the bow. Soon after I reach for it and stuff it beneath the tent I look up to the crest of a following wave, a rogue produced momentarily by a large wave from the southwest crossing a large one from the west. The wave conspires with a gentle stroke to lift the boat stern-first and launch me downhill. Suddenly the resistance between hull and water that all rowers strive to minimize seems altogether eliminated, and more than four hundred pounds of boat, gear, and rower freely surf down the face of the wave.

Like a child who's just learned to ride a bicycle with no hands I am still afraid to look over my shoulder, afraid that I might fall, that the boat will topple if I don't maintain its precarious balance. I hear the sound of spray emanating from beneath the hull, and a rooster tail of water follows the stern as if behind a motorboat. I feel the hull lean to the left—the beginning of a crash?—and so put pressure on the opposite oar to drag the boat back to a straight line. Then the momentum ebbs, the surf ends, and I welcome the sense of friction, though my adrenaline is rushing. I want more.

As I cross the bay I gain confidence in myself and the boat and soon, rather than trying to slow the hull before a following wave, I learn to choose my moment and pull hard enough to send myself skimming over the water once again. Toward the end of the day as the wind abates I notice that the metal bracket holding my left footrest has developed a stress fracture, and by the time I find a lee shore along an uninhabited coastline of marshes and treeless islands near Mississippi's border with Alabama, the bracket has nearly fallen off. I am grateful that it's done so now and not while surfing down some cresting wave, for as often as I push against the footrests during the stroke I pull against their straps during each recovery. They aid my balance on the sliding seat. But weeks will pass before I get around to finding a welder who can repair the break, and until then I'll make do with only one footrest.

I HAVE STOPPED near Pensacola at a yacht club whose cofounder I'd met last fall while working in Maine. He had drawn me a map of how to find the small harbor in case I made it that far, and his simple sketch has been imprinted on my mind ever since. I recognize the harbor immediately on the photocopied chart that I have for this stretch of the Gulf. The club itself is as unpretentious as one could find, perched on stilts so as to remain above hurricane tides, with a sandwich shop occupying a small portion of the building, also facing the water. There are perhaps fifty boats docked along the piers, and the basin beyond is so shallow that no boats are moored. Only a narrow channel leads from the docks back along the periphery of the basin to the intracoastal waterway.

It is now midnight at the end of a social evening that has left me feeling like a part of the club myself. One of the members writes for the local newspaper, and we sat outside on a raised porch amid a group of her friends talking, while she took notes. A man my age who goes by the name Rock bought me a beer and asked whether I'd like to sleep in the cabin of his sailboat, an invitation that I accepted. He described his boat and its location on the docks, and told me that in case he went home before I was ready to go to sleep, he'd leave the cabin lights on and the radio at low volume.

Now everyone has left the club and its doors are locked, and I am standing in my boat tied up to a main pier of the docks, which at low tide are the height of my chest. I organize my disheveled gear, making sure that whatever needs to stay dry will do so in case of rain, and separating out what I'll take to Rock's boat, including not only clean clothes, but valuable possessions such as my camera. As I swing my duffel up to the pier I happen to glance out toward the yacht club and the road beyond, and it is then that I realize I am not quite alone. There is a man in the sandwich shop, which had been closed earlier but whose lights are now on. In a fraction of a second, without clearly looking at him, I see that he's looking at me. Perhaps the owner, I speculate, has returned to work for some late-night accounting. Yet minutes later I hear his footsteps and see him walking toward the pier out of the furthest corner of my left eye. An aura of distrust precedes him, and I know that I am his destination; he is not out for a breath of fresh air along the docks before heading home or just curious about someone who's obviously passing through. Feeling immediately defensive I keep my gaze down, reaching into the stern to continue my busywork in the boat—a look of purpose to alleviate his doubt. At last I hear him come to a stop next to my duffel bag.

I turn my head over my shoulder to look at him, as if I haven't heard him coming, then stand up. Without delay and in a chatty voice, one guy to another among boats, I greet him. "Hey, how's it going?"

His curt nod in response allows him to maintain his position of doubt. His mind is made up. The weak lights along the dock reveal his black loafers with leather tassels, gray slacks and dark sweater above a collared shirt. Maybe he has been out to dinner with friends, or perhaps he always dresses with such casual formality. He is in his mid-forties, and sternly handsome with cleanly cut brown hair. I can't help it: I sense that his agenda is focused more on trouble than on opportunity.

"What are you doing?" he asks after nodding minimally. I register his true tone, but there's room for interpretation.

"Oh just trying to clean up the mess in this boat!" I answer amiably, hoping for a spark of chat. He stands in place, scanning the contents of the boat with his eyes, wanting straight answers.

"Who do you know here?" he asks coolly. I now have no choice but to acknowledge the nature of his inquiry, but figure I can still elaborate my answers with details about the trip. That I'm obviously traveling is apparently of no interest to him. I mention Ron, the yacht club's cofounder, assuming this will put an end to my indictment. "I'm rowing around the eastern United States," I tell him. "He's an acquaintance of mine who invited me to stop here." He's never heard the name, to my dismay, and I realize I may have only increased his doubt by mentioning the entire route. Should I have told him instead that I'm rowing from Pensacola to Apalachicola, a distance of 150 miles, living out the dream of a grandfather I never met who loved this stretch of Florida and loved to row? If only he hadn't gotten both of his hands caught in a cake mixer, never again to grasp the handles of a pair of oars. Such a combination of partial truth—I *am* rowing to Apalachicola—and falsehood might seem more plausible to him than the whole truth. For once, I realize, a description of my route may have closed, rather than opened, a door.

I name other people I met tonight, wishing I could remember more of them. I mention Rock, and tell him that there's a boat with its cabin left open, its lights on, and the radio playing, as I'd been invited to sleep aboard for the night. Another mistake, perhaps, for he might reason that I've already walked the docks and happened to see such a boat. But then how would I know its owner's name? He's never heard of Rock or anyone else I've named.

"These boats are worth a lot of money," he tells me, "and these docks are private. I don't know what you're doing here and I've never heard of any of the people you say you know." I try to contain my emotions, with middling success.

"I'm just passing through here. I've got a boat full of camping gear and if it helps any I can tell you about the coast as far back as you want. I'm not here to steal anything. I'm in a rowboat!" I pause, needing a deep, calming breath. He says nothing, and so I continue: "I didn't just make up the names I gave you. Why else would there be a sailboat down the pier with its lights and radio on but no one aboard?" I feel uneasy pressing him. After all, I am the visitor, and while I don't know what his precise affiliation is with this marina, it's certainly more his turf than mine.

He shakes his head as if to say there are no good answers in the world. "I don't know about this. I'm going to have to make some phone calls." He turns and walks back along the pier to his medium-sized sedan, and I follow him at a distance, unwilling to simply sit and wait in the boat. At what point can you claim to be a part of the tribe? How many people or what percentage of the population has to know your name, and hear that name confirmed by others? In a very short time I have gone from feeling as much a part of the yacht club community as one could hope for during a night's stay, to teetering on the edge between residence and eviction. This man had simply missed the rituals by which I'd been accepted, and now does not have it within himself, late at night and near a large city, to allow his initial doubt to give way to the possibility of trust.

He sits in his car with the windows closed and does most of the talking on the phone. I stand ten feet back, idly, a bit awkwardly, and wonder to whom he's talking. The police? Finally he opens his electric window and lowers the cell phone in his right hand.

"I'm talking to the owner of this property and he's never heard of you or any of the people you mentioned." I wonder how this is possible. The entire building, including both the yacht club and the sandwich shop, is the size of a large house. How could the landlord not know at least one name? I ask whether I can speak to him myself, and I'm begrudgingly handed the phone. The groggy voice of an older man recently awakened with a tenant's complaint responds wearily to my introduction. I wonder what he has been dreaming about. Cruise ships coming in to fill up at his gas dock? He mystifies me with his claim that he knows none of the names I've repeated. I'm stumped.

"Well," I tell him, "a man named Rock who's a member of the yacht club invited me to sleep on his boat, and left the lights on in the cabin. But I'll do whatever you want me to do."

"I'd like you to leave," he says, surely thinking also that he'd like this irksome hiatus from sleep to end as well.

"Okay. May I at least switch off the battery on Rock's boat so it won't be drained?"

"No."

As I hand back the phone, controlling myself, I ask the man in the car whether he would please turn off the batteries himself and walk back to my boat. I am watched as I row out toward the intracoastal waterway, yet find a spot in the shallows of the harbor deep enough to anchor without risk of finding myself beached at the next low tide.

I might have volunteered immediately to leave the docks, particularly as I've grown accustomed to sleeping in the boat. Yet in aiming to enlarge my welcome by two degrees I hoped to protect not just the opportunity to sleep in the more spacious comfort of the sailboat, but more importantly to protect the invitation itself by fulfilling my acceptance, and the gracious intentions of all who had welcomed me. When you are given a flower, you put in water and you enjoy it.

The following morning I return to the dock, as I'd been invited last night to have breakfast with Ron. Several hours later, after having eaten and taken the opportunity to resupply the boat, I am back at the dock and preparing to set out when the man from the sandwich shop approaches me. I am wary, yet sense that our relationship has changed. Perhaps it was simply the shift from night to day as well as my continued presence, or perhaps someone he knows confirmed my story, and he's thus become included in the process by which a stranger has been initiated into the group. Our conversation is short, but sufficient to resolve our conflict. He hands me a bottle of water and says, "I thought you could use this. Good luck on your trip."

"Thank you," I say, taken by this gesture, and without another word he turns and walks back to his shop.

THE BIG BEND OF FLORIDA begins at Apalachicola, leads northeast into Apalachee Bay, and then turns abruptly to the southeast, ending at Cedar Key. It is 150 miles of shoreline, an often lonely arc of Florida's coast protected from development by the shallowness of its depths. Two miles and more from shoreline I am able for long stretches to watch the bottom passing several feet below me, and when I stop to rest I can stand waist deep in the water. Now and then as I pass the mouths of tannin-rich rivers—the Econfina River, the Steinhatchee River, and the Suwannee—the clear water goes dark, the color of the deepest red wine or of blood as it clots. If I dropped a knife here, though it would be within my reach, I wouldn't be able to spot it through the organic dye, produced by the decay of vegetation in inland swamps.

But otherwise I watch as I row above thousands of acres of plant life, thick blades of grass, forests of what look like the miniature trees used by architects to suggest landscaping around models of enormous buildings, and varieties of other leafy growth. Here and there I float above Shermanesque scars a foot wide and extending in either direction beyond view, narrow botanical barrens carved by the propeller of some powerboat driven just barely within sufficient operating depths. Skates camouflaged in the sand suddenly dart away when they sense the shadow of the hull, though I rarely see them as more than brief streaks in my peripheral vision.

From a distance the shoreline is a blur of salt marsh with a backdrop of trees for miles on end, but I've been of a mind to row and not explore, and have watched as unpeopled points of the coast pass by at a rower's speed, emerging at first into mirage ahead of me, then slowly evolving into detailed focus, then fading again toward mirage and out of sight. It rarely occurs to me while rowing that I could drive the distances ahead of me in a fraction of my rowing time, and that thousands of people on parallel roads are doing just that. But when

such a thought does suddenly cross my mind it passes just as quickly, irrelevant. Hundreds and thousands of strokes of the oars which pull the boat through water are sometimes arduous, sometimes mesmerizing, but most often, as breath, very nearly unnoticed. I find the rate at which the occasional buoy of a crab trap disappears behind me entirely acceptable.

Particularly along this stretch I stop to look down into this separate world, and watch as a wilderness of grasses and Lilliputian forest sways in its own liquid wind. As I sit in the bow and lean my head over the side, I can see the biological and mineral seadust suspended and drifting in the tide, and, in undulating reflection precisely where the uppermost elevation of the water seamlessly meets the lowest point of sky, I can see myself leaning over the wooden gunwale. For a lucid, stunning moment, as when one is wholly distracted, transfixed in déjà vu, I am no longer myself, with a name and a history of associations and preferences, but reduced to simply a breathing, observing presence, and the feeling of the slightest breeze on my arm, the long oar whose red blade floats idly on the water, and a single architect's tree amid the miniature, aqueous forestscape below are all utterly astonishing.

· 22 ·

Ozona the Cat

AT OZONA, FLORIDA, I tie the boat up at a small marina and stretch my legs with a walk through the quaint town whose narrow tree-shaded streets and old wooden homes give it the feel of a world unto itself, though the cities of Clearwater and Tampa are just minutes away by car. I walk aimlessly, needing little in the way of supplies beyond the filling of my water jugs at the marina. I turn a corner and see people milling about at the entrance to a white clapboard building the size of a rural church, but without the steeple. Perhaps a community center of some sort. At first I think an art show is being held, but without having to ask a question I learn from a stack of flyers that I have arrived in time for town meeting. On a whim, I take a seat in the back on a wooden bench as others end their chat and seat themselves.

I like being here anonymously on the fringe of the community. I enjoy being in on the local news (one landowner who's been wishing to build and sell new homes on his waterfront lots reassures residents by offering to donate some of his waterfront land as a park if the town will agree to rezone another piece of property for two more houses), and find security among people who care about where they live. Yet I am tired too, and as much as the hard planes of the wooden bench keep me awake—I have little natural cushion left and have to shift from side to side for any comfort—I still find my vision momentarily collapsing and my head nodding in capitulation to sleep, all the while lulled by the safety of other voices.

Yet I am suddenly alert and wholly distracted when I see a half-grown kitten with a thick coon coat and white paws wander in through the doors, which are still opened to the street. I search for the posture required to attract a cat, more than indifference but less than desire, and lean forward to lightly tap my fingertips on a leg of the bench. The cat looks, but is unintrigued and rubs up against the bare calf of a woman who is at first surprised, then reaches down to scratch its cheek. The cat moves on, collecting affection. Finally it comes my way, though I am unable to hold its attention. It has clearly made these rounds before.

An hour later, as I walk back to the boat along a street faintly lit by a rare lamp, I am suddenly aware of being followed. I look behind to the left, and then to the right, and spot the kitten. It is following me at the heels like a puppy, stopping suddenly to pounce on a fallen leaf, then galloping ahead of me, then rejoining my pace. At the marina one of the employees who is just locking up recognizes the cat as a stray.

"That one's been running around for weeks now," he says. "I guess no one wants to take her home. Looks to me like you've got a friend!" I have permission to stay tied up at the dock overnight, and go about my business as usual. I ignore the cat, hop in the boat, and start setting up the tent, pulling out my two bed rolls and laying out the sleeping bag and pillow. I am pretending against better knowledge of myself, always a sucker for strays, that this cat is not going with me. Yet soon I cannot help wondering whether the cat is still near. Why hasn't anyone adopted it? What will become of it? It would be fun to have the cat in the boat at least for the night.

I climb out of the boat, follow the pier back to a marina parking lot that descends as a boat ramp into the water, and search for the feline, clicking my tongue, whistling lightly, increasingly convinced that once again it's found other sources of affection. But then a shadow leaps out of a patch of weeds by a fence, stops with abrupt alertness to look back to some phantom in the weeds, then turns again and bounds across twelve feet of pavement and, purring audibly, rubs up against my ankles. Neither one of us quite realizes it yet, but Ozona the Cat has just bought a voyage.

The following day, with Ozona at first cowering in the shade beneath the wooden thwart, I aim to reach Longboat Key, where I will stay with Urs Wonderlei, a Swiss-born importer of a French brand of sculling boat, who later tells me that he's tired of hearing that he and Sean Connery not only look but sound alike. Urs and I had heard of each other through a mutual friend in Newport, Rhode Island, and when I'd called him a week ago I'd been instantly invited to stay with him and his wife. They will meet us at the end of the day on Anna Maria Key, the next island north, connected by bridge to Longboat Key.

Ozona quickly finds all of the shady spots in the boat, and before long her nerves ease and she sleeps, lulled perhaps by the surging rhythm of the hull. I stop at a marina in order to use a pay phone—I take her with me to the marina office, and make phone calls from the side of the building while coddling her in my left arm—and as I walk back to the boat along the pier I see a manatee for the first time, looking like a large, slow-witted cousin to a seal, utterly and adorably benign. Sadly, true to all the reports I've ever heard about manatees, this particular harmless, herbivorous mammal is marked by three deep scars, all of them most likely inflicted by the skegs and propellers of outboard engines. It rolls and slowly dives among the pilings of the pier, attracted, ironically enough, to the roosts of its greatest threats, as there is little that a manatee likes so much as the flow of fresh water, which can be found where men hose down their powerful boats.

Ozona and I stop twice at small islands created out of sand dredged from the channel of the intracoastal; they make fine litter boxes. But my new companion takes a turn for the worse as we head across the mouth of Tampa Bay, whose afternoon swells have not yet subsided as dusk grows into dark. Ozona emerges from beneath the boat's folded tent looking stressed, even panicked. She wants out and ultimately there isn't much I can do about it. After I've twice brought her back from the gunwales she manages to perch herself on the wooden railing, swaying back and forth several times as the boat sways beneath her, then launches herself toward land, as if her eyes had played a trick and portrayed the lights of Anna Maria, still tingling on the horizon, as a chimera of waveless safety. She lands, of course, with a splash in the water, and showing her resolve starts swimming headlong into the waves. I head her off, drag her out of the water, and manage, while holding on to her with one hand, to dig my towel out of the duffel bag with the other. I dry her as thoroughly as I can and am relieved when she chooses her previous nest over the bay. An hour later, beneath starlight, we land at the north end of Anna Maria, where we are met by Urs and Renee and driven to their home, where we spend four days.

While in Longboat Key, I make a call to Gloucester, Massachusetts, about a race I've heard about, the Blackburn Challenge, a twenty-two mile rowing course around Cape Ann in honor of Howard Blackburn, scheduled for the middle of July. I have never been much of an athletic competitor but I'm intrigued by the idea of rowing against others who've been captured by the story of this man. How fitting it would be, I think, to arrive at the starting line of the Blackburn Challenge after rowing so many thousands of miles with Blackburn as the partial source of my inspiration. Though with hundreds of miles still to row southward before rounding Key West and heading north, I keep the date in mind.

URS HAS JOINED ME for a day's row heading south from Longboat Key. I am trailing in Urs's wake at the moment, as Ozona naps in a towel-lined wicker basket, contributed by Renee, beneath the shade of the folded tent. A plastic tray with bowls for both water and cat food sits beside the wicker basket on the aft seat. A lidded plastic dishpan filled with litter lies next to the seat in the cockpit. Urs has made a kitten-sized life preserver out of a piece of line and two dozen wine bottle corks. When I occasionally reach forward and lift the tent I find her blissfully dozing, legs stretched, head impossibly twisted and inverted.

Urs and I vaguely follow the channel of the intracoastal waterway. Sometimes we row side by side—although his boat is faster than mine—and at other times we drift apart. For the first time on the trip I see what others see as they watch me. I am impressed by his speed, as others have expressed surprise at my speed. It is calming, almost entrancing, to watch the mechanics of his body translate directly into the repetitive sweep of the long oars through and above the water. Stroke and recovery, power and glide—a cadence that works every inch of the body while freeing the mind. Every so often, as I do, Urs looks over a shoulder for a brief moment to check his route, but otherwise you wouldn't think he was looking at anything in particular, but perhaps the same transcendent nothingness that a pianist sees beyond the keyboard, or the saxophonist sees in the haze of the bar as his fingers dance and hold.

Although our boats draw no more than several inches of water, we too could find ourselves among hull-damaging shoals, and also have to avoid submerged sandbars as the wakes of a seemingly endless stream of powerboats fold dangerously upon themselves as they reach the shallows. Generally we are able to drift just outside of the channel as boats pass, but still connect the dots of the green and red markers on a curving route south. We continually contend with wakes, and I still have not resolved the question of whether I prefer a powerboat that is slowed out of courtesy to me, though it takes longer to pass and often provides a much larger wake, or the boat that ignores my presence, disappears quickly, and leaves a smaller wake. I do value etiquette on the water, and even amid the thickest traffic today I wave at anyone who makes eye contact with me, if only through a nod of my head combined with an extension of fingers while pulling the stroke. Ideally I am able, without confusing a passing captain, to wave my arm so as to communicate that he may pass me by without worry. He waves, I wave, and his wake quickly passes. In either case, however, for fun I always try to ride the wakes, and often manage to get the boat surfing for fifty yards.

The traffic today is constant, and typically consists of twenty-foot overpowered fiberglass boats driven by shirtless men accompanied by scantily clad women. The sounds of engines prevail. At one point Urs, who is now closer to the line of traffic than I am, is passed by an enormous hull with twin 250-horsepower outboards. The hull explodes the water into huge sheets of spray off to either side and is driven by a bare-chested red-shouldered man in his early fifties with wraparound bug-eyed sunglasses and hair slicked back not just by the wind. He was once strong, but his muscles have softened and his gut is growing. His wife or girlfriend or daughter, barely decent in the slightest bikini, is displayed in a lounging pose on a multicolored vinyl bench seat at the stern. As he passes us he yells out to Urs—though in cruder terms—"Get out of the way!" The woman exerts just enough energy to turn her head, then restores her pose. Urs is unfazed and continues rowing, while I think of what I'd like to yell back as the boat roars away, leaving the scent of spent fuel.

I can't help feeling a bit self-righteous, the way you would spurn the use of high-powered automatic hunting rifles (as I've seen aimed from the back of roving pickups) if you've become proficient with a bow and arrow. Or the pride you would feel as a baker of your own loaves while walking past the Wonderbread section in a grocery store. The bicycling commuter has a *right* to feel smug—whether he does or not—as he is passed by a fuming stream of cars, for he is doing virtually no harm, and happiness invariably extends from his routine work. The man on the boat just passed has been corrupted by the power of combustion, and it is precisely this mindless recreation (for he has no police siren or badge of the Red Cross on his bow to suggest that he's making an emergency delivery of plasma to Cape Haze), and this coveted right to speed that explain the multiple scars, whipping style, across the body of every manatee I've seen along the Florida coast. We would do well to apply the Hippocratic Oath not only to humans, but to fellow mammals endangered by our intracoastal recreation. Do no harm.

And what do we mean, I wonder grudgingly, by progress anyway? Here we are in the spring of 2000, amid the most extraordinary growth spurt in the history of the American economy: Car sales are up. New housing starts are up. Boat sales are surely up, with outboard engine sales in tow. Gas prices, adjusted for inflation, have never been lower. Perhaps that man grew up impoverished and could only watch from bridges as others zoomed beneath him in their runabouts. But just look at him now!

I think back to Ed Taylor and Freddy Fisher. What would they say if they were here? Rather, what would they be doing? I picture Ed fishing at the nearest public pier with a stick, a length of twine, and a hook baited with a piece of crab he would have managed to catch by the water's edge. And Freddy? His blue skiff is pulled up on some unnoticed bit of island beach, his latest camp, with a plastic bag weathervane tied to the branch of some island bush, beneath which he sits in the peaceful shade, his blue hat pulled down over his eyes. I miss the rivers and the bayous, where people seem to have less money and more time. No one, I think to myself, would have spoken to Urs that way on Bayou Lafourche.

Urs and I part ways at the end of the day, when we are met by Renee and strap his shell to the top of their car. Once again, as I had felt after several days paddling with Roy Harvey, I am newly aware of the vulnerability of traveling alone.

————

I ROW A MILE offshore from the high-rise apartment buildings of Vanderbilt Beach, south of Fort Myers, rising and falling on swells so large that the buildings disappear during the offbeat troughs between the crests of waves. A scattering of other boats are out too, all motorboats, and it seems we play a game of hide and seek amid the hills and valleys. Sometimes I'm lifted as the boat nearest me disappears, other times we're both hidden, and then we're both raised into broad view. An hour or so later as the sun falls I begin searching the coast for the inlet into Venetian Bay, at Naples. I cannot afford to miss it as I would be unlikely to reach the next inlet before dark. Not only are the inlets narrow—less than a stone's throw wide—and presumably difficult to find at night, but their entrances, with swells such as these, can be notoriously difficult to navigate even in daylight. Strong currents run parallel to the beach and across the entrances, and the swells themselves, if the tide is ebbing out of the inlets, are tripped by the exiting current and turned into breakers.

On this day of the largest seas I've yet encountered, Ozona has slept as if by a fireplace in a winter farmhouse. Occasionally she has stirred and nosed her head out, as the boat careens down a wave, only to observe that the day's ride is not over and return to her lolling sleep. Wishing I could isolate her course through space, I mentally erase the boat and the wicker basket that support her, and am left with the moving image of a lounging cat, eyes closed in zenlike bliss, floating gracefully up and down in surreal Arabian flight above the windblown contours of the Gulf of Mexico. I then spot what I think is the inlet among the repetitive seaside architecture, and angle in toward shore.

Fifteen minutes before sunset I stall the boat a hundred yards out from the mouth of Venetian Inlet, whose straight channel is reinforced by two parallel jetties of enormous boulders. I see a dozen people, mostly men, sitting or standing on each jetty with fishing rods cast into the water. But mainly I study the pattern of the waves and observe my poor timing. The tide is ebbing out of Venetian Bay and every fifth or seventh wave breaks upon itself as the tide flows beneath it, the way you would fall forward if walking the wrong direction up a broken escalator that was suddenly fixed. I have no better choice as I continue losing daylight than to pick the best window I can find during smaller waves. No matter what, however, even they might send the boat surfing, hopefully to my advantage. I study the crosscurrent as well, trying to guage its likely effect on my course, and also envision the worst-case scenario—that the surfing boat could be forced into a jetty.

Slowly I paddle closer, searching for the point from which I'll choose my moment and start pulling. Often two large waves come in a row, and the moment after a pair has passed I dig in with the oars and follow the second wave as quickly as I can before another one develops. I am acutely aware of my stroke, intent on not missing a catch in my hastened pace. I am also aware of my audience on the jetties, and know that while a rowboat emerging from the horizon and trying to negotiate passage to safety is unusual enough, it is simply human nature to hope for even more excitement along the lines of at least mild disaster. Not on my watch! I think to myself. I watch with confidence as a smaller wave catches my stern, and I pull hard on the oars to surf the boat on its momentum. The sense of friction to which I'm so accustomed gives way and the hull slides ahead for forty feet as I watch the growing shadow of a larger wave now forming.

I still have not reached the mouth of the inlet, another thirty feet ahead, and when I look over my right shoulder I realize that the current running parallel to the shore is drawing me with such strength across the mouth of the inlet that I may miss it altogether and be forced to where waves are crashing against the jetty to my left. A new wave looms and without thinking I pivot the boat into the crosscurrent, now facing north, broadside to both the channel and the rising wave. I row with all my strength and as quickly as I can, aiming to move against the ripping current and then pivot back into the channel so that the coming wave, though it may swamp me, may also help push me to safety. The wave breaks thirty feet from me as I turn the boat while maintaining my pace, and soon find myself within the mouth of the channel and rowing against *its* current. Ozona remains apparently oblivious to her precarious relationship with the sea.

The broken wave broils toward me, but eventually slows, and then rolls in place on top of the ebbing tide until it is spent. We are safe, the cat, the boat, and I, and though I still have to overcome the counter-current below me to reach the harbors of Venetian Bay and my heart still pounds, I row with elated ease as the fishermen watch me in silence. The following morning Ozona goes missing and is finally found in a penthouse kitchen with a seven-story view, which she'd reached by a flight of outdoor stairs and the open door of the apartment. She's been fed a breakfast of bacon, salmon, and cream, and thirty minutes later is curled in her basket as I row out of the inlet on a newly ebbing tide into the placid morning waters of the gulf.

· 23 ·

Toward the Brooklyn
Bridge and Home

SOUTH OF MARCO ISLAND, as an afternoon breeze rises from the west, I happen by miniscule chance to come across a bird floundering in the vast expanse of water. It appears to be a young osprey, which perhaps has dived too deeply and is now too waterlogged to thrust itself back into air. I row a half arc around the bird trying to soothe it with gentle talk, but it will not let me get close enough to reach it before it flails itself away. Eventually, first giving it a feathered oar blade to rest on at a safe distance, I am able to then lift it out of the water and slowly swing the blade over the gunwale and into the boat.

I tilt the blade, and the osprey is slipped onto the folded tent, shifting its head robotically in fear and searching for better footing. I continue to row and once somewhat calmed, the bird spreads its wings to dry, nearly losing its balance from time to time as the hull sways and surges on the waves. Increasingly I hold my head over my left, seaward shoulder, often for minutes at a time, watching ahead of me for waves building broadside from the west. An hour after acquiring the osprey, now rowing in waves whose crests are brushed into whitecaps by the wind, I happen to look back and see that the bird is gone. I acknowledge regretfully that it may have been tumbled back into the water by the pitching boat, but hope that it has flown away. Incredibly,

Ozona has slept through all of this, unaware that a temporarily flightless bird was hospitalized directly, within inches, above her.

The following day I continue south along the west coast of the Florida Everglades, a great wilderness of swamp and cypress forest. As in the Atchafalaya Basin one could wander for weeks along its less populated, wilder channels between thousands of coastal islands, some no larger than a small backyard and others hundreds of acres in size. At Naples I spoke with a woman whose father, a commercial fisherman, became lost in the labyrinth, set up his own Robinson Crusoe camp, and was finally found, by chance, fourteen months later with a shaggy beard. My growing obsession with rowing, however, cancels any impulse to explore the Everglades myself, and I decide I will pass them by.

A mile offshore in the late afternoon the boat, which is headed south, is settled for a snapshot moment in the trough between two waves rolling eastward, broadside beneath me. In this freeze-frame looking west I see a wall of water—four feet high? maybe five—tall enough that its crest is now my horizon, and I can look through its translucent face and see the light of the mellowing sun filtered by the sand and silt stirred from below. This one will not break, but it is too steep to leave room for the western oar to sweep forward for the catch, so I pause in my stroke, waiting to be lifted. Why do I notice this wave in particular, so much like the hundreds, perhaps thousands, I've fallen between today alone? What was I thinking about just moments before? I can't remember. Maybe it's a change in the depth of the light that sparked my sense of presence amid the hours of wordless, distracting repetition. The frame releases and the movement of water and wind suddenly resumes, lifting the boat and allowing me on a crest to reach for the next catch.

At the end of the day the long western shore of Florida gives way finally to the east at Cape Sable, nearly four hundred miles from the mouth of the St. Mark's River in Apalachee Bay. Still I am bound for Key West, the balmy Cape Horn of the trip, before heading north. I am curious to see that island for the first time, yet I am motivated too by the same, somewhat obsessive instinct that leads me when jogging to round the corner of a street along its furthest periphery, as if taking the inside corner would be cheating. A corollary instinct insisted that I pull the weight of the scull entirely by myself from Lake Erie to Chautauqua Lake. I would be bothered forever if I hadn't, and likewise, I will be bothered if I don't row to Key West.

The archipelago of the Florida Keys drifts southward from Biscayne Bay, within view of the skyline of Miami, and gradually to the west, like an enormous comma following the continent. Florida Bay lies between this chain of islands and the mainland, and is broad enough that I've decided to row a conservative route from Cape Sable southeast to Islamorada, and then follow the islands out to Key West. With half an hour until sunset I decide to take advantage of the lasting wind and waves, now more astern, and row four or five miles into the bay to uninhabited Carl Ross Key, which will bring me that much closer to Islamorada. I know that the sun will have set before I reach the island, so low in profile it is still beyond view, but if I can at least spot it by the end of dusk I am sure I will be able to find it in the dark. For twenty minutes I pull steadily on the oars, surfing many waves, until I am sure I should be able to see the bit of land. But I see only darkening skies on a featureless arc of horizon. I row farther as the sun sets, yet to my growing consternation see nothing. I have never needed a compass thus far on the trip, having easily managed by sight and sun alone to dead reckon my way along the open coast of the Gulf. I don't even know where the compass is in the boat. Beneath the bow seat? Or maybe beneath Ozona's perch. Instead I pull out the chart, and study Carl Ross's position in relation to Cape Sable. I look up to Cape Sable itself, then west to the retiring sun, back again to Cape Sable, and then turn to the south to where I think Carl Ross should be. I am sure I've been heading close enough to the right direction that I can't miss it. I put down the chart and, steadying myself, stand up on the wooden thwart as the waves roll beneath me. And the island appears, as if someone had played a trick on me and, at the last moment when I wasn't looking, put it back. I bend down and watch it disappear, then stand slowly up again, and it emerges through a ghost mirage into its solid self. Peek-a-boo, Carl Ross. I see you. The wind, to my surprise, continues unabated and a moonless night falls before I reach the key. I can barely see it, and can barely see the waves, which remain as potent now as they'd been hours before. Yet I feel their rhythm and the boat's speed as it glides down their faces.

I anchor in the calm lee of the island and, as I have on every night I've spent in the boat since reaching the Gulf, I take a gallon shower from a milk jug held with one arm over my head. With the stern end of the tent always left snapped in place over the gunwales, like a piece of plastic wrap only partly covering a bowl, I carefully position myself so as to stand on the rear deck (if that word can even be used for a small triangular slab of teak no more than a foot wide). With my weight aft, the bow floats in the air, and the shower water is drained by the tent directly into the salt water below. So far as I know I have always managed to be discreet, and I have yet to fall in. In fact, aside from replenishment of food and water, I could live comfortably in the boat for days on end without ever needing to leave it, though I would occasionally require some privacy.

Ozona and I have been having issues at night. I have spent the better part of the daylight hours since we met rowing. She, on the other hand, has spent the better part of the daylight hours since we met sleeping. Now when I wish to sleep, however, Ozona wishes to play, and whenever she isn't attacking the sleeping bag as it rises and falls with my chest, there seem to be few objects in the boat that she is not capable of perceiving as foe. I doubt that I've slept for more than an hour at a time over the last eight days. I can be thankful only for the mysterious fact that she has not noticed the tent, whose taut, thin cloth she could satisfyingly puncture with all of her claws and then climb. I love this cat, but now into our second week together, I'm beginning to realize that our timing was wrong. We are at different places in our lives, and I can see no way around the obvious, that these differences are both intolerable and irreconcilable. Our relationship was a great idea, it's true. But I want a divorce.

With Ozona's help, but also because I am expecting a possible windshift from the west to the northeast as reported on the weather radio, I sleep lightly through the night waiting for the wind to change. By two o'clock the northwest wind has ebbed but can still be heard in the trees of Carl Ross Key. Three o'clock: no change. Ozona settles for awhile and I sleep. Four o'clock: west wind. At five o'clock I awake with a start and both hear and feel the surrounding stillness. I quickly pop the tent, stow my sleeping bag, and yank the anchor from its grip of sand and, after a hastily constructed peanut butter and marmalade sandwich and a long swig of water, I start rowing. The glow of sunrise establishes my compass and, feeling less conservative but not yet bold, I abandon the safest route, southeast toward Islamorada, and row a course due south toward Marathon Key for several miles. As a light breeze grows from the northeast, I pull a couple of harder strokes on the port oar, pointing the bow on a beeline to Key West. Gradually as the sun rises the new breeze dies and Carl Ross Key fades out of view. Though I can just make out a set of tall radio towers rising from what the charts confirm is Marathon, I row out of sight of land for the first time since Roy Harvey returned home with his wife and I'd pulled through an early morning fog on the Allegheny.

A MILE FROM THE NORTH SHORE of Key West, Ozona, who has rarely poked more than her head out from beneath the tent while I've rowed, now emerges with a sense of urgency, as if we'd been out of sight of land for months and she'd just gotten a whiff of soil. What does she feel now that she didn't feel at the ends of other days, upon such landfalls as Boca Grande, Pine Island, and Naples? It seems she's finally had enough herself. She replays her Tampa Bay mutiny routine near the gunwales and I perform my "Don't Jump from the Window

Ledge, Think of Those Who Love You" act. I fail, she hurls herself once again into the sea, and once again I fish out a cat newly jaded by water.

Before long, and a year to the day after I left Brooklyn, damp Ozona and I are greeted on shore by a married couple, Phyllis and Laurent, acquaintances made by cousins of mine one evening years before at a birthday party. Ours was a last-minute meeting arranged when my cousin heard I would be rowing to Key West and phone calls were made. It is now lunchtime and they suggest a nearby open-air restaurant. Although dock space at Key West is at a premium, a marina manager has found an out of the way place for the boat long enough for lunch, and says I'm free to leave Ozona in his small office. But first we go to a parked car and pull from its trunk an old single-speed bicycle that I'm free to use during my visit and lock it up to a bike rack at the edge of the marina's parking lot.

At lunch I avail myself of the local culture of seafood and order a bowl of conch chowder. For the most part, I am a vegetarian. Having driven past factory barnyards in the west and having looked into the eyes of cattle and pigs, no less sentient than my own two dogs, yet packed like sardines into the trailers of semis stopped in hundred-degree heat at truck stops, I cannot insist with my money that such miserable lives be led in order for me to enjoy a Big Mac or a strip of bacon. And yet, out of respect for those who invite me to eat with them, and for the work and time they've spent to provide what is served, I do not announce this position when visiting as someone's guest, particularly when a meal is prepared impromptu and involves almost nothing but meat. I simply haven't yet found the spine and manner of diplomacy for doing so, for the risk of offending someone is also the risk of promoting antivegetarianism. My weakness is further reinforced by my rationale that no meat, including farmed fish, is more free-range or more organic than that which is caught from wild rivers, lakes, and the sea. And so I order the conch chowder.

I sit a picnic table across from Phyllis and Laurent. She is in her early fifties, with shoulder-length blond hair and brown eyes and a certain intelligent reserve amid the warmth of her welcome. Laurent, who is French, is older, perhaps in his early sixties, tall and thin with graying hair loosely swept back. He is utterly devoid of macho airs. As we wait for our orders Phyllis asks me what I do when I'm not rowing.

"I ran a small newspaper in Zuni, New Mexico," I tell her. "Before that I taught high school for several years. I started the paper with some students and always intended for it to be run by someone from the tribe, not by a non-Indian. When that became possible I cut loose and went rowing." I return the question.

"I teach at Wesleyan, in the English department," Phyllis responds. "I teach in the fall and Laurent and I spend the winter here, where I write." Though we've taught English at such different levels, we find that we've shared in the difficulty of maintaining our attention while grading twenty or thirty papers on the same topic. "But my students often surprise me," she adds, "making points I'd never thought of." Our orders are served and I answer questions about the trip as we eat. Laurent maintains an easy silence throughout, not needing to be part of the conversation, but not remote either. Finally, wishing to know more about him, I ask whether he also teaches at Wesleyan, though I'm sure he doesn't.

"No," he says with confident shyness and a lasting accent, "I write the children's books." He half-pauses. "Maybe you know Babar and Celeste?"

I control my reaction. Do I know Babar and Celeste? *King* Babar and *Queen* Celeste? I'd grown up with those books. My sister had the stuffed dolls, which she'd dressed in robes and gowns she made on our mother's sewing machine. My brother and sister dressed *themselves* as Babar and Celeste for a town parade.

"Yes, of course!" I say. He gives a smile of modest pleasure, perhaps in meeting yet another person whose childhood imagination was so engaged by the stories and primary-colored illustrations of the lives of these royal elephants. He tells me that his father, Jean de Brunhoff, who originated the stories, died when he was a boy, but that he'd already learned the style of his father's artistry and began writing new stories himself.

After lunch I resolve to find Ozona a new home before dinner. Laurent gives me directions for riding the bike to their house before he departs with Phyllis. I find a pay phone and look up the numbers for local animal shelters and veterinarians, hoping for a lead to that local angel of strays, for every town has one. In fact I am given three numbers, but each call dead-ends with an answering machine. Then I think of Hemingway's house, now a museum, and reputedly the home of dozens of six-toed cats descended from his own. In fact Hemingway did not keep cats when he stayed here, yet there are many of them now living on the grounds, some with six toes, and fed by museum staff. When I pick Ozona up and deliver her by bicycle to the front gate, however, I am introduced to the woman in charge of the pride. I make the mistake, intended as a sales pitch, of telling her how far Ozona has come by rowboat and am then rebuked for confining her so. "And what would happen if the boat had been swamped?" she asks. I tell her to no avail that it's a big boat, and lie about the terrible conditions from which Ozona was rescued. She hems and discouragingly haws about whether she can possibly accept one more cat, having just taken in five, and finally says she's sorry.

Stumped, I return to the marina, one of several surrounding a small basin created by jetties. A boardwalk connects all of them, as well as an array of restaurants and bars. As I lock the bike, unsure of what to do beyond at least checking with the marina's dock manager on the status of the boat—it's fine for the night, but one night only— a young woman in the weapons-free uniform of a security guard wants to pet Ozona. She coos and the cat purrs.

"What's her name?" she asks dotingly.

"Ozona," I tell her, feeling teased by the right kind of interest yet the unlikelihood that this is actually an avenue to adoption.

"She's so cute!" The wattage of Ozona's purring increases as she's scratched and stroked. "We just arrived several hours ago in that row-boat." I point across the docks, though the woman hardly takes her eyes off the cat.

"She was a stray I picked up in Ozona, up by Clearwater. She's come four hundred miles!" Slowly recognizing the opportunity I wind up the sales pitch again. "You want to hold her?" We trade her carefully, lovingly, like an infant. "But I'm trying to find a good home for her. I think she's had enough of my boat!" The attachment is now blossoming, and if I can just blabber away long enough it will become unbreakable.

"I've been looking everywhere and can't find anyone to take her. I even tried the Hemingway house!" The woman, who is perhaps twenty years old, with straight blond hair pulled back in a ponytail, has lit up.

"My sister's cat just died, and she's been so sad! Maybe I should take Ozona for her!"

"I think that's a really great idea!" I say. "Look, I'll be here for a few days. Why don't you take her with you and if it doesn't work out"—nearly impossible—"you can let me know." And so, as a lover of cats with no room now for a cat in my life, even such a winsome, enterprising cat as Ozona, I say good-bye to her as she is locked in the young woman's office until the end of her shift, and then ride the old bicycle through the narrow streets in time for dinner with Phyllis Rose and Laurent de Brunhoff.

I spend several days in Key West, sleeping at night in a small bungalow next to Phyllis and Laurent's house, and use the bicycle to explore the island, once a remote outpost and now a city of thirty-five thousand. Amid a crowd of other tourists I visit the marker of the southernmost point of the United States, take an obligatory picture of myself there, and then ride aimlessly through other neighborhoods, many of them Cuban-American. As I do in every town I visit, I wonder where I would like to live if I lived here, and in which houses. I lean toward the smaller homes in the quieter neighborhoods, and as I roll by on the bicycle I peer in through kitchen windows and imagine what it's like to sit at the end of a day on a variety of front steps and porches. When I return to the waterfront I find Ozona running the security beat on a leash, but mostly, to character, capitalizing on the affections of tourists and locals alike.

Before I leave Phyllis becomes the second person to row the boat, and Laurent illustrates a page of my journal with a sketch of a crowned Babar rowing a skiff, with one thick foot grasping one oar and his trunk coiled around the other. I depart after rowing the rest of the way around the island, stopping along the southern shoreline of Key West, where Phyllis and Laurent have come to see me off from the edge of a seawall. We wave good-bye, and thus begins the long stretch up the East Coast, toward the Brooklyn Bridge and home.

· 24 ·

Through the Shadow
of a Cloud Puff

FOR FIVE DAYS I rowed largely into the wind from Key West to
Miami, weaving my way through the islands of the archipelago in a
search for lee shores that seemed never to exist. In the afternoons
when the wind increased I fought the blades forward into the breeze
for the catch. I followed the Seven Mile Bridge from Bahia Honda Key
to Marathon, where the tide was so strong running out from Florida
Bay into the Atlantic Ocean that I had to keep the bow thirty to forty
degrees into the tide for the boat to make the same course as U.S.
Route 1. At Islamorada I stop at the waterfront bar, still toting the
T-shirt I'd been given minutes before being thrown out of the family
picnic the summer before on the Ohio River. But the place is crowded,
and the bartender to whom I mention the given name tells me curtly,
amid the din of music and customers' requests for beer, that people
come and go and he's never heard of the man. So I stow the T-shirt
and row toward Miami.

It was near Miami that Howard Blackburn's sailing venture
around the island of the Eastern United States had come to an end.

*I remained in Key West about a week and then sailed for Biscayne
Bay and Miami. While entering the Bay in broad daylight I run*

[sic] the boat onto a sand bar within thirty feet of the channel and about six miles off shore.

She was making about eight knots when she struck. The tide was falling, so I threw the ballast overboard, and while waiting for the tide to rise, a gale came on, and I had to lay there two nights and two days.

Then Captain Thomas Coleman, the beacon light tender, came along and took me off. I went with him to his home in Coconut Grove.

After the gale was over we returned to my boat, and after two days hard work we got her off and sailed her over to Coconut Grove, where I sold her.

Blackburn was not finished, however. The new owners of *Great Republic* gave him the questionable gift of a twelve-foot rowboat, and the man who'd once rowed for days on end with hands frozen into claws now strapped his wrists with leather to the rowboat's oars and proceeded more than half way up the Florida peninsula before deciding to end his trip. By February, 1903, Blackburn had returned by steamer to Gloucester. Far from thwarted by the difficulties of his attempt to circumnavigate the Eastern United States, however, he set out from Gloucester in June of the same year to sail a dory to France.[5]

In Miami I calculate that I've spent forty-four days along approximately nine hundred miles of Florida coastline. I've seen some of the most remote, untouched scenery of the trip in Florida, as well as the most developed lengths of shoreline, which I know will continue for most of the Atlantic coast of the state, more than three hundred miles to the Georgia border. No matter where you visit and what it's like there, eventually it's time to leave, and in Miami I resolve to leave Florida, to row every day until Georgia, a distance that will take almost two weeks to cover. It's hard to be spontaneous in a rowboat.

The eastern seaboard, with few exceptions from the Florida Keys to Long Island, New York, consists of a trail of barrier islands built from sand, inside of which the intracoastal waterway provides protection from the open ocean for both local and migrating boats. Although sometimes much longer, and sometimes shorter, the narrow spit of a barrier island might be ten or twelve miles in length, and separated from the next island by a narrow inlet. And while tides of only several feet are common in southern Florida, the effect of their ebb and flow is increased and complicated as they are squeezed through the narrow inlets and split right and left, north and south, along the route of the intracoastal. Rowing past an inlet when the tide has just begun to flood is not necessarily perfect timing. I will be assisted roughly halfway along the length of the next island, yet if that island is only eight miles long, and reaching its halfway point takes me less than an hour, I will then row against the tide, still flooding in through the following inlet. For this reason, particularly along the southern coast of Florida, I row on the open Atlantic shores of the barrier islands whenever fair weather allows, while keeping a tab on the location of the next inlet should the weather change.

But it is not for this reason alone that I avoid the intracoastal. Its shoreline and life on the water are simply, to me, less interesting. The only people I see making a living on the water are generally officers of marine patrols. Occasionally a new bridge is being built or an old one repaired, and small tugs with platform barges are stationed around rising pylons. Not that there's any shortage of traffic. Small motorboats of all descriptions exceed the speed limits, larger offshore sportfishing boats with rumbling twin V8s plow by, and the waterfront equivalent of tow trucks, with bright yellow hulls, wait like sharks in the wings for the next distress call from some hapless cruiser whose engine has broken down. I've long since learned that the more expensive a boat, the less likely its captain is to wave. At me, anyway. And the less likely he is, if in a powerboat, to slow to a crawl so as not to threaten my small boat with his wake. If he doesn't slow, he almost never thinks to turn around to see whether I've been safely passed. It's the thought that counts, for in fact I welcome all but the largest wakes for the brief rush they provide if I can surf them. Yet if I catch the wake of a boat that's slowed down for me—in which case the captain always waves—I surf it knowing that those waving will likely be as amused by it as I am, while I surf the wakes of less-attentive captains with a bit of spite. *Thanks for the fun—and I'm glad you're gone.*

The shores are lined with medium-rise condominium architecture, marinas full of million-dollar boats (yet there are virtually no public landings, and I feel I'm imposing when I ask to tie up in a corner long enough to walk to the nearest store), and miles of waterfront homes with swimming pools and fertilized lawns, their frontage reinforced by cement walls that guide the channel. It is now early May and those homes that haven't been abandoned for the summer season by their northern owners have their windows and doors closed to retain the cooled air within. At marinas and private docks boats of all sizes glisten in the sun, many of them kept polished by full-time hired crews. Yet the scene is somehow sterile, as if all ordered out of a catalog. It invites few questions, and asks even fewer, and I rarely feel curious about what lies beyond. The difference between the waterfronts of Larose, Louisiana, and Fort Lauderdale, Florida, is like that between a decades-old family-owned grocery and the fluorescence of a supermarket. In one you catch up on a bit of news, and learn how ol' Crawford got his nose stuck in his own car door. In the other you cruise methodically down the aisles, and don't stop to chat.

ALONG THE OPEN COAST I find the water so clear that I sometimes stop rowing and drop the small Danforth anchor, watching while kneeling in the bow as it tries to fly on its way down to the sandy bottom thirty feet below. With a mask and fins I roll into the warm water, take a deep breath, and dive down into the muted, gently swaying inner sanctum of a world whose moody facades, from dead calm to broken crests, I've been rowing across. I swim to the bottom, pulling my body forward then gliding serenely across the bed of the densest of the three worlds that man now inhabits: water, air, and the vacuum of space. I swim through the shadow of a cloud puff as it drifts by, and eye small schools of pastel-colored fish congregating nervously near rocks. I feel, as I always do in water, that I've been here, that I know this aqueous realm, but because of permanent evolutionary amnesia, cannot remember a thing about it. Looking up I see the ephemeral shapes of waves reflecting sunlight as if in a silent movie or a dream, and beyond the waves white clouds and blue sky. Soon to be out of breath I follow the gentle arc of the anchor rode up toward the boat, which rocks and pitches lightly, and return to the thin air.

AT TITUSVILLE I begin falling into a pattern of traffic, the tail end of the commute north by those on live-aboard powerboats and sail-boats who, having spent the winter months along the Florida coast, or in the Bahamas or the Caribbean, are now finally making their annual pilgrimage north to homes on land or simply to cooler waters. Having docked at the city marina and made use of coin-operated laundry machines while talking with other nautical transients, I return to the boat in the late evening with my meager wardrobe clean and dry and, as I walk past other boats forty to fifty feet in length, each more than twice the cost of the average home and most with a full range of amenities, I nonetheless—or perhaps more so—have an overwhelming sense of affection for my boat, so simple in design and spartanly appointed, which has come so many unforgettable miles. "Hello Boat!" I say, as I gently climb in for the night.

Ten miles north of Daytona I am passed by a seventy-foot powerboat, a cabin cruiser. It flies an Antiguan flag but its passengers, who talk to me as the boat passes, are American. The captain has slowed for me and passes cautiously. His wife, perhaps, in her late fifties with golden hair in a voluminous perm and her bronzed body

clad in a one-piece, strapless, bright yellow bathing suit, calls down to me, first asking the standard questions about the trip.

"How far are you going today?" she then wants to know. I now have the boat nestled in a fold of the passing ship's wake and so can keep up with the conversation, though her husband is perhaps wondering whether he can give it a little more throttle.

"I'm not sure where I'll end up today," I tell her. It is still morning and on a full day of rowing I rarely anticipate the day's destination until an hour or two before sunset.

"Well, we're going to St. Augustine, but that's probably further than you'll get." I now know I'm going to St. Augustine. She is kneeling on a seat on the aft upper deck of the boat, arms resting on chrome railings. She turns and calls ahead to her husband.

"Honey? How many miles to St. Augustine?" He can't hear her and so she gets up and walks thirty feet forward, collects her answer, then returns to the railing. "St. Augustine," she calls down to me, "is about forty miles. You'll make it there tomorrow." She's not the first to offer speculation about my schedule. It's always meant as a form of encouragement, but I think that there's something about the boat, and me in it, and the bare bones nature of the trip that invites judgment and comment, akin to the way men standing around the opened hood of a broken down car can hardly keep their diagnoses to themselves, wishing to be helpful and in so doing taking a form of ownership in the situation. But I like to think of the trip as divisible into stockholders' shares, available in compensation for interest shown. A child's wave from the back of a car crossing a bridge above me is good for one share. The marina dock manager that lets me tie up the boat for an hour at no charge has an option on fifteen shares. Freddy Fisher, in his blue aluminum skiff on the Ohio? At least a hundred shares, for telling me so emphatically "You're doing the right thing!" Alan, from Pittsburgh, who gave me these oars which have become dearer to me than even the boat, is a major stockholder.

But there is no end to the shares, any more than there will be an end to the trip. They will be given freely in my mind when I'm ninety-seven years old, if there's still someone then who cares to ask me what it was like on the rivers in the days of internal combustion, or what New Orleans was like before the Great Flood. Five shares for each question.

The woman asks from the deck above whether I need anything to eat or drink. I thank her and tell her I'm fine, which is the truth, although there seems no end to the amount I can eat.

"An apple?" She wants to give me something, and I want to take it.

"Sure!" She is pleased and quickly disappears to the galley, and then returns through a black glass sliding door to a lower deck. She tests her throw several times and then releases a red apple into a short arc. It plops into the water slightly ahead of me and I pluck it out as I glide by. She asks if she may take a picture, to which I accede, and her husband, whether miffed or amused I cannot tell, then throttles up his engines and leaves me behind. That evening, though they do not see me arrive from their marina berth, I reach St. Augustine before sunset and anchor for the night amid a harbor full of other boats commuting north.

· 25 ·

A Shiver Through
the Muck

THE COAST OF GEORGIA comes as a prize after so many miles
of Floridian development. I'd expected more of the same upon crossing the border, but instead enter a loose puzzle of variously shaped islands largely untouched by human development, and the channel of
the intracoastal begins suddenly to meander in a swerving route
among them. I soon learn that the tidal complexities of the Florida intracoastal are simple compared to these, which ebb and flow through
a multiplicity of channels among the many islands. Judging by a road
map alone you might imagine the blue ink between the islands and the
mainland as wide open water and bays, but in fact the gap between
Cumberland Island and Camden County Georgia, for example, consists of wide expanses of salt marsh, with fairly narrow channels running among them. Already, if only for the absence of condominium
towers and tightly nestled homes on utterly private property, Georgia
has become a favorite coastline of mine.

Along one stretch of the intracoastal I come across a small point
where an incoming tide is surging around a shallow bend, and a brisk
early afternoon breeze is blowing against the current. But there is
more to the churning water. A small school of dolphin is not quite
swimming in the tide. As I row closer I try to count them, but they roll

and twist in such a tight group that in the silty water I cannot tell whether there are five or six or seven. I expect them to hear me and dart away in surprise, but the breaking water and gusting wind, I then suppose, are too loud. I find myself rowing closer and closer, and soon am looking almost straight down at them, maneuvering the boat with the long oars. With another half stroke of one oar and caught in the wind, the boat drifts slowly across their dance, and I wonder if in their reverie they feel the hull as if it were one of them. I raise the blades out of the water and hold my breath, aware that in sudden fright a thrusting tail could fracture the boat. I let the wind carry me into deeper water as I continue to watch them, then row onward before they notice they are not alone.

Given the choice at the end of a day between rowing one mile to a secluded cove where I might shower in privacy and sleep in peace, or a mile in the opposite direction toward a town or semblance of community, I always choose the latter mile, particularly at the end of solitary days. At the end of my first day in Georgia I arrive at Jekyll Island, one of the few coastal islands with any visible development. At first I see a dock with a few boats and a pier, and what seems to be a bar or restaurant on the pier itself. And then, beyond great limbs of ancient oak trees, I see what looks like a grand old hotel painted gray with white trim. It looks like a particularly private scene, yet as I row near the dock I am greeted by two unassuming men with drinks in hand, who appear to have stepped out briefly for relief from a crowd. Having answered the obvious questions about where I am going I am told that I've arrived at the Jekyll Island Club, rented out for these several days by the Georgia Rural Water Association, a statewide nonprofit agency that is holding its annual retreat here. Why not tie up the boat, one says, and come back with them to one of the hotel bars. They're sure some of the guys would like to hear about the trip.

One of the men I meet is Robert Lovett, the founder of the Georgia Rural Water Association, who is now retired but clearly considers all of those attending the conference as family. He is perhaps in his mid-sixties, with a ready smile, sparkling eyes, and a quick hand-shake. At the end of the evening all of his questions about the trip are still not answered, and he asks me whether I would join him at 7:30 the following morning for the hotel's buffet. Naturally, I accept.

Late that evening I am told by a man my age that there are two beds in his room and I'm welcome to use the extra one, to take a break from the boat. I am tempted to accept this invitation too and reluctant to refuse his hospitality, yet feel uncertain about leaving the boat at the dock. I arrived after the dock manager had gone home for the day, and I worry that if he returns in the morning before I wake up he may be peeved by the unannounced, unattended boat. Or he may not be irked at all, but inform me that there's an overnight docking fee, typically $1.50 per foot per night at marinas, which is beyond my budget. Moreover, although there is little traffic along the intracoastal here and the grounds of the hotel are off the beaten track, I have never left the boat for long unless it's been tied to someone's private dock or at a marina under a manager's nose. There's no point sleeping in a com-fortable bed if that sleep is disturbed by worry.

So I opt to sleep at anchor, and say good night. I row out from the dock a short distance under the dark sky, far enough that I won't get stranded in the mud at low tide but not so far that I'm anywhere near the channel of the intracoastal. I remove an oar from its lock and lance its blade down into water to test the depth, and then drop the anchor.

At 5:35 the following morning I awake before sunrise and know instantly that something has changed. Something isn't right, and it's this something that has woken me up. I have become used to the sen-sation of utter stillness, when there is no wind and the sleeping water is a smooth pane of glass. Then the boat is perfectly still, the tent drapes lifelessly over its frame, the only perceptible movement is that of my chest rising and falling with each breath, and the only sound is of my pulse through my ears. But something is different now. Lying on my back, I slowly swing my left forearm off my chest and to the side, as if I were saying "Well on one hand she may not be able to make a silk purse with a sow's ear . . ." Normally the boat would slightly tilt with this gesture, but now it remains strangely still. I am suspicious. I then shudder my body hoping for a reaction, but all I get is a slight gelatinous echo of my movement, as if the boat were floating on a sea of tapioca. Distressed and already knowing what I will see, I lean on my right elbow while still lying down, pop the tent with my other hand, and peer out across a plain of mud. Every so often the tide gets to play a favorite joke, and overnight has lain me so gently in the morass that I didn't wake as it continued to slip furtively away, leaving me now no less than thirty feet from the water's edge and a hundred feet from solid shore. The punch line is the anchor rode, which reaches limply across the mud to the anchor itself, barely visible in its deep grip of the intracoastal pudding. Although the slope of the mudflat is negligible—the water, though now distant, is no more than a foot or two below my level—I quickly recall the tide schedule and know that it will continue falling before it begins to rise.

Immediately upon looking out from beneath the tent my mind concocts a scenario: of ladies attending the conference getting together for an early morning walk and seeing my stranded boat, and of new acquaintances from the night before then coming down to see if they can help, and of my having to request across the mud that an apology be delivered to Mr. Lovett's table: "I'm sorry I can't join you. I'm anchored to a mudflat." But I won't allow any of it. I don't know how I'll reach the dock, which is still clearly afloat, both discreetly and in time for breakfast, but I resolve to figure out something.

I lower the tent fully and remove an oar from its lock. I probe the bottom and am not surprised as the blade pierces downward like a knife through a stick of butter left out on a counter on a summer day. A half jump within the boat sends a shiver through the muck. I cannot possibly walk across it before falling victim to its inescapable suction and with this thought soon acknowledge that any foolish experiment that would separate me from the boat—from something to hold on to—could prove fatal upon a rising shift in the tide. I've been told that drowning is not a bad way to go when your number's up, but now surmise that any drowning that starts with a mudflat's vacuum grasp from your chest down to your toes, and is followed by the moon's release of an ebbing tide as your arms flounder an inch or two beyond grasp of your marooned rowboat, would be downright miserable.

Perhaps the mire is so soft that I can simply row my way out of it. I take to the oars and lean forward for the catch—surely an unforgettable sight for anyone lucky enough to see it, though I still appear to be the only one in sight—but the blades find too much resistance in the thick stuff and the hull itself seems trapped by the suction. I then move to the bow with the unpromising but at least fresh idea that the anchor, which lies near the water's edge, may grip solidly enough that with the right tug I might inch the boat toward freedom. But as I feared, the anchor merely dives further into the equivalent of hundreds of millions of servings of chocolate pudding before the suction holding the hull can be broken. And thus mud, from the anchor rode onto my hands, begins to invade the boat.

My seaborne honor has been compromised already, but I still believe I can save face if I can only solve this problem before anyone sees me, and in time to make it for Mr. Lovett, as well as coffee, freshly squeezed orange juice, and the all-you-can-eat buffet on the freshly linened tables of the Jekyll Island Club. Somehow I have to exert a pushing or pulling force without my own weight in the boat. Like a child who's just been told that the stove is hot, and for whom it's not enough to see logs burning within and has to touch it, I gingerly place a bare foot over the gunwale and into the cool ooze, which feels like potter's slip. I withdraw, thus extending the slime's invasion into the bow, yet it is this dumb test that leads to the door of a solution. I reach for one of my two bedrolls, a foam pad two feet wide by six feet long, position myself sitting forward on the bow with my feet resting in the organic scum, which bleeds upward through my toes, and lay the pad down lengthwise ahead of the bow, in the direction of the anchor and water. With a firm grasp of both the bow and the bowline I step with both feet onto the bedroll, quickly pivot so as to face the bow head-on, and as my distributed weight sinks slowly down I tug at the boat while trying to lift it too. My adrenaline gushes as the hull slides forward two feet. Then, nearly knee deep but not yet engrossed in the marshy batter, I sit on the bow and proceed to rescue the bedroll, which is now so slippery I can hardly grasp it with my hands. In this manner of repetition I draw the boat toward the water—eventually picking up the anchor in passing—while slathering the inner and outer bow, as well as myself, with the brownish-black half-water, half-earth.

Once afloat I retrieve an oar from its lock and, so as to contain the mess, paddle the boat canoe-like from the bow until I reach the dock. Time: 7:15 A.M. Miraculously I have no audience, and without wasting a moment I uncoil the dock hose, grab the scrub brush with which I've occasionally removed algae growth from the bottom, and hose and scour away the fine silt from my body. A white T-shirt, which I'd donned in case the lady pedestrians passed by, is quickly soaked, squeezed out, and relegated, still earthy, to its own sopping heap in the aft bilge. I scrub the boat as well, wishing to leave no trace of my tidal error, and at 7:26 rifle through my duffel for clean shorts and a shirt, dress within seconds in broad daylight, and then sprint up the runway and along the pier, beneath solid oaks as old as Monticello and past a croquet course. At 7:30 I bound up the steps of the hotel's front porch, where I find Robert Lovett casually perusing the morning paper.

As coffee is served he asks me how I slept, and I tell him that on this particular morning I slept too deeply for too long. I confess that my day has not just begun, and as I replay the events, beginning at 5:35, he simply listens, his face beaming with pleasure as I tell a story of early morning isolation and escape.

· 26 ·

More Than a Trophy

HOW MANY TIMES had I turned around with only seconds to spare before crashing the boat into some obstacle? Considering the miles now behind me, not many. I remember a cousin once telling me that she had eyes in the back of her head, that she could see me even when facing away. I wasn't entirely gullible, just too young to voice my doubt. And yet to this day I think of her as the woman who can see in any direction. At various moments on the trip I have felt that I have such eyes myself.

I had two collisions in the scull on the first leg of the trip: one with a branch that reached out of the water from a submerged log, causing minor damage, and one with a navigational marker on the Ohio River. One of the outriggers caught the red metal buoy, but the impact failed to pitch me into the water. And yet I've now rowed by thousands of other green and red buoys, and dozens of times happened to look over my shoulder on impulse and thus avoided such collisions. The intra-coastal waterway in Alabama and Florida included not only a continuing connect-the-dots channel marked by red and green buoys, but also long stretches of parallel wooden piers that reach out often fifty yards from private properties into deeper water for the docking of family motorboats. Granted, I had been more attentive to these additional, less pliant obstacles, and yet I still grew distracted by sights around me or thoughts within, and then turned around in the nick of time to either redirect the boat with a powerful stroke of one oar, or else jam both blades in the water and reverse the stroke for a quick stop. On one occasion the height of the pier and the spacing between its wooden pilings was such that the first point of collision would have been the back of my skull against a heavy wooden beam at nearly five miles per hour.

One might suggest that I've simply developed a keen sense for the rate at which I row, and that with each glance over a shoulder my eyes have come to record not only details beyond my realization, but have developed their own keen sense of distance. Distance divided by rate equals time. And so perhaps intertwined with my senses of speed and distance is the ability that allows a person to accurately guess what time it is without having looked at a clock for hours and to wake up a fraction of a second before an alarm goes off.

None of this, however, explains the times I've glanced ahead of the bow just seconds before I would otherwise have impaled the hull on a piece of rusting metal pipe just peering above the water's surface or lacerated it against some other piece of vicious, barely submerged detritus, invisible from a distance. The worst possible damage to my gear would be a hole in the boat. The second would be a broken oar. And a very close third would be an outrigger torn off by something immutably in the way.

I only just began rowing this morning, and could still hurl a rock with my wrong throwing arm to where I spent the night tied up along with half a dozen transient sailboats to a public dock at Myrtle Beach, South Carolina. As usual I simply woke up, put on a shirt and shorts, stowed my sleeping bag and pillow, dropped the tent, and after a peanut butter and jelly sandwich—I've been eating as many as ten in a day—a swig of water, and ten seconds touching my toes while sitting at the oars, I started rowing. A seven-minute routine. I started slowly, looking down and to the side, letting the cyclical, slow rhythm of the blades wake me up. The sun was rising as the tide fell in its final two hours, leaving more than enough time to ride it out to the next inlet and then continue on a newly flooding tide across the state border and into North Carolina. That, at least, was the plan.

Yet this morning any sixth sense I have developed was of no value as I pushed away from the dock. One second I remained in the still groggy haze that lingers like dawn until some routine or unexpected event refreshes the mind, and the next, with time for no more than the slightest half glance of response, the starboard outrigger, to my left, was simply ripped off by one of three wooden pilings lashed together and rising out of the water toward the edge of the channel. A bridge lies just beyond. With the lame, unsupported starboard oar in my hand, and the broken black pipe of the outrigger dangling by the oarlock from it, I find myself suddenly wide awake.

Instinctively my mind races ahead and I've hardly dragged the oar into the boat before I've imagined myself at a welding shop, not here near the restaurants that line the dock, but a hitchhike away, to an inland industrial neighborhood where someone is capable of welding aluminum. I jump to the bow and drop the anchor before the boat drifts beneath the bridge, as I'll likely have to paddle the boat like a canoe back to the dock. The anchor grips and the bow is swung upstream. Now I'll almost certainly miss the tide and will be lucky to not miss the entire day on the water, a possibility that floods me with disappointment. For lately I've become, as much as ever on the trip, obsessed by rowing. Aside from several days off in Georgia I've rowed every day since leaving Miami, averaging more than thirty miles each rowing day as far as Charleston, and forty miles each of the last two days. It might seem that I'm racing, trying to prove something. Maybe I am. But I also have limited time to reach Gloucester in time for the Blackburn Challenge. It might even seem that I'm anxious to finish the trip.

And yet this is no longer a trip to me. The rowing itself is no longer work. I go to sleep shortly after the sun sets and wake up at dawn, and each morning, though I anticipate rowing for most of the day, I feel no need to coax myself into taking the first stroke. In the same casual way you might put down a cup of coffee, open up the newspaper, and start reading at your kitchen table, I restore the cap on my water jug, reach for the oar handles, and start rowing.

The challenges that helped spur the trip and that explained the first stroke on the East River have long since lost their influence. The question, *Can I do this?* is no longer a concern. It's true, I might soon make a mistake or run afoul of luck, perhaps get run over by some power-boat. But in some ways the trip is already over and arrival at the Brooklyn Bridge is a mere formality in my mind. The trip is no longer interesting to me as a test of endurance or a question of my own range of abilities. Five miles of rowing was once a project. I now think in increments of one hundred miles and five hundred miles. If I were to find out that the cartographers had been wrong all along, and that Eastport lies another thousand miles away, I would not only remain unimpressed, but would welcome the extension of the route and the prolonging of what had started out as a trip, as an adventure, a once-in-a-lifetime journey, and has since evolved into a lifestyle.

Mine is now a life of minimums, defined on one hand by a series of three destinations—the completion of the circuit beneath the Brooklyn Bridge, the starting line of the race at Gloucester, and the final stroke of the oars at Eastport, Maine—and on the other hand by my mode of travel. Aside from clean clothes and extra food, there is no longer anything in the boat except what I use every day—a knife for peanut butter, my sandals, a pair of sunglasses—or have potential need for in distress, including my life preserver, a waterproof flashlight, and a fiberglass repair kit. Otherwise I have purged the boat of everything superfluous. On occasion I pass the time looking around me, looking for something I can live without. I am obsessed by this program of material reductions, but not because I'm trying to prove anything. It's simply a matter of practicality: the less I have in the boat the more room there is for me to live in it, and the less weight I have the easier it is for me to make the boat go rowboat fast. The useless-ness of any object begins to annoy me, and I am soon burdened not only by its weight, but perhaps more so by its mere presence, and the decision to expel it is elating. I'd been carrying four small foam blocks designed to fit over the gunwales of a canoe when carried atop a car. I'd used them twice on the first leg of the trip with the scull, but hadn't used them since. They were stored out of my way beneath the stern seat, yet even though their weight was negligible, I had gotten rid of them. At this point, there is room neither in the boat nor my mind for even a second plastic pen.

Indeed, the practicality of reducing my load by even fractions of an ounce has evolved into a defining ethic of living within the boat: the less I have the happier I am. It's as simple as that. And I have never been so consistently happy in my life. Nor have I ever been so free. Not the idle freedom of summer recess, nor the political freedom of the oppressed who've freed themselves, but freedom from the time kept by my watch, upon which I'd once depended to make myself row, yet which has become obsolete as a tool of motivation. The friction between the work of rowing and the passing of time has all but van-ished. Perhaps it's a bit like knitting, a skill that, once learned, be-comes automatic. If I were to say that I love to row it might make my rowing sound like a pastime, a diversion, a hobby, but it's much more than that. If I think of it at all each morning, I think of it as a job, al-beit without pay, which brings previously unforeseen contentment. Time is not money in this boat.

It is not only the regimentation of time that has dissipated, stroke by stroke, and been carried away in my wake. There is freedom also from a desire for possession, for material acquisition. In Miami, as sexy a city as can be found in this country, I had not been immune while on shore to the allures of what money can buy. I felt renewed lust when I saw a favorite car, whose bodacious curves and perfect slopes in the deepest shade of cumulonimbus gray were pure sculp-ture. And yet the very moment I stepped back into the boat such cravings as for an exotic car lost their currency, as if a clutch of consumerism were disengaged and they simply disappeared.

Also gone is any desire I once had to be somebody, to achieve something, to be the first or the best, or the best known. I was a very young boy the last time I cared so little about my professional future. *"What would you do if you won the lottery?"* A question for which virtually every American above the age of six has an answer. It finally dawned on me several years ago that I *had* won the big prize with conception and birth, and yet in spending the proceeds of time I'd allowed myself to become so defined by layers of associations, and purposes, and multiple identities—teacher, weekly newspaper editor, graduate, Bostonian—that these became my justifications for living. Yet, removed from the places of my history and freed from the race to accomplish, these layers of myself have atrophied with the passing miles and been shed. I'm no longer interested in getting ahead. I wish for no position and no title, not even Mister, and I will never again prepare a résumé. It's enough for me now to simply be here, a living recipient of a winning number in a mysterious lottery whose odds are breathtakingly slim.

I am reduced by rowing to my barest, observing self, and in the best of times while at the oars I do not think of myself even as Nat. The rule of time and its ticking cadence have been replaced by other rhythms, by the ebb and flow of the tides, by the solar repetition, and by the wind and the waves they create. But above all the uncontrollable cadence of the passing minutes and hours has been supplanted by the cadence of my oars, with one breath to every stroke, and every stroke is both an act of movement and a measure of self-possession. Thus, having won the lottery, I row.

I RETURN TO MY SITTING POSITION in the broken boat, studying the destruction. The outrigger was once a single tube of high-grade aluminum pipe extending from one oarlock to the other, with four bends so as to pass beneath the beam of the sliding seat, to which it attaches with two bolts out of view. In addition, each side of the pipe was lashed with a stainless-steel hose clamp to a bronze oarlock socket on each gunwale. The hose clamp on the starboard side is now torn open. The outrigger itself is broken near the bolts below, and only half an inch of pipe now extends from beneath the seat beam, ending in a vicious tear. I ponder whether I might be able to jury rig the pipe back in place, and look to the sailboats still tied up to the dock. Perhaps the couple I'd met the night before could lend me some tools.

I'd noticed one of the sailboats four days earlier as it had slowly overtaken me under power, as most sailboats must be in the narrow channel. It's a fifty-foot ketch under British registry and was clearly home to the couple aboard. I'd waved and they'd waved. Each night I'd happened to end up in the same harbor as they, although I never saw them. Perhaps it was dusk by the time I'd arrived, or maybe the couple had gone ashore for dinner as I'd set my tent and gone to sleep. And somehow on each of the following days we traveled the same distances and the same routes, yet never saw each other. Yesterday afternoon they passed me again, and this time, as on the first day we met, I watched them and they watched me. I noticed as the woman stood on the deck to gaze ahead at me, then disappeared into the boat's cabin and returned with a pair of binoculars. I studied the shore and the water and my wake so as not to embarrass her. Strangely, as they approached to within a comfortable distance for waving, they did not wave. Instead she stood next to her husband at the wheel, and they talked to each other while looking at me. I finally waved myself and they waved back, and when I saw her return to the foredeck, wanting to hail me, I edged closer to their overtaking path. She was in her late fifties, with a short bowl haircut and a dark tan beneath a white T-shirt and shorts. She spoke, as I expected she would, with an English accent.

"Are you the same one we saw near Hilton Head?" she called down to me.

"Yes," I told her. "I remember you. I saw your boat at Beaufort that night." She pauses, studying me.

"And you've been rowing this whole way?"

"Yes," I said.

"Where are you rowing to?" she asked.

"I'm rowing up the East Coast, to Canada."

She drew in her chin in silent exclamation, then turned to her husband, and called out "He's rowing to Canada!" He smiled, shaking his head.

"How far are you going today?"

"I'm not sure. I usually row until dusk."

"Well we're planning to get to Myrtle Beach, where there's a free public dock. If you make it that far we'd love to have you for dinner, just tie up and hop aboard!" Their broad hull was now abeam of me and passing, and I thanked her.

That evening across a meal of spaghetti, salad, and bread, I learned that they'd been wandering the globe for ten years in their stout boat and that they'd just recently arrived in the United States for the first time. She recounted her observations of my boat over the previous days, starting with the first time they'd waved to me. She'd assumed I was out for just a day's row and had been impressed over the following days by the popularity across the region of this style of rowing boat, for on every day since she'd first seen mine she'd seen another just like it at each of their stops. Interestingly, she'd thought—now amused in the telling—they'd all had the same tents.

The sun is now up, and no one has stirred from the boats still at dock. Among a spartan kit of tools, spares, and materials for patching fiberglass, however, I find that I have several spare hose clamps. I can easily resecure the outrigger to the oarlock socket. The question remains of how to restore the strength of the outrigger at the point at which it broke. Another spare hose clamp could be tightened over the break, but these particular clamps are too narrow in width to remain effective against the tremendous pressure of each stroke. Perhaps I can brace the pipes from within as well, with some sort of plug?

Searching for what I might use to bridge the break in the outrigger, along the embankment of the channel fifteen feet away I spot a sparse variety of flotsam, including several pieces of driftwood. I eye one piece in particular and, having removed the port oar from its lock I stand up and with long strokes paddle the boat as if a canoe upstream to slacken the anchor rode, and then edge quickly toward shore. I hope to reach out with the oar to pull the wood toward me before the rode becomes taut and the current swings me back out. I miss on the first attempt, but on the second try manage to usher the piece of wood toward me. I break it to a useable length, yet find that it fits too loosely in the pipe ends. So I wrap it with duct tape in stages, stopping several times to test the width. Eventually, after having put on too much tape and then peeling back to size, I insert the plug into the pipe beneath the seat beam and hang a slackened hose clamp over the pipe. After removing the oar from the lock of the broken length of the outrigger, I fit the end of that length over the extruding end of the plug. The fit is tight and the two ends of pipe meet. Before tightening the hose clamp with a screwdriver I resecure the outrigger to the bronze oarlock socket, and then proceed to tighten the clamp by the break.

It looks right, but is it strong? I reset the oar in its lock, take both oars in my hands, and pull moderately into the current. The outrigger pivots forward a bit. I force it back with my hands, and then with all of my strength, with two hands on the handle of the screwdriver, and applying all of the leverage of my arms and torso I can muster, I tighten the clamps as my knuckles turn white. I test another stroke and the outrigger is nudged forward almost imperceptibly. I take another stroke: no movement. It seems to have found a seat. Forty-five minutes after the dreaded collision I pull up the anchor, dunk it several times to clean off the mud, and am on my way. By the end of the day I am anchored in Southport, North Carolina, more than forty miles from Myrtle Beach.

THUS I MANAGE to continue rowing on up the East Coast, retightening the hose clamps every second or third day and feeling so content to just row that I stop ever less frequently at the towns along the way. I stop for the night at Elizabeth City, North Carolina, and at Norfolk, Virginia, where I anchor for several hours along the route of the opening parade of a multicity tour of Tall Ships. I cross the mouth of Chesapeake Bay and follow the Virginia Inside Passage from Cape Charles to Chincoteague, an astonishingly pristine world of barrier islands and inner bays protected not only through land conservation programs, but also by the shallow depths of the bays themselves, in which even I, despite the shallow draft of the boat, occasionally stray from poorly marked, shifting channels and find myself unable to proceed without backtracking first.

I anchor in Chincoteague Bay in the half mile of open water between two islands of mud and marsh grass, avoiding mosquitoes and hoping for the light evening breeze to settle, for it takes little to rock the boat and disturb sleep. This night, however, the breeze does not die, and, as on perhaps a dozen other nights, I eventually force myself out of half sleep to pop the tent, pull up the anchor, and search for calmer water—in this case closer to the leeward shore of the windward island. These moments of relocation are among my fondest memories of the trip, when the sudden opening of the tent reveals the smaller, yet deeper nighttime sky, perhaps bespeckled with stars, moonlit or not, or overcast. With the anchor reset and the tent snapped into place, deep sleep invariably follows.

In late June, six weeks after leaving Miami, Cape May, the southern tip of New Jersey, emerges through an early morning haze after I cross the mouth of Delaware Bay. For several days I follow the intracoastal channel through New Jersey, and now approach Sandy Hook, which marks the entrance to the Lower Bay of the Port of New York City. I'd imagined seeing Manhattan's skyline rising slowly over my shoulder many times, especially during the first leg of the trip. Along the Erie Canal the cityscape of New York had seemed so far away that I'd simply tried to ignore it. In heading west on the Ohio and south on the Mississippi, I'd felt a sense of progress toward the goal, and yet my compass bearings were discouraging; I'd had to row further away from the Brooklyn Bridge before I could start getting closer.

Within a short distance I should be able to see the Twin Towers of the World Trade Center rising above the skyline of Manhattan. And the Brooklyn Bridge, for so long a defining image of the trip, an image of departure and challenge, and of return and achievement, will soon appear. And yet over the more recent miles the bridge has ceased to beckon. Its meaning to me has become largely obsolete. I am now, at most, only curious to see what it looks like over the bow, but I also entertain thoughts of bypassing it altogether, and heading along the bays or open coast of Long Island toward New England. In rowing beneath the bridge, it seems, I would define the circuit at the last minute as a quest for a trophy, as a venture not worth undertaking without the carrot of a final prize. And in choosing to detour by the bridge, in leaving the circuit just barely open, I might, if only symbolically, prevent this chapter of my life and this way of living from coming to an end.

Friends and family, however, will be expecting me at the dock from which I'd left, and ultimately the continuing momentum of earlier anticipation carries me north through Lower Bay, beneath the Verrazano Narrows Bridge and into Upper Bay, which offers broad city views, though not yet of the Brooklyn Bridge.

IN THE EARLY EVENING, New York Harbor is abuzz with activity. Ferries cross back and forth from lower Manhattan to New Jersey and Staten Island. Tourists are afloat on other ferries that make stops at such icons of American history as the Statue of Liberty and Ellis Island. Sailboats carve back and forth across the Hudson and make way for a passing tanker. Above me in the sky helicopters peruse the scene below and in the distance jet planes come and go and fill the air with muted thunder.

At first I hadn't seen the Brooklyn Bridge; it blended into the backdrop of city architecture. But now the graceful sweep of its catenary emerges across the vertical lines of other buildings, and its somber Gothic towers become distinct. My eyes are riveted for a lasting moment, and yet it is not elation I feel so much as a touch of sorrow, that after so many years and so many miles a long-held dream is coming to an end and that that which I had imagined in my future for so long will soon become part of my past. On an incoming tide I row into the mouth of the East River, with the towers of the financial district to my right and the neighborhoods of Brooklyn to my left. The tide is quick, and I could simply drop the oars and still be carried by the flood. Looking further to my left I see the place from which I'd started, and a group of friends and family waiting and waving. I row toward them a bit and wave back, then nose again toward the bridge. I stop rowing for a moment, still drifting on the tide, and with perhaps a hundred yards to go before finally returning to the line of my departure, I see a former self now setting out, having passed beneath the arc of the bridge, pulling his way with uncertain strokes. I know where his day will end, as he worries about losing his grip on a balancing oar and tumbling into the spring-cold water of April 1999.

The bridge, as I am now reminded at the end of June 2000, is more than a trophy. It has evolved with every mile that I rowed as a rare lens through which I can see myself at two different times in the same place. The gift that I'd had when leaving was the presence of mind to ignore the *shoulds* of the world and just go rowing. My gift now is simply to witness that departure upon my return, through this window beneath the span of the Brooklyn Bridge and between its two stone towers.

· 27 ·

A Mariner's Dilemma

AFTER A DAY SPENT IN MANHATTAN I catch the F train to
Brooklyn with a bag over my shoulder, and walk down to the waterfront where the boat has been left pulled up on the same dock from
which I'd once departed. Ten minutes later, after routinely sliding the
boat into the water, stowing my gear, and stepping aboard, I once
again row beneath the Brooklyn Bridge on an incoming tide, this time
bound for the coast of New England, in what will be a grace note to
the original route, a five-hundred-mile farewell to my life on the water. I finally heed the directive the tanker captain had given me on the
first day to stay to the east of Roosevelt Island, and the embattled currents of Hell Gate, which remind me of the chaotic eddying of the
Mississippi River, carry me quickly toward Long Island Sound.

By the end of the day I reach the harbor at Manorhaven, New
York, which is filled with hundreds of sailboats tied to their moorings.
There is no wind at the end of the day but the boats rock ever so
slightly as an occasional passing motorboat, at idle speed within the
harbor, spreads its wake, and yacht-club launches retrieve sailors from
their boats. Now anchored at the edge of the harbor, I've assembled
the tent frame and pulled the tent three-quarters of the way over the
boat. Before snapping it down, however, I sit in the bow gazing west-

ward toward New York City, where a great display of fireworks welcomes the Parade of Tall Ships, which had begun arriving soon after I'd left Brooklyn. In the still air I hear the belated cracks and booms and try to match the sound with the light. With the Brooklyn Bridge now behind me and this display of man-made lightning in the distance, I feel a sense of peace in having completed the circuit. As I lie in the boat after the grand finale I listen to the sounds of halyards ringing gently on masts, a comforting sound which indicates that sails are down and boats are in safe harbor. It seems to come from all directions and for a moment before drifting off to sleep I can pretend that the sound is only within my mind.

UPON LEAVING MANHATTAN I'd called the Army Corps office of the Cape Cod Canal, which reaches into the Atlantic from Massachusetts like the flexed arm of a bodybuilder. The eight-mile canal cuts through the peninsula at the shoulder, and thus provides boats with an alternative to rounding the eastern reaches of the Cape, which offers few safe havens from rough seas. Though I'd grown up on the north shore of Massachusetts and know little of the coast south of Boston, I had an idea that those wishing to transit through the canal are required to do so under motorized power. I spoke with a junior officer of the Corps, who confirmed the rule for auxiliary power, but added that exceptions are made from time to time in special cases and that this might well be one of them. If so, I should expect an Army Corps boat to escort me through the canal, and I should call back within several days and hope to reach his boss, who could give the actual permission.

At Fishers Island, at the mouth of Long Island Sound, I call back and by chance the phone is answered by the same junior officer. However, if he'd been Dr. Jekyll before—amiable and interested— he is now Mr. Hyde. I introduce myself with a reminder about my trip and hoped-for transit through the canal, and say I am calling back as requested. "It's impossible," he says, followed by a reinforcing silence during which I inwardly rail against his choice of that word. I'll readily admit that some things appear to be impossible, and that I have few solutions for most of the challenges of the world, yet I can think of no reason why anything, whether by god or by man, should be thought to be impossible.

"Oh," I reply reservedly, "I was under the impression that there probably wouldn't be a problem."

"Nope. I spoke with our chief and he won't allow it."

I recall his previous mention of possible exceptions. "Under no circumstances?"

"Well, you don't have any auxiliary power on your boat, right?"

"Right," I acquiesce.

"I'm sorry. I can't help you. Boats going through the canal have to have motors. It can get very rough in the canal." And silence.

I think back on a thousand miles of the Mississippi, where currents often ran at better than five knots around the outside of river bends. Aside from several minor course deviations, the Cape Cod Canal runs virtually straight, with an average current of four knots. I recall surfing four-foot breaking waves off the deserted west coast of the Everglades and crossing the shipping lanes of Chesapeake Bay. No one had stood in my way, and I'd never faltered. These thoughts pass within my furrowed brow inside of a moment, and he continues: "Are you raising money for any cause?"

"No," I reply, regretting having not invented one in advance. I might have told him I've been rowing to free all orange-bellied newts from the captivity of pimple-nosed teenagers—I was once such a captor myself—or to raise awareness about the little known plight of the muskmelon. Or whatever else. Would it make a difference if I'd been rowing for Jesus?

"Well if you were raising money for a good cause," he follows, "then we might be able to help you. Otherwise, rules are rules."

By now I am irate in my silent way, and I know there is no point expressing anything to bureaucracy through a telephone beyond the slightest chagrin, which is quickly morphing into humiliation. Here, after thousands of miles, the domain of my own navigation would be interrupted for the first time in my own home state and on the same chart page as the port of Fairhaven, from which every sailor's hero, Joshua Slocum, had embarked in a rebuilt sloop more than a century before on the first solo circumnavigation of the world.

Worse, I know that rules are not rules. Exceptions are possible. Though safety is the general issue at hand, special permission is granted based not on experience afloat—as should be the case where consistency matters—but on the worthiness of some cause. Yes, I've been spoiled by the independence of living on the water, free from the dotted line of rental agreements and car payments, untracked by the striped pavement. And I've been spoiled too by the free access, even assistance, provided by various authorities along the way: Coast Guard boats and stations had given advice, expired charts, assistance in repair, and a chance to shower in Waterford, New York, Morgan City and New Orleans, Louisiana, and Chincoteague, Virginia. The Army Corps of Engineers themselves had offered no end of assistance. Indeed, my rowing life had been anything but a solo adventure, and yet I'd become accustomed to the way of the water, by which the captain of a ship, even of a 130-pound rowing boat, enjoys the right to determine his course. Now I am reminded that even on Hubbard's fringe of society, every so often the rule of authority pays a visit.

With minimal exchange my phone conversation comes to an end, and between Fishers Island and Cape Cod I will have to resolve a mariner's dilemma of how to pass one of the more treacherous peninsulas along our coasts.

But there is more to my frustration: At its heart is my limited schedule for reaching Gloucester in time for the Blackburn Challenge. That a government should interfere with my navigation is one thing, but to miss this race as a result would burn. Assuming passage through the canal and even just fair weather, I've been on schedule to arrive in Gloucester more than a day before the race, time enough to row the course in advance if I want. On one hand I recognize my need to race as a snag amid my evolving freedom from counted time, which has emerged as an unexpected yet essential element of the trip. Yet never before in my life had I been so mentally and physically prepared for a race, and it seems unlikely I will ever be so again. Yes, I am curious to know how I'd match up against a strong field of competition, but I am more interested in rowing any race honoring Howard Blackburn, whose presence I've often conjured during the course of the circuit: Blackburn looking down from the clouds, Blackburn sailing fingerless past me, Blackburn pulling perpetually on heavy oars with bony hands, scoffing at me in my summer warmth, as I row surely within several miles of the nearest mini-mart.

Not that I've aimed to outdo Blackburn. I might have rowed thrice as far with no more insight into the forged determination that allowed a man to row a lumbering Gloucester dory for five sleepless January days and nights off the coast of Newfoundland, hands frozen to claws, with bare bones gripping the weighty oars. Yet his story had been a wellspring of the trip. I'd given him a nod of respect, tinged with apology in acknowledgment of my full set of digits, as I rowed past the point at which he ended his incomplete, though still longer, version of my route. Of all the undersung heroes of high-seas calamity, it was Blackburn who'd inspired a young man to cut himself loose to go rowing and who'd incited an annual race in his memory, and the route of my trip and the start of the race would intersect. I've known this since stopping in Longboat Key, where I'd placed a call to inquire about the date of the race. Though my watch has enjoyed less and less prominence in the boat, I've kept track of the calendar, and I've rowed. How could I explain all this to an officer of the Army Corps? Perhaps I might have with just these words.

————

NOW I FACE the first real navigational dilemma of the trip. I can see four methods of passing Cape Cod. First, the canal, which is paralleled by a road, could be portaged. I know that no great hills, such as those I'd encountered between Lake Erie and Chautauqua Lake, exist along whatever would be the route and that this walk would be no longer than the first. Second, I could seek the assistance of someone with a truck or trailer. Third, I could row through the canal at night, as several acquaintances had suggested, for reportedly the canal is lightly patrolled, if at all, after dark. Fourth, I could row around Cape Cod.

As for the first option, the weight of my current boat is at least twice that of the scull, and even lesser inclines, should I be able to locate a dolly capable of supporting its greater weight and beam might be insurmountable. The second option is just that, an option. If I'd been taken in my determination to complete the first portage under my own power, I am now tempered steel. I will not, particularly as a by-product of someone else's apparently whimsical decision, accept assistance in passing the Cape. I would sooner be tumbled by surf upon the dunes of the outer Cape than accept the power of internal combustion.

Third, sneaking eight miles through the canal at night, even when compared to rowing the thirty miles of the nearly havenless eastern Cape in daylight, seems foolhardy. To do so would require rowing without my navigation lights, and I've been told that commercial traffic, in the form of fishing vessels and barges, travels the canal twenty-four hours a day. The likelihood of such an encounter, though I would travel within just feet of the shore, would make nighttime transit not only imprudent, but unfair to passing captains, who would surely spot me, if not also report me.

Which leaves a detour around the Cape, an option that attracts me solely on the merits that it would extend the trip and provide me with views of coastal Massachusetts I've never seen. However, I would have to row nearly fifty miles from a narrow cut between uninhabited

Monomoy Island, a narrow dune that hangs south from the chin of the Cape like Lao Tse's sage beard, around Race Point to Provincetown, with only one early chance to find refuge in Pleasant Bay, whose entrance above shallow sands is exposed dead-on to any easterly breeze. And, though I could choose early morning oceanic serenity during which to cover the first miles of the stretch, the safety of Provincetown requires a nearly complete arc around the tip of the Cape, which I would not reach until late afternoon, when a late-day breeze would be almost inevitable. I would be sure to run head-on into any wind, again without any option for retreat. Furthermore, in rounding the Cape I would add more than a hundred miles to the trek to Gloucester, extra miles for which I do not have time.

So I row from Long Island Sound uncertain of my method for gaining latitude above Cape Cod. I row along the coast of Rhode Island, and follow that smallest state's sandy shore past Watch Hill, whose Flying Horse carousel is the oldest in the country, and past Perryville, where not far behind the shoreline I'd once sat with my college philosophy professor on summer afternoons beneath his shade trees, discussing the design of an oral history course I'd been planning to teach in South Africa. After sandwiches with lemonade he reinforced his command of the educational philosophies of John Dewey and Max Black by drubbing his pupil on a makeshift croquet course. He was nearly three times my age—white hair falling against its own current toward the ball—with a ruddy French complexion, and his bent-kneed, derriere-thrusted, deadly aim hinted back to sessions of his class in which he'd employed a variety of old-school jazz recordings to bring life and meaning to the old writers still ahead of their times. "Now LISTEN to THIS!" he'd called out to the small class, nearly yelling while he searched for the play button—"Listennn!" he repeated, slowly and darkly intoned as you would caution a sitting puppy who's just seen a cat to "Staayyy!" And we listened, and we listened again, as Louis Armstrong and the Hot Fives's rendition of "Potato Head Blues" fertilized our understanding of Alfred North

Whitehead's theory of education and style. And a squarely hit croquet ball, two full strokes ahead of its competition, rolls to a preor-
dained stop eleven inches in front of a wicket, the water below my hull
is the clearest I've ever seen in New England, and a few bars of "It
Don't Mean a Thing if It Ain't Got That Swing" fall humming to the
rhythm of the oars.

Thus I find myself home in New England, where most any given
spot along the coast is known to me in some way and many points of
land bring back memories, some of long ago—for twenty years is
long ago when you're in your early thirties, and already I've felt an el-
der's wistfulness for younger days.

Buzzard's Bay carves the appearance of an armpit at the base of
Cape Cod, and on an increasingly overcast day a steady wind develops from the southwest, building waves that surf the boat slightly off
the wind to the northeast—and toward the western inlet of the nearly
eight-mile-long Cape Cod Canal. I'd marked Buzzard's Bay well in
advance as a treacherous expanse for many boats, as its winds are often strong and the depths relatively shallow. I take this favorable wind
as a gift and seek out the larger waves for the longest surfing rides, accepting what I understand within, that I am allowing the wind and its
lovely shapes to choose for me an attempt at the canal.

After a drizzling night at anchor in Mattapoisett Harbor, I follow
the bay to its head, and from a distance recognize the aptly named
London Bridge, which spans the canal for trains. It so happens that I
reach the entrance as the tide is shifting in my favor, and I eye the mirrored glass headquarters of the Army Corps and its small fleet of
hulking black workboats tied alongshore. Amid other boat traffic—a
sleek sixty-foot sailboat under the German flag has just completed a
transatlantic crossing and is also headed through the canal—I cross
the outer mouth of the channel several times, appreciate that my lunar
timing is perfect and that a slight breeze is complementing the current
for a surface so calm I can hardly sense the flow by looking at the water alone. At some point every poor slackjaw has to find out for sure if

the teacher meant what she said about no spitballs, and my number is up.

I idle my way to the further side of the canal, pull down the brim of my hat ("if I can't see you you can't see me," a persistent childhood theory), avert my gaze from the mirrored architecture ("if I don't acknowledge you I can't break your rules"), and row. Reports of four to five miles per hour of current seem accurate when gauged against the passing embankment of carefully puzzled granite stone, and this added to my own speed will easily send me through to Cape Cod Bay in an hour. I pass beneath London Bridge while acknowledging the waves of those fishing from the shore, yet also perceive among them interest less in a man rowing a boat than in what might become of him, as those who watch car races not for the design and speed and jockeying repetition of the laps, but with secret hopes for skids, sparks, and life-sparing disaster.

Just as I wonder at what point I might pass beyond the interest or at least view of the controlling authorities, I hear the brief yet piercing shriek of a siren that can only have been meant for me, and with a glance toward the Army Corps station I see the broad, glossy black steel bow of an Army Corps workboat forced toward me through the water by its rumbling diesel guts. Blue police lights flash in an absurd statement of power, as if to say "You broke our rules and we're mad!" and "You should be publicly embarrassed" and "You should be afraid." Someone has said no, and meant it. I pause in my stroke, then slowly spin the boat into the current so as both to acknowledge and meet them. The black hulk, belching blue-gray diesel breath from its stern, across which the name *Wampanoag* is painted in white letters, is slowed to an idling speed, though we both continue drifting, as the moon would have us, at nearly five miles per hour into the canal. Thus begins the end of my quest to row for Howard Blackburn around Cape Ann.

The three crew members, including the man at the helm, dressed in khaki uniforms and life preservers, gaze with interest and a touch of

amusement at the little boat, and size up the knucklehead within. I imagine I am the spice for their week and the story of my disobedience and retrieval will provide guffaws at least into next week. Others who are now off duty will later ask "What kind of boat did you say he was in?" and "Where was he coming from? There's one born every day." The captain of the *Wampanoag* speaks up first across fifteen feet of flowing water.

"Let me tell you, the Chief really loved that! You passed right in front of his nose!" I don't bother trying to explain myself, as I have only one choice, which is quickly explained by a second crew member. "We have to tow you out. Hand me your bowline and we'll tie on." This is soon done, and the *Wampanoag* labors against the current as I sit facing aft, puttering about as I can to distract myself from my frustration and suggest to anyone watching that I am unfazed. I mop the bilge dry with the sponge, reorganize my few possessions, and steal a picture of the London Bridge as it retreats to my north, rather than, as I'd planned, to my south. I take a picture too of the bow of my boat, connected by line through the belching blue exhaust to the stern of the *Wampanoag*. To my right, which had been my left, the heads of onlookers who had slowly pivoted in unison to the north are now shifting, tidelike, south. Their hopes have been rewarded, as the class titters and looks askance as the boy who shot the spitball is sent off to the principal's office. Beyond the mouth of the canal, where I can easily row against the current, I am cast off.

· 28 ·

A Race Without End

I AM STUMPED on how to get myself to Gloucester in time for the race. Though I once again entertain thoughts of portage, I also contemplate transporting the boat to the race by car—a rental car?—and then returning to row around the Cape. I am nevertheless eager to move on and distract myself. Having rowed northward into Buzzard's Bay I can now only row southward out of it and accept that however I manage to get myself to the race, if at all, I will row around Cape Cod.

As the late afternoon softens into early evening I search the shore for a protected anchorage for the night, and at Silver Beach find a broad, somewhat exposed harbor and, leading from it, a channel that opens to a quaint, virtually imperturbable cove that is circular and no more than a hundred yards across. Small sloops of various legendary designers, including Nathaniel Herreshoff and Joel White, lie quietly at anchor, and the sandy, grassy shore is lined with unimposing two- and three-story wooden houses sidled up to each other, painted New England white. Families stroll along the narrow paved road that stretches between these homes and the water, children dart back and forth on bicycles, and a pair of elderly women, who I suspect miss no detail of movement within their view, watch in tandem as I circle the snug watery recess like a dog introduced to a new yard, in search of a place that will interfere with no one and that I can call my own for the night.

Judging by the exposed beach, the tide will be out in another hour or two, and I anchor in several feet of water near the head of the channel and close to an unpaved, sandy boat launch. As the dying light lends a sense of privacy, I manage while standing behind the boat in the shallow water to bathe myself discreetly and change into clean clothes. Beyond the seawall and adjacent to the beach, the life of the village gravitates to the lights of an asphalt park, which doubles as a basketball court and two tennis courts. Beyond this, across a parking lot, a seasonal grill is selling hamburgers, hot dogs, and ice-cream. Its employees are young, teenaged, certainly local and known by all, having won what I guess is a favorite summer job. Many of their contemporaries stroll in and out through screened swinging doors, and older couples too stand in line, some with young children or grandchildren, waiting for ice-cream. Outside on the basketball court, boys loft distant shots and capitalize on the rebounds of errant aim, and leaderless escadrilles of blinded moths carve the glow of the park lamps in their helpless addiction to the artificial light. Everyone is there, it seems, and everything is all right, as the last light of the vanished sun dies in altostratus clouds above.

It is soon clear to me that an event is at hand, as families enter the park with folding chairs and blankets and coolers, and assemble in rows facing west in front of a ten-foot-tall painted cinder-block wall. I ask a man with a thermos in one hand and folded quilted blankets in the other, accompanied by his wife and two children, what is going on, to which he replies, "It's movie night. They're showing *Tarzan*." I feel grateful to have gathered this information without being asked where I am visiting from. Following the frustrations of the canal I have been pleasantly surprised to discover this hurricane-proof pond and town I've never heard of in my own, small home state. I welcome simple inclusion in this Rockwellian scene, and the distraction of the story about the purification of man in nature. I sleep that night in the boat on water disturbed only by the slow breath of the tide.

The following day I row to Woods Hole, home of the famous oceanographic institute by the same name, and confront the question of whether to race at Gloucester. I confess that there is a side of me that has given up, that reasons that the race doesn't matter enough to me anyway. After all it is only a race, and if this trip has come to represent nothing else, it is about freedom from contrived competition and from the rhythm of the clock. While one ego imagines crossing the finish line first, an alter ego doesn't wish to win at all, as merely attempting to do so would signify obedience to measured time. And yet it is Blackburn, and Gloucester, and my home waters, and the scenario I'd imagined, of arriving at the race start the night before, sleeping in my boat, and rowing my cherished hull the circumference of that famous cape, a distance only half of that I'd often rowed each day while making my way up the eastern seaboard.

It is here that frugality sticks out her wretched leg and I proceed, in slow motion, to trip. In order to transport the boat to Gloucester I would need some sort of truck or Jeep, and to rent such a vehicle, I learn, will cost me several hundreds of dollars. Having already rowed myself into debt once again—I am out of cash and relying on the last resort of a credit card—and with no certain prospects of work upon completion of the trip, I rebel against the idea of sending myself further into the red. I wonder whether the race can possibly be worth this much cost? After all, there is always next year.

Finally I realize that the scull, which has been hanging from the beams of my brother's basement in Maine, represents an alternative. If I can get myself to Boston I could, from there, make use of my father's Jeep, the roof rack of which is not capable of safely carrying the weight of this boat, but could easily transport the feathery scull to Gloucester. And so I set about finding safe storage for the boat in Woods Hole, which I find on a beachfront lined with other less traveled rowing boats and skiffs. I dismantle the juried rig and hitch a short ride with the awkward gear, including the long oars, to the local bus depot.

Having long anticipated the Boston skyline emerging over my bow, I quietly resent my arrival in Boston via the auto-clogged, regulated track of the city's Southeast Expressway rather than by wending my way among the islands of the city's outer harbor, most of which I've never explored. But I am still happy to see the skyline, including the John Hancock building, I. M. Pei's sixty-story jewel on St. James Street, whose sheer blue glass facade manages modernity in the heart of Back Bay by reflecting all that came before. Look into the glass tower and, mirrorlike, you see yourself, adorned in the background by the heavy Romanesque elegance of Trinity Church or by the early twentieth-century monumentalism of the "old" John Hancock Building, or by the stately Copley Plaza Hotel. It is a rare thing that defines itself uniquely by confirming all that surrounds and preceded it.

On Tuesday before the race I call to order parts for the broken rig. Its hose-clamp repair has held with rare need for readjustment throughout the seven hundred miles from Myrtle Beach to Woods Hole, but the scull requires the rig to be in full working order, with no option for structural simplification. Conveniently, the rig had been built by a company near Boston. My order for parts is forestalled by an answering machine, and I suppose the staff is out for lunch. A second call goes no further, however. Perhaps a day off? But the next day, and the day after too, I have no better luck beyond the answering machine. Several phone calls to those few I know in the rowing world—a small community, even nationally—inform me that there is no staff, but just one person, as I'd begun to imagine, and someone said he was on vacation. One friend in New York offers to send her identical rig to me, an opportunity that I decline as the express shipping rate seems prohibitive, and I reason that with access to a hardware store I should be able to fashion my own replacements for the missing parts.

IT IS RACE DAY, Saturday, in the parking lot at Gloucester High
School, which borders on the Annisquam Canal, the northern and
easternmost end of the intracoastal waterway, stretching from
Brownsville, Texas. The lot is full of cars and trucks, all with trailers
or roof racks, and hundreds of people are preparing their boats for the
event. Racing-class scullers are fine-tuning the rigs of their sleek craft,
hardly the width of a rower's pelvis. Traditional dorymen have little
to adjust on their simple boats, the same as that which Blackburn had
rowed to safety, and mill about feeding themselves and stowing sufficient supplies of water. Eight-person crews in Hawaiian outrigger canoes, including a team that is actually from Hawaii, boisterously build
team spirit as they prepare their massive, stabilized canoes, an odd
sight in New England. I will be rowing in the "touring" class for
single-man sculls and am busy confronting the inferiority of my repairs, which render the rig so wobbly that I'm unlikely to be able to
take a firmly balanced stroke.

Now my class has left the beach and headed an eighth of a mile up
the channel toward the starting line. I remain at the water's edge strug-
gling to tighten the rig and, for the first time on the entire trip, I find
myself wholly unprepared. Finally I slide the boat into the cool water,
resigned to whatever stroke I will be able to manage, and approach the
starting line with the Hawaiian canoes, fifteen minutes after my class
of rowers has left. I wish I'd attempted to sneak through the Cape
Cod Canal at night. I wish I'd written for permission to transit the
canal a month in advance. I wish I'd known to invent some charitable
cause. I wish for anything but this. Moreover, my father, who nearly
rowed his way into the Olympics, will be watching me row for the first
time ever in anything more than a dinghy. He's planned to follow the
race in a motorboat and must be at the starting line wondering what's
become of me. I wish I hadn't run into that damn piling in Myrtle
Beach. I wish to be elsewhere as I struggle with each stroke to com-

pensate for the insecure rig, which sends one oar more deeply into the water than the other, and the responsive hull suddenly heels to starboard at the catch, then rolls to port during the completion of the stroke. This will cost me time, but I'm sure that I'll soon master an uneven catch to result in a balanced hull. I feel delinquent and three grades behind my peers as I settle the boat near the starting line among the colorful, heavily manned canoes, awaiting the starter's blast.

The last few seconds before the start. I am filled with that mixture of adrenaline and fear and fight that I've known since before I can remember, since I was first pitted, probably in school, against another human for the goal of first place: first one over the line, last one standing, highest grade on the test—war itself in its civilized guise, tempered by the moral that no one should bleed. I wonder, if one could stop, parse, and study that fraction of a second after the gun's blast and before the body's physical movement, what would be found and how could one describe that shift from Nat, the self that an hour before had been chatting easily with a fellow entrant about the Monument Wherry he'd built, to this animalistic self whose sole purpose is to get ahead. Something snaps within, and it's neither rowing skill nor psychological preparation that is put in gear so much as something deeper, never taught but always promoted, the species' elemental instinct to prevail. Indeed, who's ever heard of a game that isn't meant to be won? While the primary premise of all practice is improvement of given skills and approach, the defining aim of all competition is victory. All games, played fully and according to their rules, whatever those may be, have winners.

Or so I'd thought. When I moved to Zuni I was given the opportunity to watch some of the tribe's religious dances, held in a central courtyard framed by the red sandstone walls of private homes as the audience looks down from the slightly canted roofs above. The dances are exotic to the visitor's eye and I understood little beyond what could easily be interpreted—for example, the mimicking relationship between younger and older dancers, reflecting the tribe's basic, modeling approach to education and to life: do what I do, then find your own style. I was happy just to be there and became half mesmerized by the disciplined repetition of song and movement. One day, however, during an interlude, I was amazed as I watched a form of dodgeball played out with an old pillow. A group of dancers split into two teams of six each and lined up against each other at the ends of the courtyard. What began as an instantly recognizable form of tag, in which any player hit by a thrown pillow is acquired by the other team, soon revealed an astonishing twist. As one team began clearly to prevail—say nine players against a remaining three—and I awaited a routine ending to a simple schoolyard game, the tide was made to shift. A player on the dominant team tossed the pillow with strength, but intentionally faulty aim, and the pillow landed as a ground ball and skidded, still spinning, into a dusty corner. Once retrieved—two of the three players mimic indecision about who should have to go get it, and the audience laughs—the pillow was sent sailing through the air again, and this time its target, who might easily have stepped out of the way, feigned the look of a deer in headlights and was hit. The audience quaked mildly in easy laughter, the way you might laugh at Wile E. Coyote reruns whose outcomes you've long since memorized. In mock dejection the struck player slowly ambled toward the other side, careful halfway to mime confusion about his allegiance, yet fear of both teams, and the audience laughed again as the pillow continued to restore the original balance.

I saw this game played out many times, always with the same result—or, frustratingly to the Western mind, with seemingly no result. It is a game without end, which no one wins. Instead it is about oscillation between balance and imbalance, and I don't recall a single event or description about Zuni that ever revealed more about the culture. Yet I had been raised with a different form of dodgeball, and I clearly remember one gym class in particular, perhaps in fourth grade, when this game was at hand. Several inflated red rubber balls were hurled with vicious intention, if imperfect aim, back and forth across the varnished wooden floor. And eventually the most agile person was left alone as victor, until he too—for it was in this case a he—was picked off and, to end the game, made part of the whole. Ultimately both games confirm the importance of the tribe, yet one tribe requires regular elimination of all but the strongest, while another survives through the tempering of individualism.

Now in Gloucester the long blast of an air horn sets us in motion, and a dozen hulls lunge forward with each stroke, the canoeing teams goaded on excitedly by their chosen maestros. Just as I had along the remotest stretches of the Mississippi, I pull in silence and am acutely aware, amid the bustling unity of paddling teamwork, of my innate solitude, both within my boat and without.

I'd studied the curvatures of the canal visible from the starting line, and immediately gravitate toward one side, whose irregular contours should break and eddy the current, and proceed with the goal of catching at least one competitor within my own class. I watch the progress of my Hawaiian company as measured against the shore, and observe the apparent wake of navigational buoys that, in addition to marking the deepest channel of this sandy inlet, tend also to mark the strongest channels of current.

Boats on moorings, like weather vanes, give silent report on the drift of this liquid wind. Those closer to the main channel indicate an unfavorable flooding current—their bows point toward the mouth of the canal, headlong into the tide—while others closer to shore point in various directions in more confused, not quite eddying current. Still others nearest to shore advise of back-eddies heading my way. I decide to stray from the shorter course for what I hope will be a faster route.

With each stroke I study the lame rig, swaying and twisting under pressure, and try to compensate for the handicap while also trying to ignore the fact that after six thousand miles of rowing, during which I'd managed to make long-lasting repairs with what was at hand in the boat—a spare hose clamp, duct tape, and a carved piece of wood—or through the unfailing serendipity of nearby, willing assistance, I now find myself hindered by faulty equipment for which no amount of skill or attitude can compensate. I try to expunge any thought that for the first time on the trip I might, because of a sudden collapse of the rig, tumble into the water, particularly if, once out of the canal and along the open shores of Cape Ann, the wind and waves arise.

Nevetheless, although much of the energy of each stroke is spent on flexing my body so as to help compensate for the rig, I manage a growing lead over some of the Hawaiians, and gain confidence that if the rig holds I should easily be able to finish with my class. My father follows from an unobtrusive distance, and I wonder whether he is struck more by my seeming lack of preparation or by the fact that I'm managing as well as I am. I scorn, on his behalf, my uneven catches and mismatched releases, knowing that this is his first glimpse ever of his youngest son, whom he'd once acknowledged in an e-mail for having certainly rowed more miles on this trip than he'd rowed in his college career. I hope he notices that occasional cycle when the blades grip with equal precision and release with understated yet unquestionable power. I am, after all, my father redux, and for the first time I had not only excelled in a realm perceived throughout my childhood as unimpeachably his, but in some ways, and by his own acknowledgment, I had exceeded him. And yet this is what he sees first, after a late start and on my way to an uncertain finish, the least promising, most dilapidated mile of rowing since I'd left Brooklyn more than a year before.

And then, with a weak snap of low-grade metal, the head of the bolt central to my reconstruction pops off and falls to the bilge, as if to say it's heart hadn't been in it in the first place. Thus released, the stays of the rig, whose own mediocre quality I'd trusted least, dissolve their obligation to support the outriggers, and I am forced to take only the gentlest strokes so as to avoid further damage and prevent capsize. My father needs no explanation. He circles the hobbled craft, distressed himself, and both catches and releases my eye as I retain tears of wounded pride. Never in my life have I been so prepared to compete, and yet so poorly tooled. He escorts me as I tiptoe with the blades to a nearby yacht club while reassessing my best remaining hope, which is now simply to finish the race, even if last of all, before the sun sets.

I regain myself and, feeling the resourcefulness and determination that had carried me since Brooklyn, I assume that on the docks and among the yacht club members cleaning and working on their boats, sufficient materials must be available to repair, perhaps even improve, my chances. Indeed tools and materials and even interest are made available, but ultimately I accept that the rig requires maintenance to its original form, and I resign.

· 29 ·

Hold the Dream Closely

I RETURN TO WOODS HOLE with a new outrigger in hand. The builder's vacation, fittingly, came to an end the day after Gloucester. He mentioned nothing about the messages I'd left on his answering machine, and I mentioned nothing about the race. With a duffel bag over my shoulders, the entire seat rig toted awkwardly in my left hand, and the two long oars in my right, I hobble along the main street of Woods Hole, amid camera-slung tourists and oxford-wearing oceanographers, past shingled T-shirt shops and across the campus of the Woods Hole Oceanographic Institute, through a blend of pure vacation and pure science.

I long to see the boat, to carefully walk its hull down the gravel beach and back into water, and, in stepping aboard, to release myself from the luckless grasp of the previous days. I'd failed to negotiate or sneak my way through the Cape Cod Canal; I was unable to restore the broken rig in time for the race; and I'd nearly missed the Blackburn Challenge altogether on account of my faulty jury rig, which ultimately failed amid an armada of giant canoes. My father, who might have seen me row for the first time at the apex of my mastery, watched what a random observer might have deemed one man's first attempt in a scull. My arrest by the *Wampanoag* had become the first scene in the final act of the trip, in which self-sufficiency within society eventually runs dry, and freedom yields to compliance. Eventually, here and there, one has to fit in.

With the boat afloat on a low tide I restore its contents to their designated places. Living within this hull has become my routine, my comfort, and like the Rainman with his baseball cards, I regain control of both the trip and my confidence as I place the flashlight on its shelf beside the bunk—a dollar store special that still works months after the switch on my waterproof light had gone bad—slide the plastic larder beneath the wooden thwart, and lay my department store knife and the bottle of sunscreen by my side. Everything has its place, a simple order perfected since leaving Natchez.

In climbing back into the boat and rowing out of the harbor at Woods Hole, I feel that I've started pulling again to that deeper rhythm whose downbeats had placed me beneath a full moon while rowing past the freighter at West Point, at a picnic table at Yummy's eating ice-cream with Freddy Fisher, and running up the front steps of the Jekyll Island Club in the nick of time for my breakfast appointment with Robert Lovett. Nevertheless I still ponder the meaning of the recent fiasco, and observe only that this single brief, discrete series of calamities, beginning with my expulsion from the Cape Cod Canal by the *Wampanoag* and ending with a broken boat mid-race in Gloucester, occurred when I'd attempted to shift from the freedom I've acquired from the counting of time to the clock-driven confines of the race. I'd embraced the very devotion to time that, though at first unwittingly, I've been purging over thousands of miles of rowing. And while I know on one hand that I'd entered the race because it was named after Blackburn, I also feel a touch of shame for having abandoned, if only for a day, this slowly acquired freedom from time, for having needed to compete at all. Perhaps it is this explanation, that in choosing to race I'd picked at a healing wound, which allows me to leave Woods Hole with restored confidence and without fear that the events of the preceding week are omens of ill-fate still to come. I am reassured by the renewed strength of the out-rigger (though I am still pleased that my on-the-spot repair at Myrtle Beach had lasted), and test its metal while reasserting myself on the water with long, powerful strokes toward the open shores of Nantucket Sound.

If you raise your left arm in a bodybuilder's pose you will have a personal chart of Cape Cod, around which I have set out to row. The town of Woods Hole lies at your armpit, Stage Harbor by your elbow, and the island of Monomoy hangs southward from the very end of your elbow. The eastern, Atlantic shore of the Cape, a long stretch of sandy beach, follows the line of your forearm to the north, then wraps around your fist, with Race Point at the third knuckle. Relax the body-builder's fist and open the fingers until they point down toward your elbow. Lying within them is the harbor of Provincetown.

The wind increases from the southwest in the early afternoon, and urges me eastward from Woods Hole toward Monomoy, still two days ahead and the last stop along the Cape's tricep before heading out and around along the open coast. Clear on the horizon the bluffs of Martha's Vineyard tempt me. My uncle and his family once had a cottage there, and I remember the day we piled into his motorboat and made a circuit of the island in several hours. Had anyone suggested to me then, at the age of ten, that I might eventually row a boat around the Vineyard I would have responded with a dumb-enough look, followed by the sort of laugh you laugh just to go along with whatever the joke might have been. Now I might easily make the circuit in a day, yet the wind keeps me on a different track and the Vineyard fades, glance by occasional glance, beyond the convex horizon. I keep a watch for Nantucket too, which lies further out, yet cannot spot its form even when I pause to stand on the wooden thwart.

Two days later I awake at Stage Harbor, near the beard of Monomoy. Monomoy is an island of sand, above water and below, and pounding winter storms erode and shift and build its shoreline like an indecisive sculptor. Occasionally it is joined by storms to the mainland, and some years a narrow cut slices through its northern end, providing a quick alley to its Atlantic shore. This year the cut is open, and thus I will be saved not only the seven miles row down its western beach and seven up the other side, but more importantly, the distance along the open coast to Provincetown will be shortened by those seven miles.

As I leave Stage Harbor, which opens to the south, before heading east toward the Monomoy cut, the sun is rising to my right, and though I do not feel its warmth on my face, the light itself is a warming promise that my bare toes will soon be warmed, I will shed my wool shirt, and the cool early morning will soon give way to summer heat. Where I'll find myself by the end of the day I can only guess, but Provincetown, some forty-five miles away, is my goal. Falling short of that, in case of bad weather, my options will be to return to Stage Harbor or to surf in at some point along the miles of beach that line the eastern shore of the Cape. Neither option would be particularly attractive. Surfing the boat on even the small, tightly formed waves of a beach could easily result in a capsize, and it might be days before the return of weather calm enough to relaunch without swamping. Even worse, rough weather might not only prevent me from reaching Provincetown or surfing into the beach, but might occur so late in the day that I wouldn't have time to return to the cut at Monomoy before dark. Today's weather report is favorable, however, calling for light westerly winds that I know will be blocked from reaching me by the tall dunes of the Cape itself. But I also know the fair conditions will likely sour tonight. I have my window, and so I row.

The deepest channel through the cut at Monomoy is marked informally by stakes placed in the water by local fishermen. Monomoy itself, inhabited by cormorants, sea gulls, dune grasses, and poison ivy, must be the most deserted slice of land north of the Virginia coast. This vacant island, combined with the makeshift channel markings, the gawking cries of seabirds, the absence of anyone else on the water, and before long, the sound of crashing surf, instills within me a sense of remoteness I'd felt only on the emptiest stretches of the Mississippi. I feel certain I will always remember having had this feeling along the crowded coast of Massachusetts. Harbor seals dart with nervous curiosity below me, and the end of the cut, with open ocean beyond, is hung with an early morning mist raised out of the surf by the warming sun.

The day evolves as if for a postcard, with clear blue skies meeting the deeper blue of open ocean to the east, and to the west the rolling contour of the dunes of Cape Cod, often well over a hundred feet high—unscalable you might presume unless you'd seen the steeper, once-scaled bluffs of Normandy. Heading north, I sometimes stray half a mile offshore, but also row at times within yards of the tightly breaking surf, and occasionally become so distracted by my thoughts, or by no thought, or by the intermittent legions of beachgoers, that I find myself rising with the final swell of an ocean wave, and nearly hurled into shore. With quick strokes favoring the dune-side blade I restore my own proper spacing between open water and breaking surf.

I watch as a lifeguard heads to the water with his board in a non-emergency run, lunges gracefully over a breaking wave and paddles incessantly toward me. I stop rowing, wondering whether I've strayed too far within swimmers' bounds, though I am now easily fifty yards out into deep water. He is watching me so intently as he paddles, not slowing down even as he nears the boat, that I am unable to read his motive. His brown arms then stop paddling, and he glides toward me, all the while locking me with his gaze. Now beside me, he reaches out a hand, and I guess that he's heard about the trip from a recent newspaper article.

"You rowed from Brooklyn, right?" It's a statement as much as a question. I answer him while extending my right hand beyond an oar-lock.

"Yes."

He shakes my hand firmly, not letting go, still looking me in the eye. He has short black hair, dark eyes, and the build of a swimmer.

"I thought it had to be you. I read about your trip, and just wanted to come out to thank you." He maintains his grip while glancing down to the boat, and then he looks back to me. "Good luck," he says emphatically, and with a final gripping shake of my hand releases my eye, pivots the board in the water and begins paddling to shore, never once looking over his shoulder. As I continue rowing I think back to all the years I'd thought of the island, and about this trip, while rarely talking about either one. The occasional mention of rowing the circuit had typically fallen upon either disinterested or skeptical ears. And so I'd learned to hold the dream closely so as to protect it from doubt. I can only guess why the lifeguard wished to thank me, and with such vigor, but I suppose that he too has had his own dreams, perhaps realized already, which were most easily kept to himself.

Toward mid-afternoon the straight line of the dunes finally hints at a gradual bend and the first approach to the tip of Cape Cod. Soon a shoreline that had been nearly barren of people aside from the occasional crowd of sunbathers becomes a sandy avenue of weekend encampments, each sprung from the back of a stocky pickup truck or small motorhome, and consisting of the widest array of wilderness and backyard gear, from the lightest weight propane stoves, capable of heating only a small pan of soup, to nearly full-sized ranges supplied by ten-gallon propane tanks. Imagine a scene of coolers of all varieties and plastic colors, and the music of dozens of stereos blending in the wind, and children flying kites and young men with reddened shoulders bounding across the soft sand to meet the downward arc of a football, spinning and piercing its way through the blue sky. Across my path, scores of filaments reach into the water, their rods propped in the sand and casually tended by rows of men and women seated in folding chairs. Some are the parents of roving children, and they monitor the play with an occasional glance, and an occasional apology to the neighbors for an errant ball or spray of sand. They talk among themselves in parental increments of two or four or six, laughing, telling stories, with cans of soda or beer in foam holders. Older couples sit by themselves, husband and wife, occasionally accompanied by the muted play of a single grandchild, or the tunes of a well-kept old radio.

The shore continues to swing around to the west into Cape Cod Bay, and a rising wind meets me head-on as I round Race Point, and though questions abound from shore about where I am coming from, I cannot afford to respond with more than the briefest of answers, assuming that the wind will continue to build. Within five miles I round the tips of your fingers and find safety in Provincetown Harbor. But the wind strengthens ominously as the sun sets behind graying skies, and sailboats and fishing boats tug at their moorings, all bows in agreement on the direction of the breeze. I seek refuge with increased urgency as I fear the night will be wet and the wind unabating. Two long piers reach out from the center of the beachside town, and people stroll along them, looking at fishing boats tied to the docks and out across the broad harbor. I imagine them soon seated at restaurant tables, or returning warm and dry to their hotels or homes as the rain begins to fall.

I row along the two piers searching for a space and method for tying up unobtrusively. Inquiries to several men hurriedly scrubbing the decks of fishing boats yield directions only to a dinghy dock at the base of one pier. "Rowboats are allowed to tie up there," says one, "but yours may be a little long." In token appreciation of his suggestion I pull a couple of strokes toward the dock fifty yards off, but can already see that it is no place to land, as small outboard engines, tilted up on the sterns of inflatable rafts and small skiffs, would gouge my hull with their propeller blades.

Eager to step on land for the first time since sunrise, yet distrusting the safety of the boat while pulled up on the crescent-shaped public beach, I scout the piers once more before resigning myself to the most protected anchorage I can find—though few options are available on the broad, wind-tousled harbor—and the prospect of remaining in the boat for the evening, even though the lights of town are all the more beckoning beneath the disturbed skies. Expecting nothing, but still searching, I row once again along the pier looking for some free spot I might reasonably interpret as public for the night. As I pass near the stern of *Two If By Sea*, a thirty-five-foot charter fishing boat, a sandy-blond woman, perhaps forty years old, in blue jeans and a heavy wool sweater, calls out to me.

"Where're you coming from?"

"Stage Harbor this morning."

"Where're you headed?"

"Eastport, Maine."

"Are you looking for a place to tie up for the night?"

"Yes," I reply. "I was wondering whether any of these slips are available." Along the row of docks several slips are empty, though I suspect that some fishing boats will soon return to their home berths.

"No," she responds. "All of those boats are still out, and they'll be in before long. But you're welcome to tie up between my boat and this one." She gestures to the gap between the bow of *Two If By Sea* and that of a similar boat tied parallel to the same pier.

"Are you sure?"

"It's no problem. Just row around and I'll help you with the lines."

By the time the boat is secure and I step carefully onto the dock, she's pointed out that the drizzle will soon turn to rain, and I should make myself at home within the protected cabin of *Two If By Sea*, whose key she gives me with the same nonchalance as if she were giving me the time. I thank her for her generosity, for having read me so well as only a captain might have done. "On the water," she might have replied had we met on the rivers. She asks for no details of the trip, knowing that these will come later.

Once again I am reminded that mine has not been a solitary venture, as many imagine, but one guided in part by the kindness of those we call strangers, a term I dislike. Any one of the hundreds of people that I've met since first leaving Brooklyn might, by another twist of fate, have been my next-door neighbor growing up. I imagine that Gabrielle feels the same way.

I soon fall asleep to the ominous whistling of wind and the pattering of rain on the deck above.

· 30 ·

That's Just the Way It Was

I ROWED DUE WEST across Cape Cod Bay on a glassy calm, and then followed the coast from Duxbury to Green Harbor to Cohasset. I bypassed Boston, as I'd already arrived there by bus en route to Gloucester, and rowed to my childhood home of Marblehead, whose rocky shores I'd last coasted when keeping two dozen lobster traps at the same age, more or less, as when I'd first noticed the island of the eastern United States. Having called in advance, I stopped at Gloucester and had lunch with Joseph and Helen Garland. Joe, whose biography of Howard Blackburn, *Lone Voyager*, had planted the idea of rowing a circuit in my mind, commented as we sat outside eating sandwiches that he "was always afraid that book might put crazy ideas in someone's head!"

Over the following week I skirted my way along the New England coast, and within two days reached the rocky shores of Maine, and the final state on the route, whose broad bays, long estuaries, and hundreds of islands provide thirty-five hundred miles of coastline, a seemingly inexhaustible landscape for the imagination of any small boat adventurer. I rowed from Turbat's Creek across Casco Bay to Small Point, and that night at anchor had the first dream I can remember about the trip, in which the boat, with me sleeping in it, was torn by waves from anchor's grip and in the darkness tumbled ashore. I passed through Five Islands on my way to MacMahan Island, in Sheepscot Bay, and from there to oceanbound Monhegan, eight miles out from Port Clyde. I paddled a short distance across Monhegan's harbor to granite Manana, now uninhabited but formerly the home of Ray Phillips, the island "hermit" I'd once met as a young boy, which was the last time I'd climbed ashore there. An old Coast Guard station, now automated, casts its lonely gaze toward open ocean, and a simple shingled hut with a pitched roof stands in its own solitude atop the island rock, which is coarsely carpeted with blueberry bushes and wild rose. But Manana was not deserted the day I rowed to it, for a group of kayakers, two families out on a picnic, had arrived shortly before me, and I was invited to join them. After four days of fog, I left Monhegan this morning and rowed across the outer mouth of Penobscot Bay, reaching the protective lee shore of Hurricane Island before a line of squalls caught up to me. In the late afternoon I arrive at Greens Island, near the town of Vinalhaven, where a family waves me into shore to include me in their evening picnic of freshly caught mackerel and mussels picked from the ledges at lowtide. Their dock, to which the boat is tied, is at the mouth of a cove where perhaps a dozen boats, mostly lobster boats, are moored. If I row farther into the narrowing cove, I am told, I will be able to anchor in safety from any traffic still to come at the end of the day. It is dark by the time I say good night and leave them. They escort me by flashlight down a wooded path to the boat.

In the still air the water's surface is a perfect sheet of black glass, which melts beneath the moving hull as if in a Dalí painting. My silent wake reflects the dream light of a half moon, and I row slowly, seemingly without effort. In this moment in the cool night air, still days away from taking the final stroke at Eastport, it is easier to row than to stop rowing. It almost seems that I could close my eyes and fall asleep, and still row onward into an endless cove.

I take a stroke and lean back, gazing upward into the jet skies, be-

jeweled by the moon and the galaxies of stars. I am profound only in my silence, and merely watch through the two small windows of my eyes. The hull glides in silence and with such perfect balance as to report no motion, and only the passing of the tops of pine trees in my peripheral vision tells me that I'm moving at all. Within moments two shooting stars flame into ashes across the sky. I sit up for another stroke, now looking down as the blades ignite swirling pairs of greenish, blueish, white constellations of phosphorescent plankton. Two opposing heavens. "Remember this," I once again think to myself, faintly murmuring the words.

I am suddenly aware of a large rowing boat, the only boat moored in the cove. I stop rowing and glide when I see it, painted white and half lit by the moon, and it slides silently by. It is similar to my boat in style, but stouter, a "pea-pod," double-ended and built in lapstrake style out of wood. Still slipping through the water, I ship the oars, move to the bow, and pull the anchor from its bag. I lower it gently over the side and then let it go, and though I cannot see it descend, its path, like those of the oar blades, is lit by a descending trail of phosphorescence. As I fall asleep the stillness of the cove is contrasted by the distant, muted thunder of surf crashing on an outer, rocky shore. My own silence, lying on my side, is broken only by my pulse, which faintly clicks my teeth together with each double beat of the heart. As I sink into sleep I feel grateful that this is all coming to an end along my own home coast.

I'm pleased to be traveling through these New England towns and islands, places that I've known before, and places I've wished to visit. The next day I row from Greens Island a short distance to the town of Vinalhaven, and from Vinalhaven to Isle au Haut, and from there to Swan's Island and Southwest Harbor, which lies at the mouth of Somes Sound. I stop at Seal Harbor and row past Scoodic Point, famous for its fog, though I find only clear skies. I visit Ripley—my first step on the mainland since leaving Turbat's Creek—as well as Jonesport, Roque Island, and Cutler, places so remote and unpretentious as to belie the common assumption among residents of the American West that the Northeast is crowded and snobbish.

With Cutler, Maine, now behind me I follow an intermittent line of cliffs occasionally interrupted by rocky beaches, on a nearly twenty-mile stretch to West Quoddy Head, the northernmost point on the open Atlantic Coast of the United States. Lying to the east in the Bay of Fundy the western cliffs of Grand Manan Island, a deep pink wall of quartzite three hundred feet high and fifteen miles long, deepens and glows through shimmering late afternoon mirage. My timing is imperfect as the enormous tide of the region, often twenty feet high—the tide that had stranded me in Georgia was no more than eight feet—is now racing out through the Grand Manan Channel, between the granite cliffs beside me and the quartzite cliffs in the distance. And so I hug the shore, at times so close that I scrape an oar blade on the ledges below, seeking eddies and gazing up to pine-topped granite cliffs a hundred feet high. I rarely pay attention to the tides anymore. I'm happy to row with them, yet intrigued also by rowing against them. I've sometimes found myself in the middle of a channel, where they run fastest and I make the least progress, content simply to be rowing. Other times I seek a route of eddies like an up-river barge on the Mississippi.

I've lost track of the miles I've rowed. The mileage of the rivers was so well marked that I could hardly have avoided knowledge of the distances, and yet at times I was obsessed by those numbers and rarely went to sleep between Brooklyn and the Gulf of Mexico without knowing how far I'd rowed in a day. Fifty-five miles, ending at Brewerton on Oneida Lake in upstate New York, had been an achievement. So had seventy-eight miles on the Mississippi, ending where I'd thrown a plum pit into the river at New Orleans. Yet now the achievement in my mind is going to sleep each night not knowing how far I've rowed since morning, and not caring.

The miles pass by inevitably on this last day to Eastport. Aside from my attention to the date of the Blackburn Challenge I have never tried to speed the trip, and I have never tried to slow it down. It's been the most perfectly paced period of my life, in which, for once, I've done precisely and with abounding selfishness what I wanted to do. Over my shoulder I can now see the bulky, rocky promontory of West Quoddy Head, beyond which a channel leading inland toward Cobscook and Pasamaquoddy Bays separates the United States from Canada. Several miles before reaching West Quoddy Head Light, with New Brunswick, Canada, still out of view beyond the point, I stop rowing on an impulse, ship the oars, and lay out a bed roll in the bow, and drift. I rock with the boat in the easy waves and look back across the miles as if through a photo album. I close my eyes and for a moment the movement of the boat in this cold water is replaced by its stillness in the mud flats of Jekyll Island. I think of Phyllis Rose and Laurent de Brunhoff, who'd waved me on as I'd headed up this coast, and I imagine them now, sitting together on a granite ledge waving me to its end. Whatever became of Ozona, I wonder, and did the osprey that found temporary refuge in the boat simply tumble back into the water and drown or fly away? I picture it now as part bird, part ghost, soaring over the coastal forests of the Everglades.

I think of the men on Bayou Lafourche who, as I drift, are now surely sitting as usual beneath their oak tree, keeping tabs on each other and all that passes them by. What antics have Thibodeaux and Boudreaux been up to now? Scoober Williams is perhaps catching a last few hours of sleep before returning to both his watchman's shift and the edge of a world that only he and few others can remember. Now when I think of the Mississippi I float in air above it, following its bends upriver, past Natchez and Vicksburg, over plodding barges and the remote sandbars that I'd briefly called home. The heat is all but forgotten. I return to the pool in the Kentucky hills where Ed Taylor had caught his fish, and from across the pool see his son and his granddaughter and myself, all huddled around Ed as he lures one crawdad out from its small cave with the tail of another.

On Chadekoin Creek Roy Harvey and I dodge branches and limbs on the swollen stream, and at Mayville Mrs. Webb whispers to me about Patton's army and a hotdog stand. On Portage Road, with a wind-torn Lake Erie in the background I am still towing the scull up the long hill, and at the base of the hill Budda and I are laughing in his truck about the wild turkey and the Greyhound bus. The long, narrow corridor of the Erie Canal leads lock by lock back to the Hudson, where Marcina is singing her immigrant's song, and the questioning light of a small freighter, having failed to spot me by West Point, is extinguished. I think back to the jogger at 110th Street, with his fist punched in the air, and a man pointing south as he tells me I am heading the wrong way if I'm going to New Orleans. I see a group of friends who are watching me as I step in the boat and uncertainly pull the oars through their first stroke.

So here I am, adrift on my last day of this rowing life on the water. It all started twenty years ago, with a question and a boyhood search through an atlas. I'd found my answer then with the canals at Chicago. The answer had been, *Yes, it's an island*, but that was not answer enough for my curiosity. I have not rowed the island route, and perhaps someday I'll wish that I had. But, as if all along I've been aiming to satisfy that ten-year-old self, I now have new answers to the same question and answers to questions I'd never thought to ask. I look to the calluses on my hands and to the worn-out rubber grips of the oars, and the salt-stained wooden gunwales of the boat, and the surroundings into which I've rowed—a lone red lobster boat plies the water and raises and lowers its traps in the distance ahead of me—and take possession of the fact that I have never once counted so much as ten strokes of the oars. This is as good an answer as any I have for childhood questions about boats and big islands.

SHALL I TELL YOU about the last few miles to Eastport? About rounding West Quoddy Head, with Canada across the way, about pulling the boat into the still-ebbing tide and the rainbow cast by a passing shower, whose timing was so absurdly perfect that I hesitate to even mention it? And what about the end of repetition, the final flight of the blades, which like the millions before it began at the catch, and continued through the powering stroke and the release from water? And yet there was no recovery, but only my hands letting go for the last time.

Or shall I leave the story here, drifting on a tide in the Grand Manan Channel, before the rain shower, with several thousand strokes still to row? If I tell you that it all came to an end, then perhaps it may as well have never started, the way a man's life is lived in vain if the last thing said about him is that he died. Instead I think back to the woman I'd met on the Mississippi, where the river bends at the city of Helena, and to whom I gave a book in which her family was mentioned. She became lost in a world that still lived on in her mind, and from time to time as she studied the pictures, she said aloud to no one in particular, "That's just the way it was."

· Acknowledgments ·

TO START AT THE BEGINNING, I first thank my parents, Nick Stone and Beverly Simpson. They raised me by the water and on the water, and it was from and with them that I acquired my love of boats. I vividly recall the hours I spent towing toy motorboats from the stern of my parents' sailboat, maneuvering them at the end of a piece of string so that they would surf on the sailboat's wake.

The atlas was the first book I needed to think of the trip, and Marjory Shaw gave me the second, Joe Garland's *Lone Voyager*, with Joe's signature on the title page, no less. Jake Page, the first person to whom I showed the route in a road atlas, said "Fantastic!"; Gwyn Isaac said "Brilliant!"; and Diana Russell set the trip in motion by offering me the use of one of her company's sculls.

A most important and difficult part of travel is saying good-bye, at some point followed by the pleasure of saying hello. Those who saw me off from Brooklyn and those who were there on my return include Janet Wu, Jonathan Lutes, the Soenens family, Seth Berry, Adelaida Gaviria, Greta Nicholas, Kristin Wise, David Cashion, Macky Alston, Diana Russell, Ala Warren, Lori Chajet, Ben Wides, Hugh Stockton, Laura Strickler, Kevin Stack, and Mike Davis.

Thanks to Megan Rice, who watched out for Grover and Hips, and to my brother, Kip Stone, and to Caroline Kurrus, who made their home my home between the two legs of the trip.

I'd like to thank Gerry Howard at Broadway Books for needing to read the paper one Saturday morning while on vacation, and Luke Dempsey, then of Broadway, who tracked me down. I now appreciate why people heap such praise on their editors. Ann Campbell, my editor at Broadway, gave sterling judgments chapter by chapter and provided encouragement and discipline with unfailing balance. Though as a novice I gave her cause to sweat at times, it never showed. And I was always pleased to hear the voice of her assistant, Jenny Cookson, such a friendly voice in such a very large Times Square building.

When I think back on my conversations and visits with Ike Williams at Hill & Barlow Agency, any talk of business is largely forgotten and I remember engaging rambles through such topics as underwater diving, the lives of dogs, and other ideas for travel. Hope Denekamp, also at Hill & Barlow, told me not to worry when the writing had come to a disconcertingly long standstill after only several chapters. "You're working on it," she said, "even though it doesn't seem like it. It will all just suddenly come out." And she was right.

Elizabeth Stone, my sister, took a handful of photographs from the trip and converted them into illustrations that, to me, seem to release the images from time, and I would gladly trade all of my trip photographs for more of her renditions.

Friends who prodded me with encouragement and commented on chapters include Anne Beckett, Joe Garland, Gwyn Isaac, Mike Lambert, Chris Keyes, Ted Sizer, Kathy Prouty, Jane Fasulo, Robin Postell, Nancy Stone, Karen Strassler, and Dave Herbtsman. For as long as I've known them and throughout the rowing and writing of this trip, Jake and Susanne Page have given their unconditional friendship, love, and support, and their company and hospitality made the completion of the manuscript a pleasure amid the last-minute stress.

Thanks to Jack Lain and Kim Strauss, and again to Anne Beckett, all dear friends who provided me with work space when I ran out of firewood to keep my old woodstoves going. Amy Nevitt and Codi Hooee of the Zuni High School Library could have just about set their watches by my arrival each morning to use their computers, whose Internet access kept me in touch with friends and family and relayed many versions of this book between New Mexico and New York.

I've often been asked if I got lonely on the trip. In fact, there was only one day that I didn't shake someone's hand, and if I were to list the names of those I did meet and comment on their generosity, this volume would be half again as long. I doubt there's been any other year of my life that I've met close to a thousand people—from most every walk of American life—and I often wish for the wherewithal to bring everyone together. I know of a nice city park for a picnic in Greenville, overlooking the Mississippi.

As I write this, I keep itching to give an example of the roles that people played along the way, of their contributions to both the nature and the continuation of the trip. But I hesitate on these Acknowledgments pages to single out even one, for I was and will remain grateful for every gesture of support and participation, from a friendly wave on a riverbank to an invitation to come in and stay for a while. The collective interest of these hundreds of people became, for me, an additional source of motivation to keep rowing, and as I met them one by one, family by family, they evolved as the cast of characters in the finest year, thus far, of my life.

· Endnotes ·

1. Joseph E. Garland. *Lone Voyager: The Extraordinary Adventures of Howard Blackburn, Hero Fisherman of Gloucester*. Nelson B. Robinson. 1978.
2. Ibid.
3. Ibid.
4. John M. Barry. *Rising Tide: The Great Mississippi Flood of 1927 and How it Changed America*. Simon and Schuster, New York. 1997.
5. Joseph E. Garland. *Lone Voyager: The Extraordinary Adventures of Howard Blackburn, Hero Fisherman of Gloucester*. Nelson B. Robinson. 1978.